Voices From the Hunger Marches

BY THE SAME AUTHOR:

The Minutes of Edinburgh Trades Council, 1859–1873 (1968)
A Catalogue of some Labour Records in Scotland
   and some Scots Records outside Scotland (1978)
Essays in Scottish Labour History (ed.) (1978)
Militant Miners (Polygon, 1981)
Labour in Scotland; A Pictorial History from the
   Eighteenth Century to the Present (1985)
Voices from the Spanish Civil War (Polygon, 1986)
The Prisoners at Penicuik: French and other prisoners-of-war,
   1803–1814 (1989)
Voices from the Hunger Marches, Volume 1 (Polygon, 1990)

Voices From the Hunger Marches

Personal recollections by Scottish
Hunger Marchers of the 1920s and 1930s
Volume II

Ian MacDougall

Polygon
EDINBURGH

© Ian MacDougall 1991

First published by Polygon
22 George Square, Edinburgh

Set in Monotype Bembo
by Koinonia Ltd, Bury
and printed in Great Britain by
Redwood Press, Melksham, Wilts

British Library Cataloguing in Publication Data
Voices from the Hunger Marches.
Vol. II
1. Scotland. Protest movements, history
I. MacDougall, Ian, *1933–*
322.409411

ISBN 0 7486 6101 8

The publisher acknowledges subsidy from the
Scottish Arts Council towards the publication
of this volume.

Contents

Introduction

These personal recollections by fourteen Scots men and women Hunger Marchers of the inter-war years extend and complement those by eighteen other Scots Marchers presented in Volume I of this book, published a year ago.

The Hunger Marches recalled below are not only the national Marches from Scotland to London in 1934 and 1936, but also several within Scotland – to Edinburgh in 1932, 1933 and 1938, to Glasgow in 1935, and one to Cupar Fife.

This volume, like the earlier one, does not constitute a history of Hunger Marches in the 1930s; it is an attempt to record and present, in their own words, the recollections of two women and twelve men who took part in one or more of those Marches, and to set their recollections in the context of their lives.

The recollections below are therefore, like those in the earlier volume, not of Hunger Marches alone; they present personal and often deeply felt experience of economic, social and political conditions – of employment and especially unemployment, including the hated Means Test, of housing, poverty and hunger, of great strikes or lock-outs such as those in 1921 and 1926, of the effects of the War of 1914-18 and the coming of that of 1939-45, as well as of the Spanish Civil War, in the last of which four of these fourteen veterans fought and a further three were on the verge of leaving Scotland to do so. These recollections add also to knowledge of the history – especially the local history – in the inter-war years of such organisations of the broad labour movement as the National Unemployed Workers' Movement, the Labour Party, the Independent Labour Party, and the Communist Party. The localities that the recollections cover or touch on include Aberdeen, Ayr and Ayrshire, Blantyre, Clydebank, Dundee, Fife, Glasgow and Lesmahagow.

The two women Marchers – Emily Swankie of Clydebank and Mary Johnston of Glasgow – remind us, often in lively style, that women also went on the Hunger Marches of the inter-war years and had particular problems of employment and unemployment to struggle with.

As in all worthwhile oral history there are in these accounts gems that sparkle. Guy Bolton, recalling that his father had gone to work down the pit before he was ten years old, with consequent bad effects on his schooling, says: 'He was fifty-six year auld afore he could write his ain name. He had

221

tae learn tae write it to go on the buroo.' And Hugh Duffy, describing the damp and holed conditions of Dixon's miners' rows at Blantyre in which he grew up, says: 'Actually, I got a frog in the room one mornin'.' It was against conditions such as those, as well as against the manifold deprivations and humiliations of unemployment, often savagely prolonged, that the Hunger Marchers marched.

These recollections tell us of many aspects of the Marches: preparations, fund-raising, footwear and clothing, food and drink, discipline, public responses, routes followed, overnight accommodation, attitudes of the police and of the press, and so on. Some commentators, says John Lochore, have given the impression that 'the Marchers were lumpen-class fodder. This is far from the truth ... The men I marched with from Glasgow to London were poor in worldly things but rich in mind ... If ever I have an epitaph I hope it says: He was a Hunger Marcher.'

Alas, John Lochore, like James Graham, John Lennox and David Anderson, Marchers in this volume, has not lived to see his recollections in print.

Any shortcomings in this volume, as in the preceding one, are to be blamed on me alone. But my thanks for their co-operation and patience are due to all those – including Marion Sinclair of Polygon but above all the thirty-two Hunger Marchers themselves – who helped ensure that these recollections are preserved for us to share.

Ian MacDougall
Edinburgh

Some Relevant Events

1905   Unemployed Workmen Act

1909   Labour Exchanges Act

1911   National Insurance Act: compulsory insurance against unemployment introduced in engineering, building and shipbuilding

1914–18 Great War 'to end all wars'

1916   Extension of compulsory unemployment insurance to certain other trades

1917   Russian Revolution

1918   Temporary 'Out of Work Donation' for ex-servicemen and civilians. Women over thirty enfranchised. Lloyd George Coalition government elected

1919   Strike in Scotland for 40 Hour Week. Increase in scales of unemployment insurance benefit. Communist International established

1920   Inter-war depression and mass unemployment begin. Rent Strike in Scotland. Communist Party of Great Britain founded. Unemployment Insurance Act: trebling of numbers covered to over 11 million, raised scales of benefit. Clash of unemployed demonstrations in London with police. Unemployed organised locally throughout Britain. Outdoor Poor Law relief conceded to able-bodied unemployed

1921   National Unemployed Workers' Movement founded. National lock-out of miners. Collapse of Triple Industrial Alliance. Red International of Labour Unions founded in Moscow. Thirty Poplar borough councillors imprisoned in struggle over Poor Law relief. New Acts first raise then reduce benefit scales and establish 'uncovenanted' or 'extended' benefit and allowance for married men's dependants. Unemployed 'Week of Agitation' (October)

1922   'Mond Scale': Poor Law scales of relief standardised. Government forced to extend uncovenanted benefit. First National Hunger March to London. Fall of Lloyd George Coalition government. Breakthrough for Labour Party in general election. Mussolini and Fascists in power in Italy. Government again forced to extend uncovenanted benefit

1923   Unemployment Sunday 7 January organised jointly by Trades

223

Union Congress and National Unemployed Workers' Movement. Hunger Marchers leave London. Franco–Belgian armies occupy Ruhr. Hitler's Munich putsch. Death of John Maclean. Joint Advisory Committee formed by T.U.C. General Council and N.U.W.M.: Unemployed Workers' Charter published

1924   First Labour Government. Abolition of 'gap' in period of benefit and exclusion from uncovenanted and many other benefits. Death of Lenin. 'Red Letter' election of Baldwin Conservative government

1925   Unemployment Insurance Act: Extended benefit no longer a statutory right; 'gap' reintroduced. Britain returned to Gold Standard. Unemployed Sunday (21 June). Red Friday: crisis in coal industry postponed. Blanesburgh Committee appointed by Government to investigate Unemployment Insurance scheme

1926   General Strike and miners' lock-out. Miners' hours increased from seven to eight a day

1927   Dissolution of Joint Advisory Committee of T.U.C. and N.U.W.M. Trade Disputes and Trade Unions Act. Mond–Turner Talks. Unemployed Welsh miners' march to London. Unemployment Insurance Act (based on Blanesburgh Report): scales of benefit reduced, 'not genuinely seeking work' clause puts onus of proof on unemployed. Stalin dominant in Soviet Union

1928   First Scottish Hunger March to Edinburgh. Women enfranchised on same basis as men. First Five Year Plan launched in Soviet Union. Communist International and Party 'class against class' policy

1929   Second National Hunger March to London. Local Government Act: elected Poor Law Boards of Guardians replaced by non-elected Public Assistance Committees. Second Labour Government elected. Wall Street Crash: beginning of world slump. Abolition of 'not genuinely seeking work' clause delayed. Trotsky deported from Soviet Union by Stalin

1930   Unemployment Insurance Act: 'not genuinely seeking work' clause abolished, benefits for juveniles and wives increased. Great rise in numbers of unemployed: 2,643,000 registered by end of year. Unemployment Insurance Fund heavily in debt. Royal Commission appointed on unemployment insurance. Third National Hunger March to London 'against the Labour Government'. Second Scottish Hunger March to Edinburgh. Coal Mines Act: $7^1/_2$ hour day for miners

1931   Royal Commission proposes reduction in scales and rights to benefit, application of Means Test to some claimants, and increase in contributions to insurance fund. Anomalies Act: benefit disallowed for many unemployed, including married women. May Committee on National Expenditure proposes cuts in benefit and in wages of government employees, large increases in workers' insurance contributions, and a Means Test on many claimants. Fall of Second Labour Government. Formation of 'National' Government led by Ramsay MacDonald. Labour heavily defeated in general election. Unemployment benefit reduced and household Means Test introduced: in first ten weeks 271,000 claimants totally disallowed. Gold Standard abandoned and pound devalued. 'Economy cuts' begin. Invergordon Naval Mutiny. Serious unemployed rioting in Glasgow. Fall of monarchy in Spain and formation of a republic. Japanese invasion of Manchuria

1932   3 million unemployed. Third Scottish Hunger March to Edinburgh. I.L.P. disaffiliate from Labour Party. Mosley forms British Union of Fascists. Serious clashes of unemployed and police at Birkenhead and Belfast: hundreds injured, two dead, many arrested. Fourth National Hunger March to London. Police without search warrant raid N.U.W.M. headquarters. Final report of Royal Commission on Unemployment: reintroduction of 'not genuinely seeking work' clause, further reductions in benefit scales, compulsory labour for unemployed in return for benefit

1933   Mass unemployment at its worst: about 3,500,000. Fourth Scottish Hunger March to Edinburgh. Government refuses to restore 'temporary' benefit cuts of 1931. Hitler and Nazis in power in Germany

1934   Socialist rising in Austria crushed by Chancellor Dollfuss. Fifth National Hunger March to London. National Council of Civil Liberties formed. Fascist attempt to seize power in France. Asturian uprising crushed by General Franco in Spain. Soviet Union joins League of Nations and presses for 'United Front' policy against Fascism. 'Temporary' unemployment benefit cuts imposed in 1931 restored. Unemployment Act: Unemployment Assistance Board set up to deal with all able-bodied unemployed other than those receiving unemployment insurance, reduction of benefit scales. United Front Congress in London. Government 'Distressed Areas' investigations

1935   Intense agitation by unemployed: Government forced to withdraw new scales and regulations. Scottish Hunger March to Glasgow. Abyssinia (Ethiopia) invaded by Mussolini: Hoare-Laval Pact. Conscription and formation of an air force announced by Hitler. Soviet-French Pact. Labour again defeated in general election. Rearmament in Britain begins

1936   Remilitarisation of Rhineland by Hitler. Popular Front governments formed in France and Spain. Outbreak of Spanish Civil War: formation of International Brigades. Moscow Trials begin. Unemployment Assistance Board scales and regulations published: some sharp reductions for unemployed. Sixth and last National Hunger March to London. Government forced to suspend new U.A.B. scales. Jarrow March. Fall in un-employment to 1,600,000 by end of year

1937   Baldwin succeeded by Chamberlain as leader of 'National' Government. Anti-Comintern Pact by Nazi Germany, Fascist Italy and Japan. Japan begins war on China. Hitler unfolds secret plans for war to his generals

1938   Austria annexed by Hitler. Munich crisis. Withdrawal of International Brigades from Spain. Fifth and last Scottish Hunger March to Edinburgh

1939   Continuation of N.U.W.M. agitations. End of Spanish Civil War. Nazi-Soviet Non-Aggression Pact

1939-45 Second World War

Emily Swankie

The Hunger March on which I was involved was in 1934. And that was during the period when the Means Test was having a serious effect on some of the people around me and especially on my own family.

We were a big family. I had five brothers and seven sisters. I was the eighth child. Two of my brothers had died before they were three years old and before I was born. My parents were both Irish, father from Antrim, mother from Donegal. Home was in Kilbowie Road in Clydebank, in a tenement house – one room and kitchen.

My mother was a member of the Independent Labour Party and she had some quite serious disagreements with the introduction of the Means Test. It seriously affected our family. My brother Charlie, who was the second oldest of the family and eleven years older than me, was paid off from Singer's in the late 1920s. My parents hadn't been able to afford to let Charlie become an apprentice in a skilled trade, so he'd had only an unskilled job at Singer's. When the Means Test was introduced Charlie was given the handsome sum of 2/6d per week, which is now 12½ pence.

At that time – 1932 – Charlie was in his middle twenties, living at home, unmarried. Two of my sisters and myself were working and so was my father. So Charlie's money was reduced because we were employed. He was not entitled to the full Labour Exchange money – it was cut quite severely. This business ended in Charlie facing the prospect of having to leave home. And at that time there were nine of us living at home, five younger than I was. That made eleven altogether when you include my parents. So it was quite a serious thing for the family when first of all we lost Charlie's wages and then his dole money.

So what was practised then was that the individual in this situation found another address and tried to move out. But that wasn't always practicable because there were so many unemployed around and his presence in the other home would have been taken into consideration in deciding their dole money. So Charlie was given an address to which he was supposed to move. He just stayed out as much as possible. It was all done so he could get back on to his full Labour Exchange money.

It was quite funny at times because the Means Test inspectors used to pay unexpected visits to homes where they thought that this ploy was being carried out. The unemployed person in the house then had to hide – as my brother Charlie had to do. Somebody would come up and say, 'The

227

inspectors are on their way. You'd better get out.' As we lived in a room and kitchen and it was a top-floor house, there was no place really to hide. So Charlie had to go out. Neighbours would tell one another when they thought the inspectors were on their way. In the Second World War Charlie was lost at sea when his ship was torpedoed in the Bay of Biscay in 1941.

So I was involved at an early stage in the operation of the Means Test, without fully understanding what it was all about. I had left school on my fourteenth birthday, in December 1929, and started work the following Monday in the shop in which my father worked. My father was a shoemaker, or a cordiner as he liked to be called – because there is a difference. The shop wasn't his but he more or less ran it. I attended to the shop and the shoe-repairs, etc. I was there for three years. It was a very boring job – nothing to do all day. So I did a lot of reading. About 1931, '32, my mother prevailed on me to help set up a branch of the Independent Labour Party Guild of Youth in Clydebank. So I had a wee bit smattering of what the Labour Movement thought about the Means Test.

In March 1933, when I was seventeen, I left my job in the shop to get married. My mother and father weren't at all happy about that. They thought I was too young. And they weren't happy either that John, my husband, was a Protestant. You see, though my father himself wasn't a Catholic my mother was and my brothers and sisters and I had all been brought up as Catholics. It was mainly because they thought I was too young to get married, but they were worried too about this difference in religion. Anyway, it was normal in these days that when a woman got married she gave up her job. It was the done thing and people expected you to do that. So I lost my job when I got married.

But John my husband was also unemployed at that time. He was a blacksmith's apprentice. He had been an apprentice on the *Queen Mary,* the 534, which was lying in dock at the time. And when the yard closed down he was just put out. And that was it. There was nothing in Clydebank. There was no work in Singer's. They had cut their staff as well.

Our Labour Exchange money at that time – that was my husband and myself – was 23/3d. That would be about £1.16 nowadays. That was for the week. Well, it was very hard to come from a family where food was always available to the condition where it was difficult to get a proper diet and to feel that you had enough food in the house at any one time.

We used to stay at home on the Labour Exchange day until my husband signed on at eleven o'clock. Home was a single-end – a one-roomed flat – in Bruce Street, Clydebank. And I used to meet John outside the Labour Exchange to buy food, because there was really nothing in the house by the time the dole money was due again. We used to go down to a shop where we could buy Polish eggs at eight old pence a dozen. In our diet then, a tin of condensed milk did for a week, and a half pint of fresh milk on the day that your Labour Exchange money came through. That was the bonus. We used to buy sausages and smoked fish, the eggs, and lots of bread and potatoes. Very little veg, but no fruit, no fruit whatsoever. It was very difficult. And we didn't have a family. So it must have been very, very much more difficult for any young couples who had young children.

But young people are optimistic and can find other things, you know. Our salvation in a way was that we were hikers. We liked to walk. And we used to go away camping at the weekends. It was a very happy time from that point of view because we were young enough to appreciate the freedom that the lack of work gave us and we were very fond of the open air. But it was the food position that we found difficult to cope with.

And we started to get interested in the political movement, just on the periphery, because my husband John was also in the Independent Labour Party Guild of Youth. We started to get a background of what was happening, that we weren't alone, there were lots of people in our condition. It wasn't like nowadays where the differences are so obvious between the employed and the unemployed. Because all around us then were unemployed. And they were more or less in the same position as we were at that time. But we were lucky in so far as we had no family. That made the difference and gave us a bit of freedom and helped us to sort of put up with the lack of things that we should have had.

Well, as I said, we were just on the outskirts of politics, just beginning to understand what was happening to us with the big unemployment that was in the country at the time. And I was interested in the marches that the National Unemployed Workers' Movement had. There was a flute band in Clydebank and it was attached to the Unemployed Movement. Big John Monaghan, as we called him, a big soft-spoken Irishman who, I understand, was at one time in the I.R.A., used to be at the front of this flute band.[192] We used to watch them going by and I thought, 'That's great. Somebody's trying to do something or at least draw attention to how the people are living.'

So when I was approached by John Monaghan of the N.U.W.M. who asked me if I would like to go on the Hunger March I said that I would. I wasn't terribly politically influenced at any time. It was only the issue of the unemployed and the operation of the Means Test, and other injustices that I saw around me for big families – the differences between big families, and those whose fathers were working and had smaller families, the differences in their conditions, etc. It did influence your thinking. So after one or two conversations with John Monaghan, whom I admired very much, as part of the I.L.P. Guild of Youth activities – they were active in the protest movement against the Means Test at the time – and I was unemployed anyway, I decided that I would go on the Hunger March. But it was for no political reason other than my strong resentment against the way that we had to live and the lack of opportunity, the lack of jobs. And the fact that my husband was still unemployed. There seemed no prospect. And the only thing to do, we felt, was, well, 'Here's a protest. I'll go.'

John, my husband, couldn't go on the March. He thought about going. But there was the fact that the Labour Exchange would have stopped his money. And we had a house and a rent to pay. Therefore it was easier for me to go. Some married men did go on the March. I don't know how they managed it. I suppose they knew how to do it. But when we thought that one of us would go we found that it was easier that I should go because he had to sign twice a week at the Labour Exchange. It kept, well, the rent and the bit of money coming in.

I was asked to come to a meeting in the N.U.W.M. Rooms in Clydebank for a discussion about the March. There were one or two of the N.U.W.M. members who were going on the men's March as far as I knew. You understand the men were going away a week or two before us. They were walking from Glasgow to London. We were walking from Derby to London. But at this meeting they explained what the position would be. We would have a send-off from Clydebank. And we'd get a bus in Glasgow and from Glasgow we'd go to Derby and join up with the rest of the women, mainly the women from Northern England, Lancashire.

They felt it would be too long for us to march from Clydebank, Glasgow and then down to Derby and on to London. They felt it would be too much. And as a matter of fact they were right. In the circumstances that arose during the March it was proved that they were right. A lot of the women weren't fit really and it was harder. The men took longer and were better prepared than we were, because there had been previous Hunger Marches for the men, from which they had learned what they could do. It was decided that the women wouldn't be asked to do so much.

I would like to say that I had absolutely nothing to do with the arrangements. I was called in as someone who was going on the March. So I don't know very much about the background of the arrangements other than I was told when we would meet, etc. We were then told that the Clydebank Co-operative had agreed to donate boots and shoes for the Marchers. And we were to present ourselves at the Co-operative and get fitted for shoes, which we did. We got one pair of shoes. And being a shoemaker's daughter, of course I chose heavy chrome leather, which in the event proved fatal for my feet! I had decided I wouldn't wear these new shoes till the start of the March so that they would be absolutely ready for going – which was also a mistake.

But from there we then met, had a discussion about the final arrangements, and that's the last I saw of them until I turned up in Alexander Street in Clydebank. And there was the flute band. And there also was my partner, a Mrs Brown, from Clydebank. There were the two of us going on the women's March from Clydebank. I didn't know Mrs Brown at all. I didn't get to know her very well on the March either, because I was part of the Youth contingent and wasn't associated with the adult members. Unfortunately, I lost touch with Mrs Brown completely afterwards.

Well, we left from Alexander Street and walked down our main street, Kilbowie Road. My father worked in the shop at the foot of Kilbowie Road. But he was so upset at me taking up this sort of activity that he wouldn't come out to the front of the shop to see me passing. And I was a bit hurt about that. But it was very understandable in the circumstances. I really understand now why he didn't want to see me leaving on this March, which he thought was not the best thing for me to do.

My husband John was there all the time, however, right from the word go. He came to see us off from Clydebank and he came to Glasgow and saw us off on the bus and was a great support. He fully agreed with what I was doing and only wished he could have come with us.

Well, after we left Clydebank we went into Glasgow to George Square. There was a demonstration from North Frederick Street there to see us off on the bus. I can't fully recollect how many women went on the bus. It wasn't very many, in fact very few – maybe about twelve or thirteen. I have a recollection of someone from Aberdeen. I was really on the fringes of politics and I didn't understand that I should have been taking notes and trying to remember. I was making a protest about the Means Test. I didn't see any reason why I should write it down or record anything. It's only in later years that I realise I should have done it.

Well, we left Glasgow and there was a great send-off and best wishes from the workers and the unemployed who had assembled there to see us off. And we arrived in Derby that same day and were bedded down in a small hall with just blankets. We were given a meal when we arrived. We also met there the English contingent of the March, mainly Lancashire women, mill women. And some of them arrived in their wooden clogs and did some of the March in their clogs. And my memories are that they didn't finish the March in the clogs because I don't remember seeing clogs further down the way. But they did arrive in clogs. And some of them started the walk next day in clogs.

We had a sort of get-together that first night at Derby and introduced one another. And we had a meeting and to my great surprise I was appointed the leader of the Youth contingent. I still don't know why. Maybe it was because I was a wee bit taller than the rest! I can't think of any other reason. I was to be responsible for seeing that everyone in the younger generation was all right. I must have been among the youngest there, if not the youngest. I was eighteen at that time. I was very surprised when I was picked out for this job because I didn't know anybody. It's still a mystery but there it was.

And of course us younger people got into a corner and started exchanging tales. And I found that the younger women were more or less the same as I was. It was the Means Test. It was a protest movement. And when you talked to them it broadened out into the general living conditions for the unemployed and for the lower paid at that time. And so we got sort of established. And you started to pick out people, or they started to pick you out as people they wanted to walk beside and so on. So that was the first night at Derby.

Well, we left in the morning. It was just about nine o'clock. We walked for sixteen miles that day. That was the longest march, that first day. We found that sixteen miles is quite a distance for people who are not used to walking. And if like me you were in a pair of new shoes it wasn't funny.

But there were some of them in worse condition than I was as far as their physical condition and their footwear were concerned. So it was decided that we would cut the length of the marches. We never did sixteen miles again. The next day was twelve miles. And then we cut it down to eight. It varied along the road. But we never went as high as sixteen again.

It was good the first day because we were all as fresh as we were going to be. And among the young people we felt we were on a bit of an adventure. We were going to London to protest. We'd go to Hyde Park. Many of us had never been out of Scotland before and this was an experience for us. Everything seemed different. The houses were different. We didn't see any tenements the way we see them in Glasgow and Clydebank. And we did march through quite a lot of the English villages, which I found were very beautiful. But the people were not very receptive to us in the smaller places.

As we marched down the road we only had the clothes we marched in, and a spare skirt, oilskins, a jacket, scarves – and a pack. We had a pack to carry our rainwear when it was dry and any spare food that we could muster, and of course clean underwear, etc. But no spare clothes in the way of extra jackets etc. We had one jacket, jumper, blouse, etc., that sort of thing – just the basic things that we had. We had black stockings which we were asked to wear all the time. They weren't in favour of anything else, although for when the stockings ran out I had brought socks with me. Being a walker I had socks and I was allowed to wear them. But they frowned on bare legs – no bare legs on the Hunger March. I don't really know why that was. I couldn't understand it at the time, this business of always having to be fully covered up. But I felt that the leaders of the March didn't want any criticism or anything untoward about the women who were walking to London. And we were asked to wear black stockings. There was a wee bit of puritanism there too, but I think it was they wanted to avoid at all costs any bad publicity – women marching with bare legs. They didn't want that. But if your stockings wore out then you could put on socks if you had them with you.

We just had one pair of shoes, oh, nothing else, not even a pair of slippers did we take with us, just the one pair of shoes. Remember, these were hard times and a new pair of shoes was a precious thing to get. You certainly didnae buy a new pair until the others were out of commission. And so it was one pair of footwear that we had on the March.

Well, when we arrived at our first stop after that sixteen mile march the first day – the women were very tired. Some of them were older women, in their thirties, early forties. The Youth contingent wasn't so bad. But we did have blisters, some of us were crippling a wee bit. And as I say it was a long walk for people who were not used to walking. We were tired and we were hungry because we hadn't eaten a lot that day. We hadn't had any receptions along the way. Our main meal was when we arrived at our destination that night. So we were hungry, a bit cold because there was frost. As I said I had these new shoes on. And the only way that I could get into them next morning was to stand in a basin of cold water, because I knew enough about leather to keep my feet in the shoes and keep the pressure down. But that didn't help the blisters much – and at least I was a walker. So the other women were tired and some of them did have sore feet. So I think that's one of the main reasons why they had to cut the mileage back for the women.

Well, what I've got to say now are the main impressions. There was long hours of walking when nothing really happened, passing through villages, people coming out to look at us, curious, interested, some of them not very receptive, as I've said. But where we did have receptions it was great. We had the Co-operative Guild women, some Church Guild women, Labour Party women and Communist Party women. They had made up reception committees for us and it was lovely. Sometimes they brought in home-baking and they got us bedded down in halls, etc., for the night. That was when things were going well. In one of the places, they had anticipated we wouldn't be very well fed the next day because they knew the area through which we were going. And they made great big bowls of hard-boiled eggs. We all had to stuff our pockets with them because it was quite on the cards that we wouldn't eat till the next night. And they sent in basins with Lysol – that was the old disinfectant for your feet, for anyone whose feet were really troubling them. I wish I could remember the name of that place, because we were very kindly received.

During the course of the March I was delegated as leader of the Youth contingent more or less to see that my people were all right. In the Youth section there must have been only about twelve or fourteen, not any more. The main section were the older women in the front. But I couldn't help seeing the people in front. And the woman that was right in the last line of the main contingent, I noticed one afternoon that blood was coming out over the top of her shoes. She was wearing black stockings. And some of the stocking had rubbed into the flesh of her heel. But she was still walking. She was limping but she didn't complain. I watched her for a bit and then I went up and asked her how she was feeling. She said that her feet were really bad. So I went to the front of the March and they said, 'Right, you drop out with the comrade and flag a lift.' They gave me the address of the next reception centre. So the woman – a thin woman, a Lancashire woman – and I dropped out. Two or three cars passed but being an old hiker I finally flagged down a lift and we got into the reception centre. They brought in a nurse to see to her feet.

I don't know what happened to that woman. She never rejoined the March. Whether she went home or not, I don't know. Someone later said that she had taken pneumonia. But I was never able to verify that. All I do know is that she never came back. That was one of the casualties on the March. The rest of us managed to get to the next reception area.

Some of the other outstanding things that happened to us on the March, apart from this comrade who didn't come back, were other occasions when we were hungry, where we didn't get any reception areas that would feed us. So there was an S.O.S. sent out one day to the men's March. It was marching down a different route from us. We requested that they send over their soup kitchen, which they duly did. It arrived in the afternoon. They fed us and gave us hot soup. Well, in the next day's newspaper there was a photograph of us standing at the side of the road with a big caption: 'The "Hunger" Marchers' – with 'Hunger' in inverted commas. The picture showed us with big bowls of soup – and unfortunately I was shown eating the soup in that photograph. I said to myself, 'Well, whatever is happening here the press is not on our side!' I remember resenting the fact that though we had done all these miles they hadn't bothered to come near us. And still, when they could get a sarcastic comment on the progress of the Hunger March, that's what they printed, with the photograph, without knowing anything else.

On another occasion we landed in an area where there was no reception committee at all. We decided that we would sleep out. It was a dry night. Apparently the leaders of the March had approached the local authorities for accommodation in the poorshouse, the workhouse. But they wouldn't agree to give us accommodation. So we had no place to sleep. It was decided by those who were leading the March that they would make a demonstration of it and sleep in the town centre. The authorities of course didn't want that. So we got the offer of a barn, part of the workhouse area. And they spread straw in the barn and gave us blankets. We subsequently bedded down for the night.

The lights had only been out about five minutes when all this rustling in the straw started. At first we thought some of the rest of the women were restless. Then we realised it wasn't us that were restless – it was the rats underneath us. The place was alive with rats!

So we hurriedly decamped and came outside. We gathered our things and went to the main door of the workhouse and rapped on the door. By this time it was about twelve o'clock at night. We rapped on the door and after a heated discussion between our leaders and this woman who was in charge of the workhouse they agreed to give us a bed.

That was the best bed we had on the whole March. We had a bed each in a long ward, clean, white sheets and a decent wash. We thought this was great because we really got stretched out and felt clean, really clean.

But we weren't so happy the next morning. We got the usual porridge and bread and tea. But what we were very unhappy about was that we had to step over these young women scrubbing floors. It was a Dickensian atmosphere: the strictness of everything, the smell of disinfectant, and these young women scrubbing the stone floors on their knees with big scrubbers and big cloths. These were the inmates of the workhouse. We didn't see any of them other than these young women that we had to pass to get out again. That was another bad experience that, well, helped to confirm us in what we were doing, and in our belief that there were a lot of people in Britain who needed help. And there was a lot of poverty in Britain. As far as I was concerned I felt justified in what I was doing after I saw these people in the workhouse. I wish I could remember which one it was but again I didn't take notes. But my memory of that is very clear. It was somewhere in the Midlands, between Derby and London.

We had walking sticks. They were very useful at times. You could lean on them when you were standing. We all had them. We were given them when we started out. I quite enjoyed having my stick because when you stopped and someone was addressing meetings you could lean on your stick while you were listening yourself. I've never had a stick since but I had one then. We didn't normally carry a stick when we were hiking. When we were doing hill-walking and that, sticks aren't so handy. I was never conscious that sticks were given to us on the Hunger March for any reason other than to help us with the walk. I've never heard the suggestion that there could be any other reason. We thought they were good to have but there was absolutely no other implication than that we were doing a walk from Derby to London.

We had no collisions whatsoever with the police or Blackshirts or anybody else *en route*. It was very peaceful. We were never in any trouble at any time. We never saw the police until we got to Hyde Park. The collisions that took place there I didn't see. They were in another part of the Park. As far as the women's contingent was concerned, we never had any problems at all either with onlookers, the police, or anything else. We walked from Derby to London without any trouble.

There were drop-outs on the way but we weren't aware, those of us taking part in the March, what the drop-outs were for. I knew about this lady who dropped out. I knew that her feet were in a bad way. But we were never told why she dropped out, where she went or what happened to her. And we didn't ask. We did hear when we got to Shoreditch in London that one of the other women had taken pneumonia and eventually had died. But I was never able to verify that. And then again I didn't ask.

The numbers did decrease slightly. But then there were always runners going ahead to set up reception committees. Some of the leaders were going ahead at different times. And as I said I had to drop out to take this lady to the next reception area because her feet were in such a bad state. When the numbers became slightly depleted we took it for granted, as was the case, that some of them had gone on to London, some of them had gone on to the next village or the next town, to arrange reception and food for us. But as for dropping out for any other reason, I wasn't aware of it.

Strangely enough, I never asked how many in the Youth section of the March would be politically active. We never exchanged this information. I think later on I found that some of them were members of the Communist Party. The leaders of the March, I think, were members of the Communist Party. There was quite a Communist element there. As a matter of fact, once some of them realised that I was a member of the I.L.P. Guild of Youth there was a bit of resentment. At some of the stops members of the I.L.P. met me and gave me their paper, the *New Leader*, to sell. I never liked to do it but I was supposed to sell this to anyone who came to the meetings. We had meetings, very frequent meetings, along the roadside. If we saw a crowd gathering to watch us somebody would get up and say a few words. Then you had to try and sell your paper. And they didnae like that, because I was selling the *New Leader* and they were selling the *Daily Worker*! And that created a bit of – well, they would rather I had been with the majority which seemed to be those selling the *Daily Worker*.

In the Youth contingent there were one or two of them had no political affiliations whatsoever. Like myself they were interested. The main reason they were there was because they resented the imposition of poverty and unemployment and hunger on the people. They had this feeling of resentment. And this Movement had reached out and said, 'Do you want to do something about it?' And I think there must have been quite a few of them. I knew of about three or four who had no political affiliation. And of course I didn't regard myself as being very politically affiliated either, because I didn't really take an active part in the Independent Labour Party Guild of Youth. There was a social part and we had education classes, things like that. I liked that. But we didn't have any real depth of political understanding at all. And quite a few of the young women on the March were the same as myself.

At one town we marched into there was a reception committee composed of Co-operative Women's Guilds, some Labour Party and some of the Labour movement. And they laid on a reception for us. But first of all they had assembled a crowd around the cross in the middle of their town. I don't remember which town it was but I very clearly remember the event. There was quite a crowd. The town square was packed. We marched in. We gathered round the foot of this statue and the leaders of the March climbed up and they were starting to address the crowd when one of the women who was in the leadership came over and said to me, 'Emily, you'll speak.' Well, I had never spoken at a public meeting in my life. I looked at these masses of people that were there and said, 'Oh, I can't speak. What do you want me to say.' She said, 'Well, why are you here?' Ah says, 'Well, I know why I'm here.' She says, 'Well, just you go up there and tell them.' I went up. I was very nervous. And when I saw all the faces I was more nervous. But I did manage to speak and to explain why I had joined the Hunger March. And that was my introduction to public speaking. The few words that I had to say must have gone off all right. It was, I thought, very well received, I think mainly because I was so young. And I think the wee story that I had to tell them went down quite well. A couple of the younger women in my contingent stood by at each side, and I think the general picture created quite a lot of sympathy in the audience that night. I know I was terribly nervous, I was shaking. But I thought, and I was told, that I had gone off very well.

On the March we had banners, but we didn't sing and we didn't march in step. I remember there were two main banners: SCOTTISH WOMEN'S CONTINGENT MARCHING TO LONDON, and WOMEN MARCHING TO LONDON AGAINST THE MEANS

TEST AND UNEMPLOYMENT. My memories were there was a youth banner but I can't recall what happened to it or whether it was used beyond the middle of the March. We didn't march in step. On the country roads between villages we would sort of straggle about, but immediately we saw anything coming into view, whether it was a small village or a small town, we would line up and straighten up and get into proper lines and walk.

We were never abused in any way by onlookers. Sometimes some would clap and shout, 'Good luck!' and that sort of thing. But there was never any exuberance on the road and I was never conscious of any hostility anywhere on the road we went. The only hostility we got was at that workhouse where we met that woman who wouldn't give us a bed! But there was no hostility from the people. There was a sort of silence when we would come through these wee villages. They would come out and look at us as if they were wondering what this was all about. But that was it.

My memory is that it was well organised and rather sober and serious. That was my recollection of the actual walking itself. Maybe of course because we were tired and some of us were sore, maybe we didn't feel like singing. It wasn't just like going on a demonstration where you were walking for a couple of hours. We were walking for days and it was tiring. If the men sang, well, that was great but maybe they were better fed than we were!

There was quite a strict discipline kept. At nights when we came to the reception areas we had to keep together. You didn't go out and wander away. We all stayed together all the time. I don't think I left the company of the women Marchers from the day I left Glasgow till the day I left them again in London – never. There was no drinking whatsoever. I didn't drink at all of course. I never saw anyone having a drink. I never saw anyone going into a pub. There was no drink whatsoever, none. And there was strict discipline in so far as we had to keep together all the time.

The young people on the March got to know each other pretty well. We used to talk to one another and the older women would come and talk to us and give us sort of slightly educational facts about the Means Test and about the March, that this was something that we were doing that the Labour movement should be doing. There was a slight tendency to political talking. Naturally, of course: we were there for a political reason. But there was no personal talks. But strict, you know. For instance, we were stopped singing one night because it was the wrong type of song – *Land of Hope and Glory*! And they stopped it. Somebody started to sing it and just because it was a good tune we joined in, and the woman came over and she said, 'Just stop that. We don't want that.'

And the other time was when one of the girls went out in the morning with her bare legs and she was told to go back and put her stockings on. They didn't want bare legs on the March. Aye, there was quite a strict discipline on the March. It was quite a serious business. Naturally we young people would laugh and joke sometimes. But there was no hilarity, no drinking, no wandering away from where we were. We kept together all the time.

We didn't send out collectors that I was aware of. There would be collectors up at the front but they were just some of the women that would take something and collect. And some of us sold Labour papers. But I was never asked to collect and none of the Youth contingent was ever asked. I did see one or two collectors on the side of the road. Where we did get collectors was where we went into reception areas where we were getting a good reception. We would find collectors who were in sympathy with the Hunger Marchers would circulate and get money. But we didn't do it ourselves, not very much, maybe one or two, but not very much.

We did get word from home. I expect the other women would be in the same position as me, would be able to get letters from home. The N.U.W.M. seemed to be able to co-ordinate where we would be and mail was sent on to these forwarding points on the March. I was able to send postcards, which I didn't do very much. But I was able to get word from home from my husband. He was able to contact the N.U.W.M. and I did receive a couple of letters from him while I was on the March. Oh, that was very good for morale! And I once got a parcel with chocolates in it. And that was great, you know. We were really delighted with that. He had sent on some chocolates as a wee sort of gesture that he liked what was happening.

Well, we finally got near London and we were received in Shoreditch Baths. That was our reception area. It was lovely. They had nurses there with stuff for our feet. They had food. They had decent beds for us. That was great. Most of us were very tired by this time. It was the middle to the end of our second week on the road. And we were due to be in Hyde Park the next day.

My memories there are very confused because there was such a lot of activity. There were loads of people going about the place. By this time the men Marchers had arrived, not at our place but another place. There was to-ing and fro-ing between the leaderships of both. We'd done what we thought was our job, and that was it, you know. For the other women who were with me felt that this was our job. We'd done it. We wanted to do the demonstration in Hyde Park and that was our job finished. So that's what we did. We marched along to Hyde Park.

There were various speakers. I think Jimmy Maxton was one. But there were no loudspeakers, it was sort of loudhailers they used. So that you could move about from one area to another and listen to one speaker and to another.

But as I say, by this time most of the young women I was with were tired. So we got back to the reception area and asked if anyone wanted to go home. Some wanted to stay on. I think some sort of discussion was going to take place about the March, etc. But I didn't stay on. I went home that night. I had a ticket, a 26/- ticket, from Euston to Glasgow, bought by the committee in London, which I duly took. We called the train the Starlight Special. And that was the end of the Hunger March for me.

I didn't take part in any other Hunger March after that 1934 one, because in 1935 my first daughter was born. So that put paid to any further activity. I don't know if I would have participated in later years, because there was an awful lot of energy expended on it. I sometimes thought in the places that we went through, especially the small English villages, that it was a curiosity rather than a political statement we were making. And I sometimes in later years have thought we might have been better going around Scotland, rather than marching through England.

That was my personal view at the time, that I wondered what the people really thought as we went through. It maybe made some people think, because at that time England was that bit more prosperous. That's where the Scots went to look for work – as my husband and I did after the March. We went to England and that's where my husband got his first job. So that England seemed that bit better off, more prosperous than I had been used to seeing in Clydebank.

I think that the overall statement of the Marches, of the fact that this body of people were prepared to go to these lengths to draw attention to their plight, was a good thing. But I don't know about repeated Marches, whether they had outlived their usefulness in the later years.

My feelings about the March were that it was a part of a protest movement. I didn't see it as a highlight at the time. I realise now with hindsight that it was a sort of highlight, that the Hunger Marches were a sort of watershed in the Unemployed Movement. But at that time for me it seemed part of this big protest that was going on about the unemployment and the poverty and the disadvantages, etc., that were occurring to working-class families not only in job opportunities but in education and dreams of a future. Because like the young people of today we dreamt of a future too. I think maybe their dreams are a bit more high flown. Our dreams were of a job, a secure job. And we didn't see that.

Personally, it launched me into what was to be a big part of my life and that was political activity. I think the Hunger March turned me from just someone who was interested in everyday affairs to someone who became very interested politically. And I remained interested politically and still am, although naturally when you're young you've got different ideas. I thought the revolution was round the corner. I thought that we hadn't far to go and got a bit impatient sometimes with those who had a bit more know-how about politics. But I thought we should be able to find a quicker road. But that's natural for young people, isn't it? Today I'm a wee bit more patient. But I think the Hunger March changed the direction in which I was going. It changed me from being a person with just a passive interest in politics to having a deep interest in politics. It was a major experience for me. It was the biggest thing I had ever done till then. It sort of pointed a road down which I went in later years. It made me put my energy into politics, into areas that I thought would change the conditions, because I still feel resentful today about the conditions and I've retained that feeling that I took on the Hunger March with me. I have retained it till now.

Well, as I say, my first daughter was born in 1935 and in 1936 my husband got his first job – in England, near London, part-time work spot-welding. So the three of us went down there and we lived at Ilford. It was just at the time of the beginning of the Spanish Civil War. I remember going to a big meeting about the War and I began to get very involved. Somebody suggested I might like to join the Labour Party down there but it was not terribly active at Ilford. So instead in 1938 I joined the Communist Party. Although I'm not very politically active now I still retain a deep interest in politics. I just cannae help being interested in world affairs. They've always fascinated me, even today.

Mary Johnston

When we got to London there were five of us were in 10 Downing Street.
Oh, we didnae see the prime minister, Ramsay MacDonald – it was his
daughter Ishbel.[193] We were shown up the stair into a big room and we just
talked to her. Oh, very friendly, offered us tea. But funnily enough, on a
point of honour, we refused it. That was the 1934 Women's March to
London.

I became the treasurer on the March. I don't know how it happened.
I don't remember volunteering. Of course I had been doing a wee bit of
work for Harry McShane on and off in the office of the National Unemployed Workers' Movement in Glasgow. It was somewhere on George
Street or near George Street, fairly near the City Chambers. But I cannae
remember the name of the street.[194]

I was very active in the N.U.W.M, Springburn branch, in Glasgow.
That was when I was unemployed, in 1933–34. Everybody I knew was in
the N.U.W.M. Actually, I think I was on the committee. We used to have
meetings once a week and there must have been about a hundred folk there.
We filled a Co-operative hall, one of their halls, but quite a good size. Peter
Kerrigan – he lived in Springburn at that time – used to be sometimes at the
meeting. But there were two brothers – Barlow, their name was, they are
both dead – they were very active. Bob Barlow was actually the secretary of
the Communist Party branch in Springburn but he was active in the
N.U.W.M. as well.

There was a kind of dry curling stones club in Springburn and we used
to get the use of their wee room and interviewed people who needed advice
about unemployment. I wasn't the only woman who attended the
N.U.W.M. meetings, though women were very much in the minority.
There would maybe be about a dozen women out of the hundred who
attended the meetings.

Most of the N.U.W.M. members who came to the meetings were
probably non-political, not members of a political party. But those who
were political were mainly in the Communist Party. I can't recall, for
instance, anybody who was in the I.L.P. It's funny, the other parties didn't
seem to exist for me. I don't even know if there was much of a Labour Party
in Springburn. Maybe that shows a sort of weakness right enough – a
weakness in my knowledge about it. I don't honestly think the Labour Party
did much in that line.

We used to have speakers up usually, the likes of Peter Kerrigan and
Harry McShane. Harry McShane was really the leader of the N.U.W.M. in
Glasgow and Scotland. The speakers, I would say, were usually members of
the Communist Party. It was rather unusual for somebody who wasn't a
Communist to be addressing the meeting, though I don't really remember
properly. But that's my impression. Aitken Ferguson addressed the meet-
ings. He actually was from Maryhill, but he did address our meetings. And
George Middleton and Bob McLennan.[195]

When I helped Harry McShane in the N.U.W.M. office in Glasgow
there were no full-time workers there, just Harry. I got on quite well with
him. He was a good organiser and an able leader. Well, I don't suppose you
would try and think critically. You know, you just accepted what they were
and that was it. I didn't go in to help Harry on any sort of regular basis, just
when I could. The sort of things I did was typing. I think it must have been
just that. I don't remember any other voluntary workers there in the office.
Maybe there would be people there at nights sometimes. It was just a single-
room office, as far as I can remember. I think the Communist Party had a
room in that building. That's all very vague.

I met Wal Hannington too at that time, of course. I thought he was
marvellous. I met him when I was working at the N.U.W.M. office. I didn't
meet him on the March, just in the office. He really was one of the best, I
think, every way. He was an impressive sort of person that I liked.

Well, as I say, that was around the time I was unemployed in 1933-34.
What happened was I had left the job I had had for seven years since I left
school. It was a painter's and decorator's office, in Springburn Road, a
miserable wee job. Nowadays you wouldn't dream of going into an office
like that. I worked nine to five, and nine to twelve on a Saturday. The wages
when I first started I think was about nine or ten bob. You'd only get a
fortnight's holidays a year, and of course you got Christmas and New Year.

Well, what happened was I would ask for a rise. I think by that time
I was only getting twenty-five bob. So I asked for a rise. I was turned down.
So I just left. I would be about twenty-two then. I just decided that I had had
enough. But the boss really was awful mean because I really did an awful lot
of work. I ran that place. There was only one in it apart from him, the
employer. And of course I was unemployed then. I left of course in the hope
I'd find something else. I suppose I did try but I don't remember much
about the effort of trying. My parents weren't shocked that I had left the job.
In fact, they supported me. They knew I wasn't getting anywhere in that
direction. But then it was difficult to get a job, and that was when I joined
the National Unemployed Workers' Movement. Of course I was already in
the Young Communist League.

Well, it really was the natural thing for me to become interested in
political matters because my father and my mother and my brother and my
sister were all in the Communist Party. My sister had joined the Y.C.L. of
course, and then the Party. So I actually joined the Y.C.L. when I was about
seventeen or eighteen. That was in 1928 or '29. I was in the Y.C.L. for quite

a while. My father was a founder member of the Communist Party as far as Glasgow or Scotland is concerned. My mother was a member but not so active as my father. My brother – he was four years older than me – joined the Party somewhere in the 1920s. My sister, who was three years older than me, had joined the Y.C.L. about the same age as I did, seventeen or eighteen. I was in the Y.C.L. when I went on the Hunger March

It was a very happy time in the Y.C.L. It was Maryhill we used to go to. There was a hall there. It was right in Maryhill Road. We used to go and hold meetings, street meetings. And there was lots of activity, selling papers, and a good social life, walking and all that sort of thing, rambling. Actually, I was a very keen cyclist. My brother worked in the Post Office and he was a member of a wee cycling club, which they called the Vikings. I joined it as well – I was only about seventeen – and my pal at that time, we both joined. We did a bit of racing at one time. We did some wonderful runs, right round the three lochs, we called it: Loch Lomond, Loch Long, and Loch Fyne. We went up by Rest-and-be-Thankful, round there. Oh, I was very fit. Oh, it was great. I used to have one of these wee registers you put on your hub and I used to keep a note of it in a notebook. Aye, I was a very keen cyclist.

The cycling club wasn't a Y.C.L. club but we used to sit and have a lot of political discussions. We had one young chap in the Vikings – in fact he was my friend's boyfriend, although she gave him up because he was a bit sort of temperamental – he went to Spain and he was only twenty-five when he died in the War there: Tommy Flynn. He was quite an erratic character but he had a lot of potentiality.[196] So when I went on the Hunger March in 1934 I was very fit, you know, with walking and cycling.

But in the Y.C.L. it was really very good. We used to go down to a bookshop in Cathedral Street. There was somebody we knew in the Party. He had a bookshop and we used to have meetings there. And that was where I met a girl, Anna Haddow, who became a very close friend until she died some years ago. We were great theatre-goers at that time. We used to go to all the operas and the plays – up in the gallery. I think we paid a shilling to get in.

We went to classes too. That's another thing – we were all Esperantists. That was outside the Y.C.L. But on the other hand you could say a lot of them were political. Some of the teachers were also Party members. It was the Esperanto Society that actually ran the classes.

And then I should say we were members of the Socialist Sunday School when we were young. And there used to be a lot of rambles. I can remember being perched up on my father's shoulder, walking along the Forth and Clyde Canal, out at Bishopbriggs. Great rambles we used to have. I was brought up completely to enjoy and appreciate the open air. We never went to church. I was never christened. My father had originally been a Protestant but became an atheist.

My father was a committed socialist all his adult life. He had actually come from Ireland – Larne – at the age of thirteen, just himself. He was born in 1885, so that must have been about 1898 he came to Glasgow in order to get work. He had practically no education. I think like a lot of others he was a message boy, and then he got into a factory and became a moulder, which was a very hard job. My father was actually quite a small person but quite strong. So he worked as a moulder all his life. He had a period of unemployment in the 1920s. I remember at that time I think he was getting a shilling for each of his children. He was unemployed for quite a while.

My father was a keen reader, and my mother, too. He went to night school when he came here to Glasgow. I don't really know all the details. He would sit at home and read aloud to us. We used to sit round the fire. He remained a keen reader all his days. He became political quite young. Long before I was born in 1911 he was a socialist. There was a man that he worked beside – I presume he was probably a moulder as well – an Irishman, a great big man with fiery red hair. I remember his name, Paddy Fitzpatrick. And it was him that really got my father interested. Paddy Fitzpatrick was a very determined man indeed.

So my father was in the Social Democratic Federation. But then he joined the Communist Party when it was first formed in Glasgow. And he was always a very active person. And as I said he was a founder member of the Communist Party, as far as Scotland or Glasgow is concerned. But they didnae class him as a foundation member in London. But he was active till the day that he more or less wasnae able. That was in his seventies.

He was married very young. My mother was a Glasgow woman. She worked as a servant in domestic service and she was only turned nineteen when she got married. My daddy had just turned twenty. So I had an older brother and two older sisters. But my elder sister died when she was only thirteen. It was appendicitis.

I went to Albert Street school in Springburn. It was really an old, antique, place. It was in three bits. The junior school was an old church. And then you crossed a bit of pavement in which was the senior part of the school. And you went past that to another old church. That was our school up until I was twelve, when you finished that part of your education. Then you moved into this great big corrugated-iron building that was what we called the Higher Grade. I went into the Higher Grade when I was twelve and stayed on the three years. Oh, I liked school. My sister and I were both very good at school. We both got the Qualy prize. She was three years older than me. We were keen readers, all our lives. We joined the library when we were five. And we used to run down this steep hill, along Springburn Road, we were in such a hurry to get to the library. As I say, my father was a great reader and my mother, too.

I was just fifteen and a month when I left school. That was immediately after the 1926 General Strike. Oh, I remember the Springburn Road, when the strikers were pushing over tramcars, and getting hold of the fellows who were driving the cars, who were mainly middle-class students. We lived in just an ordinary tenement. But at the foot of our street was about four houses. They were not quite the same: they had gardens. We did not have a garden. And there must have been a scab went to his work during the Strike, 'cause all the kids in the street went down, waiting for the police black Maria, I think it was, that used to pick up the scabs. They were escorted to their work by the police in black Marias. And we used to shout and bawl at them. I think there was only one man. But, oh, they must have had about a hundred kids in that street. There was about thirty up our stair alone.

Well, from 1933 I was unemployed for over a year. It was during that time I was on the Hunger March. That was '34. As I say, I was a member of the N.U.W.M. and I was a very active member. I suppose you realised that there were Hunger Marches taking place and you took it as a fact of life. When I heard about the '34 one I didn't need to think about it, oh, no. It was great. I was going and that was it. My parents supported me in that decision.

I remember discussions about clothes and that sort of thing before we went. And I think there must have been a lot of men went from Springburn. We didn't leave at the same time, it must have been a fortnight or so after they left. There was just myself and two other women from Springburn. One was McFarlane – Isa, I think her first name was . She got married to Bob McLellan later – she was only home from the March a week or two. I don't honestly remember the name of the other woman who went on the March. She was about my own age and height. I don't think she or Isa McFarlane were active in the N.U.W.M., though they may have been members.

I honestly don't remember if there was a send-off for us from Springburn. When the men left they had got a marvellous send-off. I don't know how many men left from Springburn but it must have been a good lot. Anyway, we went by bus from Glasgow down to Derby. I think there was a full busload of women. Of course they wouldnae just be from Glasgow, it would be all Scotland. There would maybe be about thirty to forty.

I was pretty well-prepared because I was a cyclist, so of course I was used to wearing trousers. I had decent shoes – I took two pairs of shoes with me, which was something I don't think the other people had at all. I had proper clothing – a change of underwear, woollen jerseys, a jacket and a raincoat, and a wee knitted woollen cap to keep my head warm. And I had a proper sleeping-bag too, because we did a bit of camping and youth hostelling from being cyclists.

I never had any trouble with my feet. I had good shoes and I'd prepared myself for the March: I was doing quite a bit of walking, apart from my cycling. And I think I was rubbing some sort of liquid, a spirit of some kind, on my feet to harden them. So I was deliberately training for the March before I went on it. Oh, I was physically fit, no problem.

I don't remember what sort of food we ate on the March but, oh, there must have been plenty of it. I think we were well looked after. There didnae seem to be any problem about food at all. My recollection is that we had plenty to eat. I think we were awful well treated. I remember we were staying in a workhouse one night, but where it was I don't really know. The

March wasn't the first time I'd be away from home: we went for holidays and we did a lot of Youth Hostelling. My brother was one of the first to join the Youth Hostels when they started so I was a member fairly young as well.

I don't think I took a walking stick on the March but I think some of the other women would have sticks. The sticks were just for walking, they definitely weren't intended to defend the women – no question. Some of the women were really in a terrible state with their feet, and we used actually to help them up hills and that sort of thing. Maybe it was with a walking stick that we pulled them along. I can remember that. Oh, their feet were terrible. I think there were a few sent home that they couldnae continue. Their feet were too bad, quite shocking. Quite a lot of them suffered quite badly from sore feet, because we used to see them getting bathed at night and bandages or whatever. I don't remember any of the women from Glasgow being sent home. But there was quite a few women had to go home – maybe not just bad feet but physically it was too much for them, because it was quite a trip from Derby to London. We walked maybe about eight miles each day. Eight miles for people who hadnae walked much before was pretty good. And then we would be stopping here and there for meetings, etc.

We stopped and had meetings when we came to villages and towns. And actually I did quite a lot of speaking on the March. And I don't know how that happened either. I'm very vague about it. I seemed to be doing quite a lot of it. And as I say, I became the treasurer on the March. I don't know how I did. I don't remember volunteering. I don't know how it was decided. And I don't honestly remember an awful lot about being treasurer, really. I suppose we had collecting tins and must have collected and must have counted it up! I remember adding up the money at night. The money could have went towards sending folk home.

There were about thirty women on the March from Scotland, possibly there would be about a hundred altogether. I have a vision of it, you know, stretching back quite a bit. Some of the women, me being young at the time, I would think were quite old. Some of them must have been in their forties and fifties, maybe nothing much older than that. But that seemed quite old to me. I think there was only about five or six of us in the Youth contingent. There was two girls much the same as myself from Sheffield. We picked them up at Derby. And there was a woman from London. Her husband had brought her up. She was quite middle class, a nice person. And there was Emily Swankie. She was only eighteen at the time. I don't remember Emily being asked to be the leader of the Youth contingent. I never knew there was such a thing as a leader. In fact, I think that was quite unusual. I was friendly with everybody but I didn't make any particular new friend. The wee group I was in were a very lively crowd. I think us being young, we were pretty full of beans. I think we did quite a good job in helping other people's morale.

The leaders of the March were Maud Brown – she was actually the overall leader – and there was a woman from Fife who was a councillor,

Maria Stewart. She was actually the Scottish leader. She was a very good person. I got to know Maud Brown quite well. You accepted her, you know, as one of the sort of Party people that was there to really give a lead and solve a few problems and that sort of thing. I would say she was a competent person. She was a fairly tall, thin woman with glasses, quite friendly and approachable.

I think Maud Brown and Maria Stewart were both in the Communist Party. I wouldnae class myself as a sort of third leader, as treasurer. But I think the women on the March weren't really mostly in the Communist Party. Maybe between a quarter and a third of them were.

We never saw any of the men on the March. We never had any contact with them. I don't suppose we ever thought of questioning that. I don't recollect any discussion on the point at all. And of course it would be quite a good thing, really, if the men were using a separate route. It would touch all sorts of different places.

When we got to London, oh, there was a lot of excitement. We were accommodated in a baths somewhere in London. It was the first time I had been in London actually, so of course I didnae really know anything about it. I remember going in swimming in the pool in the baths. But we used to be always out in some sort of March or other, or meetings. I think it would probably be about a week we were in London.

Well, as I say, when we got to London there were five of us, I think, were in 10 Downing Street. Oh, we didnae see the prime minister, Ramsay MacDonald – it was his daughter Ishbel. We were shown up the stair into a big room and we just talked to her. Oh, very friendly, offered us tea. But funnily enough, on a point of honour, we refused it. Well, it wasnae discussed but we all seemed to say, 'No, we wouldnae have tea.' I don't even know if it was that we felt it would be weakening our position if we accepted tea. Maybe it was just pride or something. There was no discussion about it.

I think we actually told her our own particular story, you know, of being unemployed and of how bad it was and all the rest of it. Each of us spoke in turn about our personal circumstances. We asked her to just try and have some influence with her father. I think she was quite sympathetic. I don't think she really had much influence on her father and his policy. Oh, it wasn't a heated discussion. I wouldnae even say it was discussion in that sense. I think we just talked about how serious a thing it was to be unemployed. I had a cutting – I suppose it was in the *Daily Worker* at that time – that shows us outside Number 10. I think we were inside there for quite a while, at least an hour. I think probably Ishbel MacDonald was quite a nice person. She was just there to fulfil a hostess role or whatever because his wife was dead. But we didn't see Ramsay MacDonald himself or any other Cabinet minister – just Ishbel, and then we were ushered out.[197]

I remember after we came back to Glasgow there was a meeting in the City Hall and I was speaking at it, along with some of the rest of them. And it was packed – that's when you could fill the City Hall. It was just telling them about our experiences on the Hunger March.

I didn't go on any other Hunger March. My father knew some of the men that worked in the baths at Springburn and the result was I got a summer job in it. They took on somebody during the summer when there was a lot of kids. You were supposed to be a bath attendant but really and truly you were a right skivvy. I only got the job for the summer – it must have been '35 – and then I think I was laid off. But then I actually got in as permanent. I don't know how I stuck it! There were piles and piles of towels. You had to drag the big basket of towels up a stair. You had to put them into a great big washing-machine. And then you had to drag them out dripping wet into a bogie. You had to put them into a spin-dryer. Then you had to take them down, shake them and fold them and hang them up and dry them. It was heavy work. It just shows you how bad the situation was. That was just one of your duties. You had shift work. One week you were early and one week you were late. So in the late week, after the washhouse was closed, you had work to do in that.

In 1936 or early '37 I went to work in London. By this time I had met my future husband. He belonged to Fife, Newburgh-on-Tay. He was a bricklayer and he was going down to London to work. So I thought I would go down to London as well. And I actually got a job there to work in somebody's house. I don't know why I did it because I had never worked in anybody's house in my life. We got married in 1937. But my husband was killed in the War in the Far East in 1945. I've been a widow since then. Oh, my husband had a great future. He was working for the Communist Party before he got called up. He was very capable. I've got a son, just one son.

Looking back on the Hunger March, it was a very important experience in my life. I don't see it as the high point of my life. But I would say it was one of the really good things that I enjoyed. Well, I probably enjoyed the walking, that was one thing. And then I must have enjoyed the feeling that you were doing something. And I enjoyed the companionship too. It was something worthwhile. Well, the whole idea that all these millions of folk were unemployed, couldnae get a job. And of course we were concerned about the poverty.

Thomas Davidson

I was born in Swanston Street in Bridgeton, Glasgow. I lived there tae I was about fourteen and then we went from there to what they called the wooden houses, in Buddon Street. They were huts they built tae keep us alive then – temporary accommodation built by the town council. And when they were finished we went to a house called Lord Newlands' House, that was opposite Celtic Park. That was jist after I had left school.

Oh, I had plenty o' brothers and sisters: five brothers and three sisters. I was the third youngest. I was born in July 1912. We lived in a room and kitchen – nine o' us and my father and mother. Even when I was growing up all my brothers and sisters were still at home. At that stage there was nobody married at all. As far as I was concerned the nicest o' the family was my oldest brother, Robert. He was on the railway, and he left there and went into the army, the H.L.I. Well, he volunteered and went right through the First War. He was never right efter that: he was shell-shocked. I think it was that, aye, he was very bad. He died when he was seventy-odds.

My father belonged to Glasgow. He was an ironmoulder. He was very active in the union – I believe it was the Associated Iron Moulders of Scotland. He was an I.L.P.-er. He led the marchers to the schools protesting against the rents. They marched up and doon the streets when they were goin' tae the school wi' torches. Ye didnae hae lights then, it wis torches. I remember my old man very well. He was quite active. He was with Jimmy Maxton a lot, oh, they were very, very close. He used to talk to me all about the political men. He had been politically active since he was a young man.

My grandfather, my father's father, was frae Belfast. He finished up a Bible thumper in Bridgeton. He used tae walk along the streets singin' hymns. And that's the kind o' man he wis. But my father wasnae a religious man. There could have been a bit o' conflict between him and his father, there could have been. It's a funny thing about my father. His brother was an organist in the church, but in Rutherglen. And my father used to play an organ like him, and yet he turned away frae it a'. I don't know why. I never got any details about that.

I went tae a church in Dalmarnock Road, because the wee boys went to that. Well, in actual fact I was non-religious, I never felt religious. I used tae sit in the back seat and I was listenin' to the minister and I would say, 'What is he talkin' aboot?' I mean, that is the way I spoke, quite honest. I used to say, 'What do they mean? What the hell are they talkin' about? If

249

they listened to what I've seen they would understand different.' It was the life, the bad life that we all had. I was disgruntled.

I cannae remember noo where my mother come from. She was ninety-six when she died. Her name was McNealy. But, oh, it was horrible for my mother, the conditions we lived in. Eleven o' us in a room and kitchen, oh, heavens we were like a block in a box. The six boys, we slept together in the one bed, and the girls had a curtain across for them in the same room. That was how I grew up. We had an ootside toilet, but we even had an inside toilet, a bed-pan in our house, because ye couldnae get tae the toilet in time. Ye'd tae rush. Sometimes we had tae wait tae get outside. Ye jist couldnae get movin' anywhere. It was an ootside toilet in the stair, but ye still had an inside one for yersel' – the commode, they ca'd it, the commode. It was hellish during these conditions, oh, horrible.

When I went out I was always fightin' wi somebody. But it wisnae jist ma nature. I think it was the conditions that made me like that. I felt terribly depressed in a lot o' ways. If I had been playin' as an ordinary lad outside I would have been different. If I had had a different place tae stay it would ha' made me different. But I couldnae get anywhere. I was jist runnin' aboot and fightin'. Ye'd see somebody over a dyke that would want tae fight me! I would go and fight them. And there were a lot o' gangsters there. One lot was called the Redskins. They were jist round the corner frae us. 'Oh, don't go near them. That's the Ridskins roond there.' The Billy Boys, the Norman Conqs, and there were a lot o' Orangemen tae. They were all bad. It was terrible.

Ye left school of course when ye were fourteen. I didnae want to stay on. I didnae give myself the idea that I had any knowledge at all. I felt that I wis a dunce. Teachers used tae send me wee messages or hae me cleanin' up the classroom. and I was back wi' ma writin' and various things. When I was writin' my name I used tae write 'Thomas Dictation' instead o' Thomas Davidson, My brain was away. See, this was the way my brain went. I think everythin' was goin' through ma mind, everythin' about my family, everythin' about everybody. And I said, 'There's somethin' wrong wi' me here.'

When I left school I couldnae get work. The first job I could get a chance at was in a cobbler, a boot repairer's. Somebody had spoke for me, see. And I took the job but, ach, I was disgusted. I wasnae interested in the job at all. I didnae feel that there was anythin' in it for me. I was only goin' out in the motor and collectin' boots for repairs, that's a'. But I stuck it for three months. Then I left there, I jist gave it up, I chucked it and came home. And I didnae know what I was goin' to do next.

So I got a job in Tennent's Brewery, Wellpark Street – the Wellpark Brewery, it was called. I was about two years and seven month there. And after two year and seven month there I got my books for fightin'! It wis jist wi' a boy in the work. It wis a lark, jist for the boys, you know. There were nothin' bad about it. It wis jist a friendly fight. But because I was fightin' the man that looked after the place he reported me, and of coorse the two o' us got wir books.

So I said to my mother I'd like tae go abroad. She said, 'Oh, don't go abroad.' She put me off. And ah says, 'I'll need tae try the merchant navy or somethin'.' I tried a number o' things and I still couldnae get anywhere. So I was leavin' the house a lot. I left the house then came back again, I left it again and came back again. I did this two or three times in my life.

During that time I was in the Unemployed Workers' Movement. I joined them because I was unemployed. I was attendin' a lot o' meetins, ye know, I wisnae too fully versed in meetins or anythin' like that. But I went wi' some men and we chalked the streets and whitewashed the streets, tellin' people where the next meetin' wis. Well, we did this durin' the night, we did it on the nightshift. And sometimes the police used tae take wir names. That's what happened durin' these days.

It was Bridgeton branch o' the N.U.W.M. I was in. We'd a few dozen members, but I cannae remember clearly. They werenae a' active o' course. Some o' us took part in the meetins or did somethin', you know. I wisnae on the committee, I was like a group member. Among the young fellows I was a group leader. I went to meetings and went to the people that were being evicted. Somebody says, 'Where's Tom?' 'Aw,' they said, 'he's away tae an eviction, somebody's gettin' put out a house.' Well, that's the work I did. I went to the south side and I sat in a house. I think it was Maclean Street. But I sat in that house along wi' another lad. And we were the members of the Unemployed Workers' Movement, ye see. So the band was playin' in the street and we went up tae keep him frae gettin' put out the house. And the band were playin' a' the time. While we were in the house we were killin' bugs. That's how we passed our time – killing bugs. The bugs were all over the place. It was terrible.

Bridgeton branch o' the N.U.W.M. had some women members. I remember one o' them was a nurse. I remember her very well, because her daughter was at the meetins too that I went tae. Her daughter was young, but she herself was a nurse and, oh, she was quite active.

The only members o' the branch that were connected wi' the I.L.P. were in the Guild o' Youth. Well, I got in wi' them because I used tae go tae their camp up in East Kilbride. They had a kind o' school up there and I cycled there. But I can't remember members o' the N.U.W.M. branch who were in the Labour Party or the I.L.P. apart from them. I can't remember them at all. It's helluva hard to go back. Any in the N.U.W.M. that were politically active tended to be in the Communist Party, rather than the I.L.P. or the Labour Party – that's the way I see it.

I joined the Communist Party masel' about two year after I'd joined the N.U.W.M. The group o' people that were around were all that way inclined. It was how they felt, you know. Tommy Flynn was one o' them. Ye see, he was my pal. Tommy was about the same age. Tommy was a scientific-instrument maker. He wasnae unemployed all the time, jist some o' the time. And his father had a good job in the *Express* papers in Glasgow. He was a foreman there.

It was the Bridgeton branch o' the Communist Party I joined. Oh, it was a very active branch, very active. I remember once we had a place they called The Coffin and it was in the Gallowgate. The Coffin was a hall shaped like a coffin and you'd to go up the stair to it. And they asked me to go and be like a doorman, along wi' another chap. We took part in meetins – jist watchin' the door a' the time. Men would come to the door and they would be mad and threatenin' ye wi' gettin' your throat cut! That wis the kind o' language – they were kind o' rough. They werenae Orangemen, they were nothin' at a', they were no religion. They were jist bad, jist bad in theirsels, that's what, jist wantin' tae carry on.

I cannae remember who wis the chairman or the secretary o' the branch but there would be maybe a couple o' dozen members. Ye see, it wis jist like a branch union meetin': you could get jist two or three men in but there could be a lot o' members, quite a lot o' members. But they didnae a' come.

I remember in those times I went tae the berry pickin' wi' Tommy Flynn in Perthshire, Blairgowrie. That's when I met the wife there. She was in domestic service at that time and went there for a workin' holiday. She went there for about seventeen years a'thegither. We went tae the berry pickin' jist for the season, that's a'. But there were strikes there and I led a strike. It was for more money. We were getting a farthing a pail, a farthing a pail. The pail held about twelve pounds, a big pail. Ye see, I used to go up there tae the place where they weighed it and jist shouted. So I got them a'thegither.

Well, I learned about the Hunger March because I was in the N.U.W.M. at the time. I mean, I learned about it jist wi' goin' about wi' them about the streets. We were a' grumblin' a bit. My home life was terrible. I mean, now I can talk about it because I'm old, but I can see that I was so active and I was very serious-minded that everything that happened in my home I noticed. Now can you understand that? Every little thing I noticed. Oh, it was terrible in every way, terrible, it was awful. So I was always agitated about that. I could see a connection between things at home and things in the outside world. And goin' on the Hunger March was a lot to do wi' Tommy Flynn too. I went about wi' Tommy Flynn a lot.

They told us wi' leaflets there were a Hunger March. But as soon as I seen it, 'Oh,' I says, 'this is it, I'm gaun tae do this.' So my mother says, 'Oh, please yersel' what you do.' She started grumblin' aboot it. I says, 'Eh, well, ah'm goin' anyway.' I said, 'Give me that old haversack.' And I put the haversack on and just made off. That would be the 1934 March.

We set off from Glasgow. My wife remembers she got socks made for me by a woman in Coatbridge. She knitted them specially for me to go on the Hunger March. The wife and I werenae married at that time. This woman was a neighbour o' hers and she knitted socks and wee hats. So I got two or three pairs o' socks and jerseys and wee hats. I was a'right that way. I dinnae remember whether I had a raincoat or anythin', but the wife remembers I had an oilskin waterproof. And heavy boots, aye, we had walking boots, jist the one pair.

I had the walking stick. We jist took a stick because we thought it would jist help us on the road, jist the walkin'. We never thought about violence or anything like that, although we could have thought about that later. But ye didnae think about that then. Ye jist took it for walking, that was all. And I only remember once – and it wasn't through me, it was through the police – when we marched through Birmingham. The policeman came intae the ranks and he came towards me! He got my shoulder. I thought he was goin' to arrest me. He kept pullin' me. A young lad next door to me jist put his stick up and hit him on the chin. Well, he was quite right to do that, he was quite right. The policeman was only interferin' wi' the March. We werenae doin' anything wrong.

Every place we went tae Harry McShane had arranged before we went there. They had arranged for sleeping places, a wee hall o' some kind or a school, anything. As far as I remember, there were twenty left on the March from Bridgeton. Tommy Flynn wasnae on the March at a' because he wasn't unemployed. I cannae remember the name o' our Bridgeton group leader. He was a wee fellow, smaller than me, very small. He led the March along wi' us. All o' us were members o' the N.U.W.M. When we set off from Glasgow, oh, they were marching on the side o' the road to give us a send-off. Oh, there was a mass of people there. When we got to Kilmarnock I jist remember goin' to the Cross. There were an awfu' crowd there to welcome us.

I jist remember old Harry McShane a' the time, he was always shoutin' and bawlin' at the side o' the road, where tae go and where tae march tae and where we were goin' next. I remember that. I cannae remember what hall we went intae. I only remember as we went along the road we were well fed. The people were plying us wi' a lot o' food. And the Hunger Marchers had a cook, a man frae Rutherglen, ex-Scottish boxing champion – I forget his name, I think it was Skilling, it was something like that. I remember years ago, when I came back, meetin' him on Cathkin Braes here walkin'. Oh, we had good food on the March, good food. I was surprised at the food. We had soup, stew – a lot o' stew. Oh, I cannae describe it but everything was good no matter what it was. There was nothing bad about it. We had sandwiches and tea too, plain food. Oh, I was eatin' quite good. I think I was better off on the March right enough.

I don't believe there was any trouble on the March. It's good things we had. There was a good feelin', you know. No hostility, no Blackshirts. We practically sung nearly a' the time along the road. It was mostly marching songs. *The Internationale* was one o' them. There were a lot o' other songs. I didnae whistle because I'm no' a whistler.

In my mind every place was good. It was only when we come near Birmingham that we doubted the police then. Because when we were going towards Birmingham we were all got together. Harry McShane got us all together, and Kerrigan and McGovern. And they said there were a danger o' some police interferin' wi' us. And they advised us what to do, and

how to arrange ourselves on the road. We said, 'Well, we'll do that.' Then
I remember we went tae a school. When we got intae the school police
came in and they started questionin' us in the school. Some o' us lyin' in
bunks, wee boards on the floor, we said, 'What's wrong here?' And Johnny
Docherty, well, he was an older man than me and he started to quiz about
the police bein' in. So our leaders had a good talk wi' the police and they
talked the police round tae preventin' them attackin' us. That's what would
have happened. Well, we made them go back out the school and we started
tae get thegither and we started tae lift our sticks then. And we said, 'By
God, if they're gaun tae do that we're gaun tae give them it back again.' We
were jist prepared for it.

Well, the wife and me werenae married at that time when I went on
the March. We had known each other about three years before then. We
were jist goin' steady. I used tae write tae her tae tell her every place we
stopped at. She wrote to me about once a week and I wrote back about once
a week. So she kept the letters. We have them yet.

When we got to London, oh, the crowds were massive. We went to
Trafalgar Square. I remember a young fellow stopped me. He says,
'Tommy!' He shouted to me and came towards me. I says, 'In the name o'
God what are ye doin' here?' He came from Glasgow. He says, 'I've been
on the run from the army.' He was a Regular. He had deserted. And here
he'd met somebody in Paddington and he had a place tae stay there. I went
tae see his place. But I didnae go intae any o' his business. He wanted me tae
tell his mother in Glasgow that he was goin' tae be a'right. So I said I would
let his mother know. I mind he came from Springfield Road.

But, oh, in London there were big demonstrations in Hyde Park, oh,
massive, ye couldnae get movin', ye couldnae. There werenae room tae
move. It wis jist a mass o' people, ye couldnae go anywhere. I don't
remember how long we stayed in London. I think it was roughly about a
week. I think we got a train back to Glasgow.

When I came back from the Hunger March ye heard it everywhere ye
were goin' – no jobs anywhere. Well, ye used tae go round everywhere tae
see if ye could get a job but I got disgruntled. I jist said, 'Well, I must go
somewhere.' I met Johnny Docherty and he says, 'Tommy,' he says, 'you
got a job?' Ah says, 'No, no' yet, Johnny.' He says, 'I know where you can
get work,' he says, 'if ye're wantin' tae go. But ye'll need tae walk it.' I says,
'Where have I tae go tae?' He says, 'Kirkcudbrightshire.'

I got my Hunger March haversack on my back and I says, 'Ach, I'm
gaun away.' And I went away tae Kirkcudbrightshire. And when I walked
tae Kirkcudbrightshire it was the Glen Lee tunnel that I arrived at. Well, I'd
never seen a tunnel in my life. But I asked the manager at the office. He says
tae me, 'Where dae ye come frae, son?' Ah says, 'Glasgow.' He says, 'How
did you arrive here?' I says, 'I walked up.' He says, 'You walked up? Go over
there and see that man and see if there's a bed for ye. Ye'll start in the
mornin'.' Well, I stayed there for two and a half year. It was near Dalry in
Kirkcudbrightshire. It's on the road tae Castle Douglas. They called it the

Glen Lee tunnel. It was diggin' through the mountain to another part o' the glen. There were an awful lot o' Irishmen there. Our wages was eleven pence an hour.[198]

I'd been doin' a little boxin'. I was a lightweight. They were startin' a boxin' club. They asked me one night if I would do a wee bit trainin' in front o' somebody. So I did that. They asked me then to go and put on this bout. I was boxin' a man the name o' Howard frae Leith. I won a'right. So I had a few fights up there and made a few bob back and forward. Sometimes I had about £6. Well, that was a big lot for me at that time. We were only gettin' 11d an hour. But after about two or three year I got disgusted wi' the job. I wis jist navvyin'. You would call me a cod labourer because I got a lot o' easy jobs. A cod labourer is a man that's like a ganger. Ye're no' a ganger, you're a leadin' man, that's a'. When we were doin' the dam, ye see, at the top o' the dam it was parts like concrete but we put tar into that, and then it was concreted over and above that. There were wee bits here and there in the dam that was concreted, and ah got these wee jobs to do. Then I was helpin' the joiners – various things. It was all odd jobs. There was nothing particular. But ah finished that and went away frae there.

I was in that many jobs I couldnae tell ye. I remember I came back frae Kirkcudbrightshire and I got a job on the railway. Somebody spoke for me. So I got the job and it was £2.3/9d. a week. That was in Coolairs. And I left and I went tae a pit – Auchengeich pit – and was six month there. And then I went tae another one for a fortnight. But the next one I went to it was £2 a week I should ha' got, but they gave me a pound. Ah says, 'Ah'm leavin'.' This was the way life went on. I wis jist trampin' frae place tae place, livin' rough. I was in the model lodgin' houses too. I was in one in Edinburgh and one in Stirlin'. I remember that.

The wife and I got married in 1936. We were only about five months married when Tommy Flynn come along and asked if I'd be interested in going to the International Brigade in Spain. I volunteered. It was George Middleton that interviewed me for Spain. And I think that's why they stopped me, because they heard I'd got married recently.

Well, lookin' back on the Hunger March, I think we helped a lot by marching. Our March is maybe in the past but through our struggles we've helped. It was a major event in my life anyway, it was a major event there a'right. I was quite proud of what I'd done. I have no regrets at all. It should be happenin' now, that's what I think.

James Henderson

My father came to Lochgelly about 1910. He started workin' in the pits, in the Minto colliery. It's away now, it's what they cry Brighills. But he worked there a' the time I was a lad. He was always at Mintae colliery. He never had nae other job. He was an Edinburgh man. He had worked in the rubber works at Fountainbridge there, and hotel work and things like that. And then he come ower here tae Fife. I was born in Murdoch Terrace in Fountainbridge and ah wis only months old when I come here tae Lochgelly. I had two brothers and two sisters. I was the eldest, born in May 1910.

There were a great demand for men in the Lochgelly pits at that time, accordin' to ma father. I had an uncle, he was frae Edinburgh tae, and he'd come first tae Lochgelly tae the pits because there were always a wee bit mair money for them. And then he got ma father tae come across, because he was married on ma father's sister. My mother was a quiet woman, jist an ordinary working-class woman frae Edinburgh.

As soon as I left school I went intae the pits. I was fourteen. It was jist before the 1926 General Strike. I first started in a pit cried the Peeweep at fillin' and drawin'. I didnae work wi' my father: he was on the surface at the Mintae, I wis down below in the Peeweep. When I started there the shift wage I had was 3/6d a day. And then ma father said, 'Ah've got ye a job in the Mintae at 4/8d a day.' That wis in the pit bottom tae. That wis where a' the fresh air was – pit bottom, 4/8d a day. So that wis a'right and that wis me in there up tae I was about twenty, about 1930.

I mind o' the 1926 General Strike 'cause we were oot there for six month. I wis sixteen at the time. I mean it was a gigantic holiday tae us, you know. Och, it wis a terrible struggle for ma parents. There were soup kitchens and everythin' like that. But I got ma job back at the end o' the strike and went back intae the Mintae. Father went back tae.

About 1930 we started to get what they cried three days a week. They werenae gettin' the wagons in. There werenae a great demand. I cannae really mind what was happenin' at that time but the pits was on three days a week, ken. I was never a face worker, always on what they cried the oncost, that wis keepin' the hutches and everythin' gaun, workin' on the motors and everythin' like that. I cannae mind how long our three-day a week wis. But eventually it got that bad that ah wis paid off. It would be aboot 1931 or 1932.

I was on the dole: 15/3d a week, that's what we got. I was livin' at home and my father was still workin' in the pit. Ma sister Nellie was workin' on the pithead and ma other sister Isa was in domestic service. Ma sister Nellie remembers she worked on the pithead for 1/11¹/₂d a day. It was either that or go to service. So that was about 13/- a week, eleven-day fortnight. Ma two brothers werenae workin' then, they were too young. Well, we come to the Means Test. We got six month o' oor benefit and then we were telt we were cut off benefit. We had tae get what they cried at that time an accommodation address. Ye couldnae stey in the hoose and get your money, your 15/3d, ye had tae get an accommodation address.

Well, that meant gaun roond some o' the neighbours, 'Wull ye say that I'm steying wi' you like? 15/3d and I'll pay you so much like.' And that's hoo that went on. Well, I'll tell ye what I steyed wi', and this is the funny thing aboot it. There wir another boy that I kenned, he was on the dole tae. And I dinnae ken how it come aboot, we didnae ken what tae dae, but eventually ken where we went tae? On the outskirts o' Lochgelly, gaun towards Glencraig, there were a lodgin' house. We cried it the Model, the model lodgin' house. It was run by a family cried the Hugheses, Pat Hughes and that. And we went doon there and went tae see Pat. There were three o' us, me and another two boys: 'Could we get you tae …? Is it an accommodation address, Pat?' He says, 'Aye, and I'll charge ye four shillins a week. And if any o' the inspectors and that come and ask, you're steyin' here.' So that was a'right. We got oor buroo money and that. But Pat says, 'What ye'll need tae dae is come doon maybe two or three times a week and stay in the lodgin' hoose.' So that's what I used tae dae. 'Jist two or three nights a week,' he says, 'in case anybody comes. And tae let the rest o' the men ken ye're stayin' here.' The other nights I stayed at home. Ye ken, it was a' a sort o' big adventure. But it wisnae an adventure for the people in the hoose. I maybe jist went doon and steyed the night at the Model and listened tae a' the auld boys' crack. Then I went home and got my food. And at the weekend I jist steyed at home.

Well, maybe compared wi' some others we were one o' the better off families in Lochgelly, wi' ma father and ma two sisters workin'. We got our food. It wis jist the usual – mince and tatties, tea, margarine, oh, nothin' fancy, soups and things like that. Oh, no, we were never really hungry, ye ken. We managed a'right. And then my father – well, when I was younger – my father used tae dae a lot o' overtime tae boost his wages up, him being what they cry jigger engineman, looked efter the tables and everythin' like that. Him and Nellie worked at the Mintae pit, jist on the road to Bowhill and Cardenden.

I was unemployed aboot two year. The time we were on the dole my pal Tam Simpson and me used tae go doon tae the pits – and there were the Jenny Gray pit only about a quarter o' a mile away fae us. Of course there was nothin' for ye. Ye would go to the pit maybe aboot two o'clock if they lowsed then, and see the gaffer when he come up: 'Any jobs ?' There were nae jobs. We went aboot two or three times a week. And then we used tae go away for walks. We used tae like to get oot in the fields and things like that.

I never joined the National Unemployed Workers' Movement. There were nothing really at that time. And we werenae politically motivated. But ah can mind in Lochgelly Institute there were a great lot o' Labour activities. The I.L.P. was strong in Lochgelly – Will Crooks and Michael Lee. They were a' a wee bit older than me. And then there were another boy cried Jimmy Stewart. He was in the Communist Party. He was a great boy during the miners' strike. I can mind o' Jimmy Stewart, 'cause he used tae hold meetins along at The Cross.[199] But we really didnae bother much aboot it, well, I was only sixteen efter the '26 strike. But we used tae go back and forrit, maybe tae meetins and that. There were only one thing I think I was in. Along at the Institute there I joined the Young Communist League, when we were unemployed. I wisnae that long in it, jist two or three month. The branch sort o' collapsed. But I can mind o' goin' and playin' fitba', one or two o' their matches down at Glencraig. But that fell away tae. And along at the Institute I think that's really where I met up wi' Harry Houston. He jist come frae the same place as me – the Happy Land, the miners' raws. There wis Melville Street and Hunter Street, Russell Street, and there was Craig Street and Minto Street. I couldnae say why it was called the Happy Land. I wisnae born there but my sisters and brothers were. The Happy Land's away noo.

I never joined a political party. But I jist had always thae views. When I was young, the books I used tae read was Jack London. And I've got the poems o' the other boy there, Robert W. Service.[200] Well, they were a' boys that wis left wing. And Lochgelly was a very left-wing place – oh, some o' the greatest boys. And I mean we used tae talk. We didnae run so much aboot what they do noo like. At that time it was only corner boys, boys standin' at the street corner when you finished your work at night like, more so during the week. The weekend when ye got your wages, that was the only time ye maybe went up the street tae the cinemas or tae hae a pint or anything like that. But durin' the week it wis jist a' meetin' the corner boys, talkin', and then the guid weather – 'Come on, we'll hae a walk.' And there would be a certain amount o' politics would come in – but I cannae mind o' a great deal o' it. One o' the boys I ran aboot wi', a special pal o' mine, John Erskine, his father was in the I.L.P. And then there were another old boy that steyed along where we steyed, he was another great boy at the I.L.P. But we never thocht nothin' much aboot politics, ye ken. Maybe somebody would raise it at night but there were never great arguments.

But we heard aboot the Hunger March. And me and this Tom Simpson we said we'd go on the March. Well, it must ha' been Harry Houston and them we went tae. I dinnae ken if it originated frae this Young Communist League. I cannae mind if Harry Houston that was oor leader was in the Communist Party or the Young Communist League. But I mind o' bein' in the Young Communist League and bein' at one or two o' their fitba' matches. And then we heard aboot this Hunger March. I think it wis jist something that had started along there at the Institute, maybe a meetin' or somethin'. It was the 1934 Hunger March.

I can mind we went doon tae the first-aid hall. I cannae mind whether they enrolled you or that. They jist said we were tae gaun at a certain time for tae go on the Hunger March. I mind gaun doon and tellin' ma father and, oh, 'What do you want to go on that for?' Ah says, 'I'm gaun tae go.' And he wasnae very pleased about it. Well, I couldnae really say why I was so keen tae go. Ye ken, it must ha' been at the back o' us that this injustice, havin' tae come oot the hoose like. We werenae politically motivated. We used tae always argue about politics and that but no' very deeply. I dinnae ken what really drove me to it, whether it was the idea o' marchin' tae London or no'. I'd never been away frae Lochgelly, never went on holidays or anythin', and I wis twenty-four.

There were nae big send-off frae Lochgelly for the March, nothin' that I can mind o'. We jist left frae that first-aid hut doon there. We must ha' marched into the centre o' Bank Street – that's the main street in Lochgelly. And then we marched doon into the Happy Land. That's where we come frae like. Ah come frae there, Harry Houston come frae there, ma friend Tam Simpson come frae there. And then we come oot on tae the main Lochgelly-Kirkcaldy road. We marched tae Kirkcaldy. That's about eight to ten mile. We steyed the night there.

The Cowdenbeath men had marched tae Lochgelly so we'd joined up wi' them and we a' marched tae Kirkcaldy. There'd be maybe fourteen or fifteen o' us a'thegither. I cannae mind for sure but we either got the bus or the train to Glasgow to meet the main body. That's where the March was really startin' frae. We got into Glasgow and I landed in the Gorbals, stayed the night in the Gorbals. I cannae mind whether it was a hall. That was the first time I had been in Glasgow. I cannae mind o' gettin' nothin' to eat. I can always remember I thought there was an awfy lot o' Jewish boys knockin' aboot, ye ken. Because I seen a lot o' the boys wi' the beard, auld Jewish men wi' the beards and that.

Harry Houston, he would be meetin' Harry McShane and that. We maybe seen them gaun aboot but we didnae meet them like. We didnae ken whae was actually gaun tae be the leader. I couldnae mind where we set off frae in Glasgow. And I cannae even mind o' the crowds, if there were crowds. And then we marched. We must have stayed the first night in Kilmarnock. Then we went through Cumnock, that was the 400 o' us, the Aberdeen boys, Dundee and a' the rest. They a' had their banners and everything like that, ye ken. And then I think it was frae New Cumnock we used tae get ten minutes' stop every hoor on the road.

When we left Cumnock – I think it was Cumnock – we stopped on the road. That's when the stick come in. Harry McShane telt us: 'A' cut sticks!' So I mind o' goin' over to this rose bush and cuttin' a stick. The reason they telt us tae take the stick, he said that he had an idea that somewhere on the March the police would try tae break us up. And when we got intae England Harry McShane would tell us, 'We're comin' in tae a sort o' big town. Now just watch yoursel' and behave yoursel'.' I think he was more worried aboot us goin' into England than what he was worried aboot Scotland. There was always a chance the police would maybe try and break us up, ye ken. That was the feeling. I think the stick was mair jist for a defence. A' the boys was swingin' them, you know.

I cannae mind the route. I can only mind o' comin' tae Penrith and Kendal, ye ken, and then over the Shap. Well, they got the bus over the Shap. I don't actually ken why. It was good enough weather like. I can mind o' them sayin', 'We're gettin' the bus ower the Shap Fell', from Penrith tae Kendal like. And then I cannae mind much aboot that, ye know, gettin' intae Kendal. I cannae mind o' a' the different stages as we went doon in England. But we went through Birmingham.

When we'd left Lochgelly we didnae hae a medical. We didnae sign a paper or nothin'. They only telt us what to get, just wear; a good, stout pair o' boots, a big coat, and a blanket and a cap. I cannae mind if I had a cap or no'. We didnae wear caps at that time – we'd plenty o' hair! But I had a small pack for cairryin' the blanket. I cannae mind o' change o' underwear or nothin' like that, ye ken. And really a' the time we were goin' doon there I mean it wis jist rough washin' – ken, jist stripped tae the waist. I cannae mind o' showers or anythin'. There might ha' been showers but we wis always clean enough. We also washed oor feet, ye ken ye always attended tae them whenever ye could get intae a place. I cannae mind the name o' this place that we got intae but there were a big Co-operative Society there. We had a meal and everything and then it was announced frae the stage: 'Anybody wants their boots repaired take your boots off.' So we took oor boots off. And ye just sat there or knocked aboot in your stockin' soles. They took a' oor boots away, ye ken, and they were back in aboot a couple o' oors efter that, soled and heeled and whatever you wanted done tae them. We didnae have a boot repairer wi' us on the March.

What I can mind o' it, it was only about twelve or fourteen miles a day. And as I say, we used tae get ten minutes' stop every hoor on the road. We always got haversack sandwiches, maybe aboot fower slice o' breid, maybe cheese an' that on it, ye ken. That wis tae keep us goin' durin' the day. And we must have a' had a mug for oor tea. And then the van used tae come up and doon wi' the tea like when you stopped, just an urn on the back o' a wee van.

Efter we got our lunch or oor sandwiches during the day like, there was always a forward party went on for tae arrange accommodation and where we were gaun tae stop next. And usually when we went into thae different toons and places it was I.L.P. halls, Labour halls, or schools that wis allocated tae us like. The Co-operative tae, they always had a meal laid on for us when we were comin' in. And I can mind in West Bromwich everything was laid on for us, ye ken.

Well, the food on the March, it seemed to do us. I think there were only one bit where it was difficult. I think it was when they first went into England. I mind o' one diet we sat doon tae, sort o' tatties and meat. The meat was underdone, ken, half-raw. And I didnae like that. But it seemed they liked it. There was always a great lot o' blood on the plate, sort o' underdone steak. I didnae fancy that one. But a' the rest it was a' right. I wis never hungry nor nothin' on the March. The meals was jist more or less aboot the same as at hame.

Me and my neebour was smokers. We werenae great drinkers at that time, ye ken. I cannae mind o' any rule on the matter o' drinkin' on the March. But I mean we were always meetin' people. See, as we went doon the March there were some o' the boys oot o' each contingent went wi' the collectin' cans. Oor boy that done it for us was a wee boy cried Sinclair. I think he come frae aboot Lumphinnans or Hill o' Beath. He used tae go. And then we would tell him we'd gie him maybe tuppence or fourpence, 'Get Woodbine, Tim' – we cried him Tim Sinclair. 'Get five Woodbine or ten Woodbine.' We'd gie him the money and he'd go intae maybe a paper-shop or a confectioner's shop and he come out, 'Ah got the Woodbine and they didnae take the money!' Ye ken, they didnae take the money.

And then at night maybe when ye come oot for tae hae a look roond aboot the toon there were always people oot there that wanted tae take ye in for a drink an' that. People were very friendly wherever we went. I cannae mind o' any hostility or any trouble wi' the police a' that time doon there. Any time we went oot, there were maybe two or three people aboot, 'Are ye gaun for a drink, sir? I'll take ye for a drink.' Or maybe they'd come ower and gie ye money, ye ken: 'Buy yersel' a packet o' fags.' Things like that. I think there were always plenty o' people watchin' the March gaun doon the road. That was the reason for the collectin' cans, the boy jist gaun up and doon.

I wisnae a collector mysel'. I was usually carrying the banner. Oh, that banner! That took a bit o' strength if it was a windy day! Ye ken, ye were never very pleased when Harry Houston said tae ye, 'It's your turn for the banner.' We jist carried it bits o' the way, goin' through the towns you unfurled the banner. We didnae carry it along the country roads. It was pretty heavy.

We had a band on the March but I cannae mind what they were playin'. They were always playin' wi' a mooth organ. I mean there were boys had bugles and boys wi' mooth organs and things like that. I cannae mind o' singin' mysel'. I expect they would sing a' the old War songs and things like that, *The Red Flag* or *The Internationale*. When everybody settled doon at night thir two Glesgae boys used tae sing and they were good singers tae. One used tae sing an auld song:

> When life's sun is setting
> And your hair is turning grey,
> I will love you jist the same
> As on our weddin' day.

It was braw, ye ken, tae hear him. And then the other boy used tae sing the Irish song *The Four-leaved Shamrock from Glenore*.

Thae two Glesgae boys always landed up on the stage when we got allocated tae a hall. It was maybe a dance hall or an institute or that, and we'd get telt: 'So much o' ye go in there and get settled down.' So we jist went in. And if there were a stage in it there were usually a rush for the boys tae get up on the stage. They always thought the stage was a bit warmer. It was above the floor and away frae the door, so that ye wouldnae be bothered, you know.

What I can mind o' it was a' I.L.P., Labour people that was always lookin' efter us like. And then I mind o' gaun further doon efter Birmingham – I cannae mind the name o' the place – but we couldnae get accommodation. So we were telt tae go to the workhouse. And what I can mind o' this workhouse was that it was up on a hill. We jist cried it the spike and the grubber, that's what it was cried in thae times. And I learned later on that the auld hardened tramps o' the road jist used tae cry it the spike. So we were telt, 'They've got tae take ye in there,' because we had nae place for tae rest. And they did take us in there. And then the next place I mind o' there were a big Co-operative Society. Ye ken, the Co-operative was always daein' their bit. And we got intae this place and went tae the Co-operative, the Royal Arsenal Co-operative. And I mind o' us sittin' doon, everything was laid on for us. It could ha' been St Albans.

I cannae mind where it wis as we were comin' doon on the March – it must ha' been in aboot the Midlands – but there wis one boy I'm gaun tae tell ye about. I mind o' goin' in one mornin' tae the wash-hand place for tae get a wash. It was only an ordinary tap. And the boy that was in front o' me was stripped doon to his semmit and that, ye know, and his galluses hingin' ower the end o' his troosers. D'ye ken whae it wis? John McGovern, the M.P. I mind o' them tellin' me, 'That's John McGovern.' He had a limp. John McGovern M.P. was washin' his face at the tap.

The 400 o' us were the Scottish contingent. We always seemed to be on our own. But I think there were a big contingent come frae the North o' England too, for tae take in the English boys, but I cannae mind what route they took.[201] On our banner it said, 'The Cowdenbeath contingent o' the West Fife Miners march against the Westminster Monsters.' And there was a Nessie, the Loch Ness Monster, on the banner. So the Lochgelly lot – there would be about eight o' us. And then there must have been about seven or eight frae Cowdenbeath. There was one wee boy frae Lumphinnans, a wee boy cried Sinclair. He's dead noo. I dinna ken if Eddie Smith come frae Ballingry, he was two or three year older than me. Harry Houston was the leader o' the whole Cowdenbeath and Lochgelly contingent.

We were a' jist near enough in aboot the same age, in oor twenties. I was twenty-four. There would only be about four or five years o' difference between the lot o' us. There werenae any old men. The two main men as far as we were concerned were Harry Houston and Eddie Smith. I dinnae ken, but they might ha' been politically active. I dinnae ken aboot the Cowdenbeath boys, whether they were. But Harry Houston and Eddie

Smith done a' the business and come and telt us what ye had tae dae. Eddie Smith was frae Lochgelly tae. In oor contingent they would be a' miners. The Lochgelly lot and the Cowdenbeath lot would be the same because it was a' pits round aboot here.

I think the March only took aboot a month or maybe five weeks. The weather seemed to be a'right 'cause I never mind o' us complainin' or nothin' aboot it. I never mind o' snow or nothin'.

Sometimes I was gettin' sent about five shillins frae my mother, five shillins or about ten bob. I wrote home, like. And I can mind o' her sending five shillins and that. She knew where ye were gaun tae be on the March. I cannae mind o' much writing home but I must have wrote home for tae let them ken. So the money was very handy at that time, because it was only cigarettes we were bothered aboot. Woodbine was tuppence for five and fourpence for ten.

I can mind we got intae St Albans and then I think oor next stop must have been gettin' into the suburbs o' London. We were billeted in Deptford or New Cross. It was a place cried Nine Edge Street. It was a school we were billeted in.[202] I can mind one o' the nights goin' up tae the New Cross Empire. It was only aboot sixpence tae get in. The only turn I can mind o' on the stage was an Italian boy playin' a big melodeon, Ernesto Jaccanelli.

They arranged the marches frae Deptford or New Cross. They said, 'We're goin' tae a demonstration at thingmie, half a mile or a quarter o' a mile frae the Houses o' Parliament.' This was oor demonstration for Parliament. I cannae mind much aboot it. But I can mind o' goin' through the West End at that time. There were always plain clothes men wi' us, they moved wi' the demonstration a' the time. They marched alongside ye. I dinna ken if it wis the Aberdeen or the Glesgae boys but they had bugles, somebody had a bugle. And they were blowin' it goin' along this street. And I can always mind o' this plain clothes boy – he had a big burn mark on his face, a big blue mark – come alongside us and telt us, 'They've never heard the like o' this before.' He says, 'Ye ken where ye are?' He says, 'Ye're in Harley Street!' So we got tae Parliament anyway. I dinnae ken if we went tae Hyde Park first but we got tae the demonstration. We marched in tae Hyde Park and we wis a' marshalled in roond aboot this platform. I can mind o' a great crowd there. And then this demonstration come in frae the Rhondda Valley. And the people was runnin' aboot, showerin' them wi' everythin', the Welsh contingent – cigarettes, money, and everythin'. I can still see the banner yet, the big red banner, frae the Rhondda Valley. And then the speakers: one man sticks oot in ma mind. And he was a Communist, a boy cried Wal Hannington. And the foam, the foam used tae come oot his mooth. I thought he was a great speaker.

We steyed in London for about a fortnight, I think. There were different meetins. A' the time we wis in Nine Edge Street. But I mind there were one rumpus. I dinnae ken if it was the Glesgae boys or whae that had went oot. But I think they had caused a bit o' trouble when they come in. I think there were drink and that concerned in it. They'd went oot one night and there had been a bit o' a rumpus, drinkin' and fightin' like, ken. The committee, the boys that wis lookin' efter us, they had a meetin' and they said that they were gaun tae disown them, didna want nothin' mair tae dae wi' them. I dinnae ken if they paid their fare back home nor nothin'.

We come back on the train. They telt us they had a big meetin' and they'd been collectin' for to see we were gaun tae get hame. They had us a' in the meetin' and asked us how would we like tae go hame. The biggest majority put up their hand, 'We'll walk up back up the east coast.' I mean, we were a' fit enough and everything, ye ken. I wanted tae dae that masel'. It was always a bit o' a novelty, ye ken. Because there wasnae much good o' comin' home — we'd nae jobs nor nothin'. We had a' the time in the world. So – 'We'll march back up the east coast.' There were a lot o' boys in favour o' that. And I was in favour o' it masel' because I had always a guid pair o' legs. I was always fit enough that way, never had nae bother. But it was decided we would take the train. So we got the train back. We come in tae Cowdenbeath and there were a welcome party waitin' for us, the local Labour, the Communist Party and that. As we come off Cowdenbeath station there were a big reception party waitin'. But me and ma mate didnae bother like, we just come away. I think we got the bus or the tramcar back hame into Lochgelly.

I was unemployed for about a year after the March. I went through to Edinburgh. I met a boy there that was on the March wi' me, Willie Gildea. He'd been an auld professional fitba' player in his time. We looked roond aboot for yin o' thae bed-sitters where they'd chairge ye five bob a week and ye cooked yer ain meat. We used tae hae a wee gas-ring. I mind o' stayin' down in Rose Street for a wee while and I was in the Greyfriars Model Lodging house. The Greyfriars was a'right. The rooms wis braw–cubicles. There were two o' us in one cubicle and ma neebour was an Edinburgh newsboy. He had a pitch doon at Register House. Then I met another Lochgelly boy and it wis jist gaun intae bed-sitters, cooked your own food.

I mind o' goin' doon tae Tollcross Labour Exchange and it was still 15/3d a week. Every Thursday I remember gaun intae the butcher's at Tollcross – a pund o' sausages, 6d! And then there were a scheme come oot, more or less a rehabilitation scheme. So I put my name doon for that. I was telt tae get on the train for Hawick and tell the driver you want off at Lewisburn Halt. There were a big van waitin' there. They took us to Kielder, for the big forest. [203] We used tae go oot and dig the drains and everything for the plantin' o' the young trees. We lived in huts, wooden huts. There wis a guid lot o' Glesgae boys there. It wis just like the army. There would be about twenty or thirty in a hut. I just cannae remember how many in the camp but there would be a guid lot. But that was oor job at that time. We jist got oor buroo money for that, 15/3d a week. I don't think we ever handled the money at that time. We got our food and jist a bit pocket money. I cannae jist remember how much.

We were at Kielder aboot a month and then we were shifted doon tae Carshalton in Surrey. Well, it was more or less jist like the labour schemes they've got there the noo. It wis jist labourin' a' the time. We were put intae digs. Three or fower o' us were billeted wi' an Italian woman, Mrs Tortellani. And where she steyed was 1 Goat Road. We didnae stay at Carshalton that long, about a month. But efter aboot a month the word come in that they'd got us jobs. So we were sent oot tae Braintree in Essex.

They got us fixed up wi' digs wi' an auld spinster woman. And ma mate nearly a' the time was a boy cried James Osgathorpe frae Doncaster. And we started wi' Crittals, them that made the metal windae frames. That place was hotchin' wi' work, it was hotchin' fu' o' work. There was Crittals, there was Courtaulds. Plenty o' work there. It sticks in my mind to this day, gaun tae that Labour Exchange in Braintree – and there were naebody in it! In Lochgelly here when I was on that 15/3d and they brought oot the Means Test, big queues o' men, big queues o' men.

Well, we were about two or three month at Crittals, labourin' first. And then eventually they put us on the bench, makin' thae metal windae frames. It was easy, it was like a meccano set. And we used tae get our dinner there. That was the first time I found a canteen in the workshop – canteen, showers, games rooms and everything. And the wages I got was aboot £2 somethin' a week

There was an urge on a' the time I was there, I wanted tae go. This Billy he come frae Newcastle, so me and Yorkie – that's what I cried James Osgathorpe – and Billy gave up our jobs and went on the tramp. We went marchin' as far as Winchester. I can always mind o' gaun ower what they cry the Hog's Back, that's the road between Guildford and Farnham. We bocht a tent and we had the tent up and cookin' and drummin' up – it was jist a holiday. We got the idea that we were gaun tae try and get on the ships at Southampton but here we got as far as Winchester and we met two or three boys and they jist telt us, 'Boys, ye'll no' get intae Southampton docks unless you've a seaman's caird.' So right about turn, away back into London! We walked intae London. I mind o' sittin on thae steps at a bridge in London lookin' at the Thames. We'd got the tent, it was gettin' a bit o' wear and tear so we flung it in the Thames.

We were sittin' on the Embankment, me and Yorkie. The next thing a polisman come up. He says, 'What are ye daein' here?' 'Oh, we're intae London lookin' for work.' 'Have ye naewhere tae go?' 'No,' we said, 'we've naewhere tae go.' So he took his book oot and he wrote, 'Go to the hostel at Gray's Inn Lane, Gray's Inn Road.' 'You go up there,' he says, 'you'll be a' right up there.' So we went up there tae the hostel. It was jist like a workhouse. And ye done a certain amount o' work, breakin' sticks, sometimes you cleared up. You had to be in at a certain time at night. Then efter aboot a month ye got putten oot o' there. It was jist more or less a centre for unemployed people comin' in tae London. Ye were supposed to be oot lookin' for work like, ye ken. And I believe at that time I could ha' got plenty o' work in London. But we didnae really bother like. Ken, there were that many boys like us walkin' aboot.

A great place for us at that time wis at Nelson's column. We used tae go away doon there and sit in Trafalgar Square. I can always mind o' meetin' a big seaman there. He used tae sit beside us. And ye would listen tae a' thae boys. One time I was sittin' in Trafalgar Square. There was one o' the worthies sittin' roond aboot and he says, 'Right, get off your mark. Get off your mark! Get away frae here! Away up tae the British Museum oot the road!' We wondered what wis wrong. The next thing here two big police vans come in tae Trafalgar Square. We could jist rise and run. But there were aulder boys than us. The polis were shepherdin' them intae the vans. So efter they'd cleaned up Trafalgar Square we met another boy and said, 'What was the idea o' that?' He says, 'That's them takin' them in tae the workhoose for tae delouse them. If you'd sat there you'd ha' been roped in tae for delousin'.

Efter we left the place in Gray's Inn Lane we went tae Rowton House. It was a big hostel for men, somethin' like the Salvation Army. And then there were another place, doon the Waterloo Road, what they cried The Coffins. What ye got tae lie in was jist like a coffin. It was a kind o' black leather thingmy that you lay on. You had nae blankets nor nothin', jist a black leather thingmy that you lay on, and a black leather thing for pittin' your heid on and ye set your coat ower the tap o' it. It was a kind o' bed in a box, that's the reason they cried them the coffins. It was only aboot four bob a week.

I can always mind o' this big lodging hoose we were in and there were one day a boy come marchin' in wi' a case. You'd see some boys comin' in wi' cases, auld claes, ye ken, shirts and everythin', lay them a' oot and the boys used tae pick what they wanted oot. But this boy come marchin' in this day wi' a big case, opened it out – and d'ye ken what it wis full o'? Fag ends, cigarette ends! He got them at a' the big hotels. He was one o' the unemployed but that's what he did. He went roond the hotels in the mornin' and when the cleaners, ye ken, put the cigarette ashes in the bin he went and filled his suitcase wi them' and then he come back tae the lodgin' hoose and unravelled them a' oot. He made big heaps o' shag and then he had thon cigarette maker. And he selt them – ten cigarettes for so much. I cannae mind what he chairged but it wis coppers. And then he had cigar ends. He had them set aside if the boys wanted tae buy cigar ends.

Well, we were in London maybe jist aboot two or three month. And then we got fed up wi' that. The boys would tell you, 'Away up to the Sisters o' Charity. Chap at the door and ye'll get a piece or something.' Ye'd come back and buy a cup o' tea. We were gettin' a bit fed up so Yorkie said he would like tae go hame tae Doncaster. A boy says tae us, 'Go doon tae so-and-so pub and ask for so-and-so boy.' And d'ye ken what we were in there for tae get? The return tickets o' boys that wasnae gaun back. Ken a boy bought a return maybe frae Doncaster tae London and he would jist sell this. So Yorkie got a ticket for Doncaster and I got one for further on, but different trains.

I came back home first. Then I went to Edinburgh for a bit. That would be about 1935, jist comin' up tae aboot that time. I worked in the North British Hotel, down in the plate room – £1 a week and your food.

And I steyed in the Greyfriars model lodgin' hoose. I think it was only aboot fower or five shillins there in the Greyfriars.

I was about a year workin' in the North British. We were washin' up the dishes and the silver. The best thing in the North British, workin' there, the waiters used tae slip the plates through to us and sometimes they'd put a plate through, ye ken, wi' a full fish on it that hadnae been touched, lemon sole, wi' a' the greenery a' roond aboot it. So we used tae pit it on the shelves – 'We'll eat that efter.' And we were gettin' well enough fed. But you often thought that was waste. You ought to have seen it. It was some o' the brawest stuff in the world – never touched. Oh, terrible when so many were hungry.

We started away in the mornin' maybe about half-past seven. We didnae come oot tae aboot maybe three o'clock again. We had tae wash up the lunch dishes. And then we had tae go in at night tae aboot six or seeven o'clock, maybe aboot that. It was a broken shift. But the heat in the kitchen was killin' me. I used tae go oot in the Princes Street Gairdens and take ma shoes and socks off, ma feet was that rid hot. It was thae cheap socks that wis daein' it.

We had our £1 a week but ye got aboot three or fower railway passes a year. Ye could go to anywhere in Britain but I used tae jist get one for comin' home occasionally. And then me and this boy Jimmy McKinlay that I ran aboot wi' – he worked in the grill – we went up tae Cruden Bay and got a job in the plate room in the railway hotel there. I was there durin' the summer season, six months. Then I got a job on the railway, and then I come back and got a job in the pits. That would be aboot '37, afore the War broke oot. I was doon in Glencraig for a wee while but I didnae like it. It wis what they cry steel drawin'. That's efter they take oot the coal ye draw the steels and the whole thing comes doon. And then I had a job in the Aitken pit, drivin' a stane mine. And then I left and went back tae Edinburgh again and wi' the outbreak o' the War I went doon tae the Labour Exchange at Tollcross and I got a job wi' what they cried the Rescue and Repair Service. Oor headquarters was doon by Powderhall, civil defence work. Everybody had coats, oilskins, wellingtons, helmets and everything for anything that wis breakin' oot. But we never did anything a' the time I was there. Boys used to sit and play at cairds, darts. That was an eight-hour day and then the word come oot – 'Twelve hours a day'. They were pittin' us on a twelve-hour shift. That was it. We were no' wantin' nae twelve-hour shift. I dinnae ken if we were peyed off or we left o' oor ain accord. I must ha' went back on the dole. But the next thing I got my callin'-up papers for the army. I was five year in the Royal Artillery, never oot o' Britain at a' till the latter end. It was field artillery and at the end o' the War we went tae Belgium first then Germany. When I come back in 1947 I went to the buildin' trade and I done aboot two year in that, labourin', and then I done twenty-eight year wi' the toon council, jist the same – labourin'. I retired when I was sixty-five, in 1975.

Well, lookin' back tae the Hunger March I would think we did make a protest. I thought it was a great success. I think we started tae get mair money. It was efter the March I went tae that thing I was tellin' ye about, Kielder, and things seemed tae pick up.

Hugh Sloan

The big pit, the Wellesley pit, that I worked in at Methil on the north side of the Forth, was affected by the general depression. In December 1930 they paid off 400 men. The men paid off were selected by the Wemyss Coal Company – the ones they wanted to get rid of. My father, my brother, my two foster brothers and myself were all paid off. And then we were immediately ordered to evacuate our Wemyss Coal Company house. I was unemployed for four years, until January 1935. When the Means Test came in in 1932 I only got about 4/2d (21 pence) a week off the dole.

I have no doubt that we were victimised on account of my political activities. I was openly active not only in producing pit papers but selling them at the pithead every Friday. So the whole family were sacked because of my militancy.

Seventy Wemyss Coal Company tenants in Denbeath, where we lived, who were the most militant or sympathetic to the militants, a' received eviction orders. Ours was the only one that was carried out. Despite the fact that my father offered to pay the rent – about 7/2d a week in old money – the Wemyss Coal Company turned it down and ordered our eviction. The rest o' the seventy stayed on: an agreement was reached in time and they got off wi' it.

I had left school at fourteen, during the miners' strike in '26. Shortly after leaving school I started work in the Wellesley. I travelled to the face as a pan motor laddie. The pan motors were pans that jigged the coal produced by the coal hewers or strippers down on to a tub at the level, where they were taken out the section and then up the pit. So I was the laddie who controlled the jiggin' pans.

The access roads then were very scary at times. The proppin' system was wood and wood was really treacherous to the maintenance of good roof conditions for workin'. And you were workin' under the sea, under the Firth o' Forth. The pit shaft o' the Wellesley was on the shore. You landed in the pit bottom. The depth to the pit bottom was just over 300 fathoms. And then the sea mine turned and went direct out underneath the Forth. The sea mine itself was the main access to the workings. It would be coming pretty near to a mile long. And then you branched down into deeper sections. The coal was always taken from the high ground first. The furthest down was maybe about 2,000 yards, because we talked about explorations to try and find where the coal basined out under the Forth which never was established yet – and I think that was about 1,900 metres. So that's a pretty considerable depth. The further you went doon the hotter everything got.

Eventually I came on to other work. There was development work taking place and a private cementation company was brought in tae use concrete blocks as a means o' creating a tunnel effect. I was sent on to that work to supply the workers wi' their tubs that went up the brae pulled by a tail motor. Then the last job I was on before I was paid off was wi' the wire man as a form o' apprentice trainin' for an electrician's job. I had just started that and I was to attend night school and learn electricity when they paid off the 400 men and I lost my apprenticeship.

It was at the beginning of this century that the laird Wemyss, who was also the Wemyss Coal Company, sunk the Wellesley pit to extract coal from underneath the Forth.[204] It was a large modern pit and he needed miners. So he built the raws of Denbeath to house miners who responded to his advertisements in the national press. The miners' raws were euphemistically known as the Garden City. So miners – in the words of my father, 'A' the off-scourings of Scotland' – congregated in Denbeath. Now my father wasnae demeaning the character of these people. What he meant was they were part o' the displacement o' people that had taken place since the Highland Clearances, and he was talking in that sense.

But the people who came into Denbeath were rough-cast people who eventually coalesced into a very robust community, almost a ghetto. And the raws emerged in the 1920s, after the 1914–18 War, as a very politically militant place. Denbeath threw up its own political leaders who became very important in the miners' struggles in '21 and '26 and in the fight for trade union rights and representation and Scottish trade union unity. So Denbeath was very significant in that sense. It got a little bit of notoriety because of its rough-shod people and ways and was referred to frankly by others as 'that awfy place'.

Denbeath is exactly a mile from Leven on the way to Buckhaven, which is also a mile away, and down on the lower ground from Denbeath lies Methil. So over the years they a' sort of integrated in a conurbation.

My father came through from Ayrshire maybe 1910 or even earlier, and then he sent for my mother and settled in Denbeath and there I was born in August 1912. My father had left school at ten year old and went to work at the coal face wi' his father. In these days coal was got wi' the father working his own place and taking his son. So my father worked in shallow hole-in-corner pits, as he called them, in Ayrshire but I don't know where exactly the pits were.

My father volunteered in the 1914 War. He became a Cameron Highlander in 1914. He lost his leg at Cambrai in 1916. He had a field guillotine operation that wasnae very clinical. He was in hospital and had to have further part-amputations until well after the War. The result was he was bothered with nerve pains in his legs that required a certain amount o' dopin' for the rest o' his life. He got a fifty per cent disability pension.

When he came home from the War he took a spell o' learning a trade as an electrician at Cowdenbeath. But because electricians had to be very mobile to get about the pit he couldn't find a job as that. So his job was merely as a haulage motor attendant. Although the basic wage then was eight shillings per day, he was getting less because he was merely a motor attendant. That wasnae a very encouraging thing to happen. So we never had plenty o' anything. And his fifty per cent disability pension was really needed to keep us going: it would be about twenty-five shillings in the later 1920s. He was on constant backshift, that was from 2 p.m. until 10 p.m., five shifts a week. Only on special occasions did he work at the weekends. So he had about £2 a week from the pit.

My father was sympathetic to militancy but he had become a little bit cynical over losing his leg and how it had incapacitated him. He was a physical person, an athlete. So he became a very angry person.

My mother was an Ayrshire woman. Her father was a miner as well. I had a sister older than me who died young. After me there was Jackie, Richard and a young sister, all still living. I had a third sister but she died a few years ago. But there were also two orphan laddies related to us in a way. They were in the poorhouse but my father took them out and reared them at his own expense. Later on one of them – George Smith – went to Spain and fought in the Civil War. He died at the beginning of 1986.

We were the first generation of children in Denbeath. We arose out of what I have characterised as the first invasion of miners from the West of Scotland. I think there were three invasions up until the Second World War Methilhill also arose out of incomers, mainly from the West. The first development took place just prior to the First World War, the second after the War, in the 1920s. The third took place when they built the houses up in Kennoway during the Second War.

Denbeath was a very rough place. School was utterly primitive. We only learned the three Rs, that is, if we learned them at all. And schoolin' was quite frankly a kind o' bore to youngsters, well, to me anyway. Both my brother Jackie and I were very good at drawing. Art wasnae a word in our vocabulary then – drawing. And at school I was regarded as the best drawer in Denbeath. When I first went to school I got Excellent for drawing, until the Educational Board decided there wasnae such a thing as Excellent so I always got Very Good efter that.

The peripatetic art teacher would come one day every month and only spent half an hour in the classroom. He would sit down beside me and all I was allowed to draw was maybe an apple and an orange and a tumbler or something unexciting like that. He would say, 'Hugh this is very good. I couldn't have done better myself. Here's a threepenny piece.' As my pocket money was a ha'penny a week I always thought I was going to get a threepenny piece from him. I was always taken in: he gave me a peppermint sweetie tae shove in ma mooth. He stuck it in. I could have killed him.

Jackie, my brother two years younger than me, was very good at drawing as well. When he was eight or nine years old he asked his mother

for a loan of a half Bradbury, a ten shilling note. And he got margarine paper
and drew on it an exact copy of a ten shilling note. As a joke Jackie and my
other young brother Richard sent a wee laddie to the ice cream van and told
him to get three chocolate wafers wi' the 'note'. The wee boy came back
wi' three wafers and change. Eventually the fraud was discovered and father
had tae attend wi' Jackie before the forbidding Sheriff Dudley Stuart, who
was notorious in these days in Cupar.[205] People thought it was I who had
done this dastardly deed and even today will not be convinced it wasn't me!
I understand that that ten shilling 'note' still exists in the Cupar museum.
Jackie got only six months' probation.

Anyway as a result my notoriety grew. The militants in Denbeath and
around that area after the '26 strike produced pit papers in which political
cartoons was a big feature. They needed a political cartoonist. It would be
about 1928 and I would be coming on for sixteen. They asked my father's
permission to allow me to do the cartoons. So I became the cartoonist for
the militant trade union pit papers opposed to the scab unions and fighting
for the unity of the Scottish mineworkers that resulted about 1929-30 in the
United Mineworkers of Scotland.

They were duplicated pit papers, produced by the Gestetner process,
with the stylus pen and the typewriter. For the Wellesley the pit paper was
The Spark, obviously taken from *Iskra*. Some of the more significant other
pit papers were The *Pan Bolt* at Muiredge and *The Flame* at the Michael.[206]

The Spark was significant because the Wellesley was the first great big
pit probably in Scotland. I don't know how many miners would be
employed at it during the First War but there be over 3,000, I'm sure, during
the Second War. And there was over 3,000 miners worked in the Michael
pit, three miles along the shore further up the Forth. But even in the 1920s
there was a considerable number o' miners, though after '26 there was a lot
of miners never got their jobs back. Frae '26 onward the coal-owners
blacklisted whole numbers o' men who never started back. Many o' them
lasted throughout the '30s until the Second World War before they came
back into the industry. Some o' the men never started back at a'. I could
think on the neighbours that lived next tae us in Denbeath. There wis the
Hallidays that lived downstairs from us. One o' them was arrested for
putting oot the biler fires at the Wellesley in 1921. He did a bit o' time in
jail for that and I'm quite sure it must ha' been pretty nearly the beginning
o' the Second World War before he started back in the pit.

I've strong recollections of the '21 strike. The troops were sent in and
first of all came in the marines. They were billeted in the school hall in
Denbeath. The hall was central to a' the classrooms. So we had tae step over
the marines to get into oor classrooms. We were fed then at the soup
kitchens. There was a Mrs Bell who held a wee dairy shop where she
supplied the milk 200 or 300 yards from the pit, and who looked after the
feeding of the schoolchildren, supplemented to some extent by parish relief
feeding at the school. We got all our meals at the school, our breakfast, our
dinner and our tea at night. For breakfast we got tea and jist bread. For

dinner it was always soup, different kinds o' soup according to the things that the active strikers could forage for. We never missed a meal. At tea time I think we got a cup o' tea and a piece on jam. I'm no' quite sure.

The Wellesley pit stood out in the open then and directly across from the miners' raws. The troops were a Scotch regiment because they wore the kilt. And machine guns were mounted on the pithead facing into the raws. They were never used. According to Jock McArthur, the troops augmented the strikers' rations wi' their military supplies.

There were three scabs in Denbeath in '21 and the women burnt their effigies in the gardens. I witnessed it. I witnessed Tam Kirkcaldy having his effigy burned – he was a Labour councillor and remained one until after the Second World War.[207] Labour representatives then were despicable characters. That was one of the reasons why young people like myself were attracted to the militants like John McArthur, Davie Proudfoot and Mosie Murray, and not to the Labour Party.[208]

In '26 we got fed at the soup kitchens again and it became more a distinctive experience for me. There was no troops brought in this time. But the General Strike was very, very strong in the Methil-Levenmouth area. We had the railwaymen, Councils of Action, Young Pioneer groups who sang songs and paraded. I participated as a schoolboy in the march to the Thornton poorhouse in the summer of '26, after the General Strike but while the miners were still locked out. And I can remember during the strike A.J. Cook addressing one of the biggest demonstrations on the Ness Braes at Buckhaven just above the harbour, where the ground rises. The whole area was filled wi' people like a big amphitheatre. There must have been about 30,000 people there, wi' me standin' watchin' frae the top.

I was a member of the Young Pioneers, the Communist children's group. I'd be thirteen when I joined. There would be at least forty o' us in the Methil Young Pioneers. I remember on one occasion we paraded up and doon Methil singing songs, wi' an adult in charge o' us. As far as I remember our activities were jist bein' indoctrinated, marchin' up and doon, singing songs – revolutionary songs – and things like that. An adult, Fluck Allen, was given the task o' lookin' after us and he would take us around. He was a tallish boy. Ye wouldnae say he was a hunchback but he had a bit o' a bent shou'der. He's dead noo, big Fluck Allen.

I joined the Young Pioneers because I jist think it was the thing to do. My father bought the militant papers. And then there was the situation when we had the Reform Union. And he paid a' his dues then to the people that came to the door. So there was a political attitude prevailed in our house. I don't remember if my father had been a member of the Reform Union from 1922-23. You see, he was a pigeon man, secretary of the pigeon club. Jackie and I, because my father had that disablement, looked efter the pigeons when we were laddies. And the men accepted us. We sent the pigeons away, took a' the documentation, supplied the rings, entered a' the nominations. So Jackie and I had to look after the pigeons and practically run the pigeon club. We even helped ma faither in makin' oot the velocities and printed them on a primitive duplicating pan wi' a wax stencil and delivered the results tae a' the pigeon members. This was more concern to me at that time until we were evicted from Denbeath, doing this kind of work. The old boy was a strong disciplinarian and workmaster. For instance, we had tae clean oot the pigeon loft, fly the pigeons for half an hour without lettin' them land before we got oor breakfast and went tae school. So there was an indoctrination o' discipline that obviously was distinctive to oor trainin'. I'm afraid it didnae happen in school. I never paid attention to lessons. The teacher would say, 'Waken Hugh up. He's away in a brown study again.' And when I got my exercise books I would fill them wi' cowboys and Indians instead o' sums and things like that.

I never had an adolesence. First of all, I was working with the pigeon men before 1926 and efter, and then I was working wi' these very advanced political activists like Jock McArthur and Davie Proudfoot. If you were an activist you were taken with the big men. Ye see, miners' raws and the nature of the militancy in their organisations were purely macho. The question not only of women but of youngsters was an irrelevance to adult people. So there wasn't concentration on trying to build up a Young Communist League. There wisnae a Y.C.L. in our area in those days so when I became politically active very young with McArthur, Proudfoot and Johnny Boyle and we co-operated in the production o' the pit papers, they made me an honorary member of the Communist Party at seventeen. For membership of the Party then you had to be twenty-five. And then I was involved in the general political work of the Communist Party, advertising meetings, chalking streets, and became known as a member of the Party.

After I became unemployed in 1930 it got to the point where we spent three days in getting a' the pit papers produced. It was a very primitive and to me rather depressing technique of producing the cartoons for them. You had to cut the cartoons at first with a little stencil cutter that was just a little serrated wheel. It was like somebody marking the lines on a football field. You had to guide it round and perforate it as you went. Then the next technical development was we had a plate that had a grain in it and you used a blunt stylus pen. It was a very difficult and discouraging business. I wanted to do my own line work and that was clearly impossible and reduced the quality of the cartoons to a crudity. But I had to do the cartoons.

It was in David Proudfoot's house and under his supervision that I began drawing the cartoons. The first cartoon that I drew I had a bit o' a confused political attitude, naturally. I was only beginning to get initiated into political work through drawing cartoons for the pit papers. McArthur comes and looks at it over my shoulder and he turns away and I heard him sayin' tae Davie Proudfoot: 'Davie, ye're no gaun tae let him dae that?' And Davie says, 'Let the laddie be, let him please hissel'.' I blush every time I think on that cartoon, wi' my political simpleness.

Selling *The Spark* and our other pit papers at the pithead was obviously a target for the Wemyss Coal Company, so as I say I have no doubt the reason why my father and my brothers and me were victimised from the

Wellesley and evicted from the Company house was on account of my political activities. We were involved as well in the United Mineworkers of Scotland from about 1930 on. And the other 400 paid off then from the Wellesley were men who had joined this union and who were selected for pay-off and eviction.

Something else that happened to me when I was eighteen and not long after I was paid off at the Wellesley was I got arrested and got twenty-one days in Perth penitentiary. It was disastrous for me. The day I was arrested Pat Devine, John McArthur and big Peter Kerrigan were arranging to have me sent to the Lenin Institute in Moscow for political and art education and then to become the cartoonist for the *Daily Worker*. It was immediately cancelled.

What was happening was that after I was paid off I was starvin'. I was still living at home. My clothes were becoming threadbare. Jimmy Hope from East Wemyss, a militant who had played for Raith Rovers and Blackpool and became a first-class public speaker, worked for an I.L.P. tanner-a-week man—Birrell o' Dunfermline – and he agreed that he would hae us measured for suits o' claes.[209] Wi' the money aff the pit papers we would pay a shilling a week to Jimmy. Well, Jimmy was paid four shillings within four weeks. Then – this is the discipline o' a Communist Party – the Party decided that Communists should not act in any gainful way in doing political work and they stopped our payment to Jimmy Hope. At that stage two other young fellows I knew who lived in Denbeath were up against it. Poverty prevailed in the miners' raws. And one of the two says, 'Hughie, I'm needin' tools. Ah could make money. If you get me the tools and if I make money we'll help you to pey your claes.' Ah says, 'Well, I'll tell you where you'll get the tools. You'll get them in the joinery department o' the school.' I knew the school and I told him how to get them. Well, they went and got the tools. They got theirsels arrested and then they implicated me: I think the police had threatened them that one of them – who had a record – would get more time unless he told the whole story. I guessed that by implication of what they told me when I was arrested and we got thegither.

So I got myself into that situation jist oot o' impoverishment. The other two were arrested on the Friday selling the pit papers at the Wellesley pit. Then I learned the police were looking for me. I went to the police station to find out why and was thrown into a cell beside the others. We were sent post haste to Cupar Sheriff Court on the Saturday morning. A lot o' comrades turned up tae bail me out if I pleaded not guilty which I had told them up until I went into the court I was goin' to do. But as the other two were sentenced first I had the realisation that they had betrayed me. One got, I think, aboot thirty days. The sheriff, an auld man ready for fa'in' intae his box, come to the other one next. He got fourteen days. And then he come to me and said, 'Guilty or not guilty?' And this thing caught into my mind that if I pleaded not guilty I was gaun tae discover my two friends had been treacherous wi' me. I hesitated to the point where the judge became very angry wi' me. I was switherin' in my mind for if I pleaded not guilty they'd be brought as the evidence against me. And I couldnae face the idea o' acceptin' that in oor relationship. So I just said, 'Guilty.' They couldnae believe it. Of the three o' us I was the young boy, the laddie at eighteen: I got twenty-one days' jail.

I remember in Perth jail the warder asked me, 'What age are you?' 'Eighteen.' And there was a wee prisoner sat by, he says, 'You'd be better optin' for the Borstal.' I says, 'Get lost. I'm doing twenty-one days here.' Well, the kind o' experience I had in Perth jail was scrubbing stone slab floors. In the Block 'C' I'd be scrubbin' the flairs all day and they had these big windaes right away up. Stray pigeons would come in strutting and cuck-cooing, their neck feathers iridescent in the bright sunshine. And I used to love just to watch these pigeons coming doon. Pigeons were my favourite birds.

There wis strong enough discipline: you werenae allowed to talk. There was only one quarter of an hour in the day when you were allowed to talk. But you had conversations in the passin' because some worked in the workshops and things like that. It wisnae as brutalisin' a place as the long sentence men up in Peterhead suffered. But it was a most humiliating experience. When you were sittin' in your cell you were given stuff tae towse oot, a soul-destroying job withoot any end result. You was brought oot in the morning and given breakfast – porridge – made to scrub floors jist back and forward, back and forward, no end to it. When they released me they flung me oot withoot giein' me a shower. I didnae have a comb, I had a tie but nae studs – it was these detachable collars then. And ma claes – ye'd think they'd crushed them a'thegither, put a steam roller on them. They were half-way up my legs wi' crinkles. I had no money. And this is the way that I had tae come hame. There was no other way out o' it. If I had been in a reasonable condition I would ha' cleared out, I widnae ha' went home. But there was no alternative but to go home.

Immediately we'd been paid off at the Wellesley in December 1930 we went on to the dole – the whole family. Then we come under the Means Test. It was a ten per cent cut and operated on households, so that any money coming into the house was taken into consideration before you qualified for any kind o' benefit payment. My father's disability pension was counted. So I only got about 4/2d off the dole. In other words, my father was made to keep me. That's despite the fact that my father, me, my brother and my two foster brothers had all been paid off and were all on the dole. I decided to clear out.

Friday was pay-day at the dole. I had drawn my money, I had this four-and-odds in my pocket. I hadnae yet given it to my mother. Jock Clark, who was in a similar situation, came to me one Friday afternoon on a lovely July day in 1933. He had a gruff voice: 'Hughie, are ye gaun tae the berries?' I looked at my mother and I says, 'What about this four-and-odds?' She said, 'Jist keep it.' So Jock and I set out at four o'clock on the Friday afternoon for the berry-picking. We walked a' the road tae Blairgowrie, sixty-odd mile, and landed wi' the risin' sun at the berryfield. As we were walking along frae Perth to Blairgowrie, I was the only one that had money and cigarettes. So we had rests through the night. At every milestone we'd sit on the milestone, smoke a Woodbine and then march off to the next milestone. We were doing this through the night. We finally arrived at one milestone and discovered we had left the matches at the last one. So that did away wi 'our smokin'! Jock, who was about the same age as me, had sandals on and by the time we arrived at Blairgowrie as the sun was risin' – a lovely mornin' – his feet were raw, he was stiff, and he couldnae walk more than two or three steps at a time. I was very good at walkin'.

So we stayed the season at the berries. In Fife it had been a long practice wi' the unemployed tae go tae the berries – raspberries. The berries was the form in which they took their holidays: 'Are ye goin' tae the berries?' This was the first o' me goin' although I knew others who had gone before. There was a whole host o' people I got to know that summer at the berries. There were three Glesgae boys who lived in the tent wi' us and we got close together. We stayed at Blairgowrie until September; I remember that quite clearly because I had my twenty-first birthday in August at the berries. And then four o' us, in the same situation as mysel' under the Means Test, a' decided tae go tae Dundee.

The three others were Johnny O'Brien and Danny Kelly – they came frae the Gorbals – and Paddy Gilmour or (he had aliases) Paddy Garriss. He came frae Cambuslang and he is the most significant one in my experience. He was thirty-four. He had never been insured in his life. He was a kind o' father figure to us. He was a very remarkable person. He had never been in employment in his life. He knocked about sellin' a clean-off powder. Everybody called him P. I presumed P. stood for Paddy or Peter. He had these aliases but we just called him P. Now P. and I got very, very intimate. He was a very smart boy but in the down-and-out sense.

As I say, P. knocked about sellin' a clean-off or scourin' powder. Well, it was an undeveloped commodity at that time. So what P. would do was buy a twopenny packet o' whitenin' powder and go oot to the Lawhill or a brick workers' yard or a building yard and get sand. He always carried as part o' his basic equipment a fine sieve. He would sieve the sand fine and then mix it up wi' the black whitenin' pooder, put it in little packets and sell it off as a clean-off abrasive powder at 4d a packet. He went out every day and did this. He even tried to develop it. Then there were mair ambitious people than P., who would buy bankrupt stock and employ people merely on a commission basis to sell it. So we indulged in that game in Dundee. There was a Major Burbitt, an ex-military nurse – this is what he had on his packet o', for instance, shampoos – and it was P. that introduced me to him. Major Burbitt shoved any kind o' stuff, I think, intae his packets, but it was supposed to be a shampoo.

So Major Burbitt involved the four o' us and we were to get fifty per cent o' the price we were sellin' this commodity at roond the doors. We didnae have any official licence and we got stopped by the police on one or two occasions. But we would spin them a story aboot takin' orders. Major

Burbitt drove us out to the places – Carnoustie, for instance. We discovered that Carnoustie wasnae the kind o' place that ye could sell this stuff. P.'s favourite expression was, 'To sell that stuff you've got tae go into the scruffy quarters.' Dundee was ideal but not a snobbish place like Carnoustie. So the only one that sold anything was me: I gathered half-a-crown. P. hissel' had only selt aboot a tanner's worth, the rest practically nothing. So they depended on ma half-crown to get their expenses. So we went in and had a cup o' tea and maybe a scone for the four o' us. I bought a twopenny packet o' Woodbine in a wee slim packet. And by the time we deducted what we spent on our meal and our expenses there was nothing left. Major Burbitt was supposed to come back in the evening to Carnoustie and pick us up. But then it would only be about two o'clock in the day and there was no prospect o' sellin' any mair in Carnoustie. So we decided to walk home to Dundee, maybe aboot seven mile.

At that time I was lodgin' wi' an old granny in Dundee who lived hersel'. I was payin' 3/6d a week tae her for lodgins. I had to pey my ain meals. My dole money then was 12/6d a week, say 62^1/2 pence and I was spending 17^1/2 pence o' that on the lodgins. That's how we eked out things. Well, because the Major had gone out in the car in the evening but couldnae find us at Carnoustie he got into a tizzy, came back to Dundee and demanded the stuff that I had in a suitcase. That upset the auld lady. She got her son in and I lost my digs and that's when I went to Rose Street to an awfy bloody garret place.

The garret in Rose Street up the Hilltown in Dundee had three beds. And besides the four o' us – P., Johnny O'Brien and Danny Kelly and me – I must admit they had also two other people in the garret as well. So that was six all in one garret. One of the others worked as a street fruit merchant. The other one, a relative o' Freddie Tennant the boxer, what he did I don't know.[210] And as we discovered, the garret was lousy. I soon put a stop to that. Well, we werenae associated wi' these other two. How we managed the three beds was the fruiterer boy was there at night and had one bed but the other one was a night-shift worker. So we had two beds for the four of us. I slept wi' Danny Kelly in one bed, and P., and Johnny O'Brien in the other. That's how it was.

We paid 3/6d a week rent, that was the whole six o' us. And we had only a gas-ring on which to cook. On the Friday, when we drew oor 12/6d frae the dole we bocht mince and onions and then we went up to Warnock's pub in the Overgate and got a fourpenny Snowden pint and a threepenny gless o'wine.[211] These were the first things we did every Friday. We fed on bread if we could get it. We then went up to our garret, put a frying pan on the gas-ring, mixed the mince up wi' water and onions, a little salt, and dipped our bread in it. And that was the only cooked meal we had in the week. What I remember mostly is no' eatin' at a', no' eatin' at a'. Dundee had 23,000 unemployed then, out of a population o' about 220,000. The unemployed would a' be on the Means Test. There was boys that I knew who, because they were outside their own parish, couldnae get parish relief, went into the poorhouse, worked the whole week in the poorhouse for their meals and were only let out on a Sunday or during the weekend to meet their friends.

We were starving. We ate the mince and onions once a week, on the Friday. On the Monday we wouldnae have anything. Ah slept on the Law Hill. Johnny O'Brien and the other boys would get so wearied and fed up – nothing to eat and nothing to smoke – and we'd go up the Law Hill, lie doon and fa' asleep for maist o' the time, or wander round. They were Catholics and they would come to a chapel and Danny Kelly in particular would go in and say his rosary beads round the stations o' the cross. I would go in and sit and wait on him finishin'. Then we'd go for a walk and get oorsels lost again, or maybe up the Law Hill and fa' asleep. That was the kind o' way we lived.

It was absolutely compulsive in me to be politically active. So almost immediately I landed in Dundee I went down to the Unity Hall and acquainted myself wi' the Communist Party people who operated frae the Hall, at the fit o' the Hilltown. That was their headquarters for the whole of Dundee. I become acquainted with the leadin' comrades there: Jim Hodgson, an immaculate little man who was the Party secretary, and his assistant, Jimmy Connacher, and Arthur Nicoll, who eventually went to Spain to fight in the Civil War – one of the most solid, natural little working-class activists, militants and agitators I ever met.[212] There were young Y.C.L.-ers in Dundee but there wis no proper organisation. So they suggested that I should become the secretary of the Y.C.L. In these days you had to be twenty-five to become a member o' the Communist Party, and I was only twenty-one, although as I've said already I had been made an honorary member o' the Party aboot 1929 when I was about seventeen year old because there wasn't a Y.C.L. in my area in Fife.

So we got a good Y.C.L. goin' in Dundee. We had no trouble gettin' young people and there was a lot o' promise in them. Some o' them actually went to the Spanish Civil War later. I remember two o' them that I had recruited into the Y.C.L. One was killed at Jarama: McGuire.[213] Then there was Kennedy – I think that was his name. And at Jarama he received a bullet through the side o' his jaw. It went right through his head and although it disturbed his sight a little bit he was recovering from the wound when I went into Spain. I met him in Albacete. I don't know what happened to that laddie efter that.

This brings me on to the Hunger Marches. Whenever I became unemployed at the end of 1930 I had joined the National Unemployed Workers' Movement. The unemployed signed on at given times and there were always unemployed at the Labour Exchange in Leven. They signed on in groups every quarter of an hour, and they had to sign three days a week then. So there were always masses of unemployed at the Exchange. That was the only one in East Fife, from Wemyss to Cupar. It became a famous public meeting place. And ye could deal wi' a' the issues – something that disnae happen now. Ye have nae access tae the unemployed now. But it was there you a' signed on. And the N.U.W.M. people collected on the Friday, a penny a week, and that gave the expenses for winning cases and appeals. Unemployment was always a big problem even in the '20s, and in minin' areas in particular, wi' the payin' off o' miners as a result o' the depression – the Great Depression they called it: a euphemistic term for poverty created by the crisis o' capitalism at that time.

The first March that I was on against the Means Test was a March tae Cupar, the county town where the Fife County Council was located. The March went from East and West Fife to Cupar. And it was led by Alex Moffat. I'm no' quite sure what their demands were in gaun tae Cupar but I think it was related to gettin' relief from the parish council. It was either the beginnin' of 1932 or the latter end of 1931.[214] The March took in the West o' Fife people, the Kirkcaldy people, Milton o' Balgonie and further inland, but mainly from East Fife to West Fife because forward you have the fishing areas and they werenae implicated. They were always regarded as sort o' non-industrial and very little political activity took place. The Marchers were predominantly miners because the whole o' this area in East Fife and West Fife was predominantly minin'. I could count fifteen pits; now there is not one left. But it shows you the domination.

So Alex Moffat was in charge o' the March. And then the local leaders were activists in the trade union struggles which dominated the whole o' this minin' area here: Johnny Boyle, for instance, and Jimmy Meek. Jimmy Meek was a miner and he was treasurer in our group o' people that produced the pit papers. Now the strange thing is that Jimmy never joined the Communist Party. George Middleton came through to Fife and wanted to know why a man who could co-operate wi' us in that close way could not join the Communist Party. We never raised the question. Later, Jimmy Meek was killed in what we called the Dubbie pit, the Frances colliery at Kirkcaldy. Jimmy Meek and Johnny Boyle, like myself, belonged to Denbeath. Denbeath was the hub in which a tremendous amount of political activity took place. Jimmy and Johnny along wi' other local activists carried on the N.U.W.M. and on Fridays took turns in standing the whole day at the Labour Exchange and collecting the pennies. They were continually holding meetings outside the Labour Exchange.

The March collected on the way, starting from West Fife and along down to the coast here from Kirkcaldy, I reckon maybe about three or four hundred – which was a considerable demonstration. Cupar for the people in East Fife was only an eleven-mile walk. There are very few villages ye could pass through. We went up Dangerfield. There was only the country farmhouses and farm labourers. We had Frank Pitcairn, pen name o' Claud Cockburn, on the March, reportin' for the *Daily Worker*.[215] Well, when we arrived at Cupar he described that area to the north and the west as the edge of the bible belt: in arriving at Cupar we had entered the bible area. When we got to Cupar we stayed the night in a wooden scout hut. Quite frankly I was a bit raw at that time – I'd be about twenty – so the political things that happened I'm no' too clear about. But nevertheless that was the first March we had against the Means Test and the economy cuts.

And then I was on two Hunger Marches to Edinburgh frae here in East Fife, before I went to Dundee. The first one must have been about 1932, after the March tae Cupar and after I had been in prison.[216] How I got involved in it was, well, being a member o' the Communist Party and discussin' a' things. The Communist Party really was the organisin' factor in a' these things. I knew what was takin' place. I was a party to the decisions so I was very intimate wi' the thing. We even had Wullie Gallacher doon there then to appeal to the unemployed tae jine in the Edinburgh Hunger Marches. I mind o' Wullie addressin' the unemployed at Leven. He didnae bore people. He said things in short, very distinctive statements. 'You either march against the Means Test now or you march to war later.' Now they understood what he was sayin'. I always remember that. He put these two things in juxtaposition. They said everything that need be said.

I mind that first March to Edinburgh was in the winter-time – cold, cold weather. The Fife March started from Leven. We marched tae Kirkcaldy then Inverkeithing. We stayed the night in Inverkeithing. There were women on this March, because at Inverkeithing I met Tommy Bloomfield's sister and his mother. They were on the March as well.[217] We come over in the ferry from Inverkeithing. It was a big Hunger March organised for the whole of Scotland. After we'd landed in Edinburgh and when we were marchin' round about, in the distance comin' towards us is the group frae the West o' Scotland. They come past and as they passed, auld Adam Hamilton, who'd come frae the West to live in Buckhaven, recognised his friends frae the West. And there was a terrific cheer went up. It must ha' been heard a' over as the twa groups, West and East, met passin' each other.

We landed in the Waverley Market. It was an iron structure wi' a gantry round about. There was Johnny Boyle and big Jimmy Meek and me. We were a' sleepin' there and the cauld was unbearable: stone floors. We couldnae suffer the cold. About the back o' twelve o'clock three laddies had their sticks and they're marchin' up and down shoutin', 'We want a bed!' And I said tae Boyle and Jimmy, 'This is for me. We're no' gaun tae sleep here. It's too bloody cauld.' So I went doon and jined the three boys whae were marchin' up and shakin' their sticks, 'We want a bed!' And then eventually before it finished, between twelve and one o'clock, every Marcher in the Waverley Market was marching and shoutin' at the top o' his voice, 'We want a bed!' It must ha' been everywhere gaun aboot Princes Street and these places. And there was panic wi' the police, and even wi' Harry McShane and these people, about what was gaun tae happen.

I also participated in the Hunger March to Edinburgh in 1933. We were unable to find accommodation one night in Edinburgh, so Harry McShane, the leader of the March, took all his men on to Princes Street to bed down for the night. We all bedded down on the pavement just at Princes Street Gardens. That night a huge crowd of people turned out to watch us bedding down in Princes Street. I slept between old Maria Stewart from Methilhill and an old Miss Smith from Dundee on the pavement in front of the Gardens. Oh, there were plenty of women on the March, Tommy Bloomfield of Kirkcaldy's mother and his sister were on it again. The women marched alongside the men. We all bedded down thegither in our clothes on the pavement. We didnae have any pyjamas in these days!

With the sun rising in the morning some of the Marchers went across to the shops and shaved themselves. But there was one big woman we knew as The Amazon, who came from Vale of Leven. She was sleeping across the tram line. When the workman's tram came along in the morning before the traffic started, the workmen had tae get out and lift The Amazon, a big, strong, fair-headed woman, bodily off the lines tae get by.

At dinner-time our field kitchen came along and the police chief told Harry McShane, 'This is Princes Street. You can't feed here.' Harry told him, 'It was good enough for us to sleep here, it's good enough for us to feed here.' We all got two bananas the piece. The word went along the ranks in front of the Gardens: 'This is Princes Street. You must keep it clean. Put all your banana skins on the top of the spikes in front of the Gardens.' This caused quite a lot of interest, particularly amongst the reporters and photographers. They all wanted to take photographs of the display of banana skins on every spike in front of the Gardens. Old Maria Stewart said, 'Well, put a half-crown in my box and I'll let you take photographs.'

When we were on Princes Street I was collectin' on the side across from the Gardens. An auld lady drew up in a black car. She was dressed in a black dress. She asked me a number o'questions, why I was there and how I was feelin'. Then she took oot bags o' silver and she put a half-crown in the collectin' box. Then she asked me another question, went back into her coat, brought out another two half-crowns and put them in. Later we discovered that somebody had been manufacturin' half-crowns and quite a number o' them were bein' put into the collectin' boxes. And although I associated this wi' the auld lady I couldnae believe that she was shovin' in counterfeits!

Early in the following year I went on the Hunger March to London. I think it began in January 1934. By that time of course I was living in Dundee. Well, the N.U.W.M. in Dundee had a hall in the first street that run up on the left parallel to the Hilltown, a broken-down, squalid place. It was near Rose Street, where we got those digs in the garret. Most o' the leading members o' the N.U.W.M. in Dundee were also members of the Communist Party. And they organised the Dundee contingent that left for London.

We were continually having meetings and appealing to the people. We held meetings every Sunday in the City Square. Although as a result of police trouble in 1930 or '31 marches and demonstrations through the town were banned, traditional meeting sites were still open. The meetings were probably organised by the Communist Party. But the N.U.W.M. was related in a very close way so that was the instrument that was used, the organisational form that was used tae make the appeal. But the Communist

Party was the central political organiser in Dundee. The I.L.P. as far as I know was non-existent. The Labour Party wasn't an activist party in the sense of having open arousal public meetings. They had their premises just off Murraygate. And we – the Communist Party and the N.U.W.M. – used these premises also on occasions for night meetings.

You could never describe the Communist Party in Dundee as a mass party. But it was a very highly significant party. The proof o' that seems to lie in the fact that Bob Stewart, the prohibitionist who to some extent had been associated wi' Scrymgeour, polled 10,000 votes in the elections, which was a considerable vote for a Communist candidate.[218] But obviously personality counted very greatly because Bob was a very well-known public figure. We had a very good lively and cohesive party and it had tremendous political significance in regard to Hunger March propaganda and the demonstrations and activities against the Means Test.

There were about thirty Hunger Marchers in the 1934 Dundee group. The boy who was in charge was Jimmy Stewart. Now Jimmy Stewart was also a member of the Communist Party, but he had the image of an N.U.W.M. man, not a Communist. He was a public street orator or agitator. I don't remember him very well from his involvement in the general politics of the Party. But he certainly was one of the leaders of the National Unemployed Workers' Movement. Arthur Nicoll, whom I menioned earlier, was in the Dundee contingent. Earlier in the '20s Arthur had actually worked in the pits in West Fife, though I think he was a Dundee man. Then he had worked in the jute industry, but also in the Caledonian shipyard on the Tay. I don't think he could have been a skilled tradesman, it must have been general labouring. Oh, he was a rough-shod man, a little man, stocky build, maybe fractionally smaller even than me but robust. And I remember Tom Clarke bein' on the March frae Dundee as the first-aid man. He was distinctive in that. I didnae know him personally.

All the Dundee contingent were in good physical shape when we left Dundee, except Jock Tadden. Jock had been a soldier in the British army in India where he had contracted malaria. I've seen Jock on a burnin' summer day at the fit o' the Hilltoon wi' his teeth chitterin' and shakin' wi' the effects o' malaria. Later on Jock was killed at Jarama in the Spanish War.

You went on the Hunger March with whatever you were wearin'. Really, there was the Green Market doon in the dock area where a' the puir folk went at the weekend. It was where a'thing was sold. Well, my shoes had gone done and I bought mysel' a pair o' shoes for a shilling, and a pair o' socks for a tanner at the Green Market in order to go on the Hunger March. I got a big motorin' coat there too, an overcoat. I don't remember what I paid for it. I find it difficult to describe but it was one o' these bulky coats wi' the wide armpits. So it came in handy when we run intae inclement weather. I never wore a hat: I had a head o' hair then! I had two shirts, because there was an incident on the March at Birmingham when we rested in which a boy aboot my age named Small – we called him Smallie – and I were larkin' aboot sparrin' and I accidentally struck him on the brow wi' my head and he had to go to the hospital to get his brow stitched. And of course my shirt was all blood and Littlejohn, who was prominent in the Dundee N.U.W.M. and was on the March, made a sarcastic remark. He said ah wis forced to change ma shirt because o' that blood – a kind o' aspersion against ma cleanliness. I got annoyed wi' him and I was very near doing something physical to him because he was a scruffy character. Well, people could be excused for being scruffy because we had no money to buy anything, living off o' second-hand clothes we got oot o' the Green Market. Well, I think I had a change because I had to put my clean shirt on after that. But quite frankly that first shirt had been worn from Scotland, maybe about a fortnight. So there could be something said against that. But there was no way I could do any washing. I had a change o' clothin' then, but most o' the Marchers from Dundee didnae.

I had a scarf. I didnae carry a walking stick but everybody else did – well, most o' the Marchers had sticks. Ye've got to understand the kind o' incidents that had been happening up till then. The police had been interferin' in a' the meetins and demonstrations and protests against the Means Test, frae the beginnin'. Baton charges were takin' place in many towns. No doubt about that. In such a staid place as Kilmarnock, where my father came from, there was a baton charge. In the big demonstration that took place in Kirkcaldy there was a baton charge, and I witnessed that. This was in the early '30s.[219] I'm illustrating the conditions that prevailed that explained the attitude toward carrying sticks. The sticks were tae help in the walkin' but at the same time they could be used as weapons if the Marchers were attacked. I didnae carry a stick because there's an arrogance in young people, the arrogance is that you didnae need a stick. Ye could walk to London. Anyway it wasnae a real consideration in my mind: aggressiveness was not a part o' my psychology. There was a wee bit o' ambivalence in my nature: while recognisin' the need for force on occasions, I was basically a very placid person and was opposed to violence.

Well, when we set off from Dundee we gathered at Ninewells. I don't think there was a band. We didn't get any publicity. I think we must have taken the train from Dundee because we certainly didnae march to Glasgow. But for sixteen miles we marched out o' Glasgow and then we got on buses and were driven intae Kilmarnock. We had a parade through Kilmarnock. The last time I had been in Kilmarnock was in 1924 when I went wi' my father to stay for a fortnight: we had relatives there. I was very keen to see if any o' them turned up to the Hunger March: I never saw one.

We left Kilmarnock and I remember passing through Riccarton and seeing Burns' monument. Then we went to old Cumnock or New Cumnock but it was then I become aware that John McGovern, the I.L.P. M.P., was on the March.[220] He marched parts o' the way. He was relatively better-dressed than the Hunger Marchers, which wasnae a hard accomplishment. I remember him being interviewed on that March by the radio people. I remember on one of the earlier Hunger Marches to Edinburgh, McGovern burnin' the *Daily Express* at the Meadows because o' misrepresentation.

Goin' over the Leadhills, comin' I think it was intae Sanquhar there was a blizzard. And when the blizzard came on I had my haversack wi' my spare clothes in it, I put the motorin' coat right over my head and bein' a short person ah must have seemed like a little bundle gaun through the blizzard. Big Peter Kerrigan he comes up behind me and looks doon tae see who this little bulk is, wi' this big motorin' coat over my head and my hunch back as a result o' my pack and whatnot. And going over the Leadhills there was a boy named McKendrick from Dundee. The wind was blawin' pretty stiff and we were carryin' the banners over the hills where the only occupants were sheep. The wind was racking the banner around and McKendrick and I fell oot because the two o' us wis carryin' the banner and we couldnae maintain oor balance. But why the hell we were carryin' the banner is simply beyond me. It was the main banner. It just said, 'The Scottish Contingent'. But why we were carryin' the banner in a bloody place like that wi' strong winds blowin', I don't know.[221]

We were in Sanquhar, Gretna and Annan. I think we missed Dumfries. Now I cannae mind how many crossed the Border but it was quite a considerable number o' Marchers. It was quite an impressive army we had. I would say we were maybe comin' up for about a thousand.[222] The first stop over the Border was Carlisle. Then we went over the Shap. And the Shaps then were these auld primitive roads. It was quite an experience for me goin' ower the Shaps. Sixteen miles o' nothing through the hills, then there was a slope doon and we arrived. It was dark. And auld Tom Mann came up and joined us on the rest o' the March down into Kendal. We were then billeted in the poorhouse, the only place they could find for us, and it was very, very cold. Big Frank Hillhouse frae Dundee, who drove a little van like a pickup but it didnae have any sides on it, he had nowhere else to go in this poorhouse but the morgue. And in the mornin' he confessed to us that he couldnae ha' been caulder or he would ha' been a corpse hissel'. He was lyin' on the slab where the corpses usually lay. Well, we were luckier. We were put into a little room, maybe twelve feet by ten feet, and it had these inset wooden bricks on the floor. We had straw tae sleep on. That's a' I remember. We never got food there. We never got tasks to do there, we were only billeted there. They had to find us somewhere and that's where we were docked.

We took a diversion on one occasion and went intae Blackpool, which wasn't on our route. We were taken in in buses and went to the baths. This was to give us the opportunity for a wee bit recreation and also get ourself cleaned up. I remember big George Middleton, who was a member of the Communist Party then, was there. We were a' in the nude and he was gettin' pot-bellied. And George was a lovely person. Arthur Nicoll, who had quite a nice sense o' humour said, 'George is the only person who could whisper in his ain ear', because he had the most magnificent ugly face.

When we were passing through Crewe I was in my usual white shirt. It must have been a pleasant day. And when we were marchin' through Crewe it was at the time when the Reichstag Fire trial was on. Dimitrov was standing up to the threats o' Goering and became a folk hero during the March. So, many o' the people in Crewe were shoutin', 'Long live Dimitrov!'[223] As I was passin' along the street, a reasonable lookin' young laddie, suddenly a baker's shop door opened and a youngish motherly type o' woman looks at me, stares at me, wonderin' what the name o' heavens is gaun on. And suddenly she realises what it is. She has a poke o' cream cookies in her hand and she dashes forward and hands me the poke o' cookies. I'll tell ye I've loved that woman ever since.

When we rested for the night in a place we had little social events all together. And we would learn the different songs o' the struggle. There was an Aberdeen comrade who sang a song that I learned then, *Stenka Razin* and then there was the *Irish Rebel*. McKendrick, wi' whom I'd got a wee bit annoyed goin' over Leadhills wi' the banner, was a busker. In these days people had to augment their dole money in various ways. McKendrick had a lovely strong tenor voice. And he learned me one of his buskin' songs, nothing to do with the struggle. While we were marching we sang songs like *We're Going to Fight the Means Test*. McKendrick would sing any kind o' song but mostly we began to learn the songs o' the struggle, *Joe Hill* and songs like that.[224] I remember once we were passing a graveyard on the March and Arthur Nicoll starts singing, 'Arise, ye starvelings...' – *The Internationale*. *The Red Flag* wasnae so much sung. Wee Joe Mathers, who sold the *Daily Worker* at the fit o' the Hilltoon, a wee stunted man because o' the poverty o' his upbringing – and not only his family – he would sing:

> The people's Flag is deepest pink,
> It's not as red as people think.
> And ere their limbs grow stiff and cold
> The Dundee workers will be sold.

So we had that kind o' attitude tae the *Red Flag*. When we were gaun intae Birmingham somebody started singin' 'Pack up your troubles in your old kit bag'. And Kerrigan blew his top: 'Cut that bloody...!' And, being the puritanical kind o' Scots Communists that we were, big Kerrigan put an end to that song. It was a jingo song – pack up your troubles, nothing to worry about.

But talkin' aboot singin', we began to associate and come close together as a group o' people and we developed oor understandin' o' things and we developed friendships that sustained us possibly for the rest o' oor lives. And singin' was an important part.

We stayed in Birmingham for the night. I think we stayed for two days. There was one or two places where we stayed for two days. That was to give us a wee bit of rest. I never had any problems wi' my feet. But many o' them had really very bad blistered feet. Tom Clarke was fully engaged the whole time into the late night treatin' their feet. I had the shoes I had bought for a shillin' in the Green Market. Well, when we landed, I think it may have been about Kendal or Penrith, the shoes had given way. So the Co-operative gave me a new pair o' walkin' boots, good, heavy walkin' boots. And I never had any problems wi' my feet. But there were many who really had feet in a horrible state.

I cannae remember anybody droppin' out the March.[225] There was a boy who, when we were well down in England – I think we were gaun near to St Albans – and walking through the dark, was struck by a car. Tom Clarke had to treat him and he was taken into hospital. By the time we set oot in the mornin' and by the time we got tae oor destinations it would be dark, really dark. For instance, after we crossed Shap Fell we looked down and we could see lights down in the low ground as we were comin' off the hills. Tom Mann came out from Kendal to join us and it was utterly dark. There wasnae the same traffic on the roads then. We didnae have lights or a lamp with us on the road.

On occasions the reception we got was sparse. But at central points you would maybe have a reception group. In a place like Crewe, for instance, you would get people on the main streets where the shopping was. And maybe they were unaware o' what was happening. But then we had a reasonable reception. When we got into Rugby, I think it was, Jimmy Stewart, who was in charge o' the Dundee contingent, came to me and says, 'You and I have got an invitation to the Working Men's Rockabye Club.' They were havin' a party. And for the first time I witnessed families in a workingmen's club havin' a social evenin'. Because we werenae members the members stood up tae get us drinks. We couldnae buy drinks oorsels. So we spent a social night there. It was my first experience o' that. The clubs in Fife or Dundee were always macho, and the pubs tae.

On the March there were no incidents either by the police or the Fascists. When we arrived in Coventry there was a meeting held in which we were told to be careful because we expected interference by the Mosleyite Blackshirts. No incident as far as I know happened there, except what happened to Smallie and me. We drifted away from the meetin' in the dark. We were jist wantin' a look around. We became aware that three young men were followin' us. So I told Smallie – he was hopin' to get bouts and earn money as a boxer – 'I think there may be bloody Fascist elements comin' efter us. Stand wi' yer back tae that wa' and I'll stand beside ye, and jist be ready.' So we stood and they spoke to us, 'What are ye doin' ?' 'Oh, we're lookin' for work.' They eventually left. I had made it clear that Smallie was a boxer. And he looked it. I think they were Fascists. There was nae Fascists interferin' wi' the meetin'. But there may have been a number in the crowd. Because o' the strength o' the meetin' that we got they maybe decided not to interfere because they wid ha' got chewed up.

But there was nae opposition or abuse, nor provocations by the police. Well, there was a situation at St Albans that was created by the police. St Albans was our last stop before London. On the previous March somebody had thrown a brick at the Marchers, I think it was in Oxford Street, and it created an incident that caused the police to interfere. So the police must have been very concerned about what was goin' tae happen and we got an ultimatum from the Metropolitan Police that we had to give up oor sticks. Naturally this created a lot o' resentment amongst the Marchers. They claimed they needed their sticks as part o' their walkin' equipment. And possibly some of them did need sticks. McShane, Kerrigan and the group leaders said, 'We're here to demonstrate against the operation o' the Means Test and the economy cuts and not to have a diversion or fight wi' the police which would misrepresent the whole idea of the March. We're here to protest peacefully and wi' discipline.' And they said that we should give up oor sticks. But the bulk o' the Marchers refused and they were led by two people in particular: Jimmy Beecroft, from Bellshill, I think, and Norman Kennedy from Dundee. Beecroft was a very significant person in the miners and Unemployed Workers' Movement but he was what we called anarchistic, an out-and-out physical protester. Well, he took the hard line, he took the hard line that this was part of the struggle. He opposed the giving up o' the sticks in a very, very strong way.[226] The other one, Kennedy, was not a workin'-class lookin' type, more sort o' lower middle class. For instance, he wore plus-fours when I knew him in Dundee. He was a cultivated kind o' a person. I don't know what he had done for a living. But he was on the March. He was one o' these sort o' people it was in the fashion then to become a political person. He was opposed to giving the sticks up. He didnae represent in any way the sort o' anarchistic, violent type. He represented the very educated type o' person. So McShane, Kerrigan and these boys had quite an argument before the Marchers finally agreed to give up their sticks. Now that was one o' the most dramatic incidents in an otherwise well-organised, well-carried through demonstration. So the leadership took over the sticks. Whit happened to them then I don't know. We never got them back. They would be used for firewood. But I didn't have a stick myself anyway.

On the road we had a field kitchen. And the cook was I think a person named Skilling, I remember at one place – I think it was Kendal – Skilling for some reason had been unable to present us wi' a proper meal. I don't know what the stuff was made o'. It was raw. How he had contrived it I don't know. But we called it skilly. We got fed wi' skilly. It was a repulsive kind o' meal we got. It wasnae even a stew, it was like a kind o' porridge but it wasnae oatmeal. I think there was a ground cheese in it as well. It was something we stuck to. We manufactured a new dish.

Another thing I remember was that big Frank Hillhouse who drove the little van like a pick-up had the *Daily Worker* cartoonist with him. He had chalked along the whole length of the van a cartoon o' 'The Loose-Mouthed Monster'. At that time the Loch Ness Monster was news. But the cartoonist drew Ramsay MacDonald, who belonged to Lossiemouth, as 'The Loose-Mouthed Monster'. It was Nessie, wi' Ramsay MacDonald's features painted white on it. He was the prime minister but he was beginnin' to babble 'On, on, and on. And up, up and up.' It was quite clear that his brain was beginnin' to go.

I didnae correspond wi' home when I was on the March tae London.

I wasnae a great letter-writer to my family. Oh, we were close. But we didnae talk aboot the intimate experience of things. And I didnae receive any letters frae them either.

Well, we marched into London. There we began to get a big support from the people gathered in the streets. There was no incidents like what had happened on the previous March. The main incident was that one night Donald Renton and me held the meetin' in Tottenham in the dark. The lightin' wisnae the same then as it is now so we were mair or less addressin' the crowd in the dark. I spoke first. It wasn't the first time I'd spoken in public. But I wisnae an experienced political platform man. I mind I spoke about the menace o' Fascism, about the situation wi' the Means Test, and the crisis in capitalism. Donald come efter I finished and complimented me on the material that I had used. So that gave me a wee bit hert. Donald was a really experienced speaker. He was a wee man wi' a big voice. The first time I ever met him, I think it was a discussion on the miners that I attended in Falkirk in connection wi' the N.U.W.M., I marvelled at the sound o' his voice.

We went to the Houses of Parliament to lobby oor separate M.P.s. And the Dundee group had Dingle Foot, a Liberal M.P. His wife came out and he then took us into the foyer to meet auld Isaac Foot, his father. While we were talking to him Lady Astor comes rushin' into the foyer. She looks at a boy frae Lochee – I knew him very well but I forget his name – and she looks at the rest o' us, and we were a' sma'ish men, and she says sarcastically: 'So you're all the big bad Scotsmen who've come down to murder us all? Why don't you wait on a Labour Government?' And Hughie, the boy frae Lochee, says, 'We're no' wantin' a Labour Government.' 'What Government are you wantin'?' 'We're wantin' a Soviet Government.' She got off her mark.[227]

Dingle Foot said tae us, 'Ye cannae get intae the House of Commons. But if you promise to behave yourselves I'll see if I can get you into the House o' Lords.' So we agreed that we would not create an incident and Dingle took us in. It was one o' the Cecils that was talkin', aboot some laddie that had been birched.[228] And ye see the dozin' auld lords actually sleepin', half o' them. And then we see the younger types, and one in particular – immaculate black hair wi' a baby face. And none o' them seemed to be payin' ony attention to this Cecil. Oh, Christ, they're the people who rule us!

We stayed in London I think it must have been a day or two then we came home by train to Dundee.

I think the Hunger March undoubtedly drew attention to the hunger that existed. But I think the main effect was to develop the consciousness o' people. Being a Marxist you know you're no' gaun tae get any immediate results. It's a process o' development and it takes the form of struggles and the class struggle in a' its aspects. I didn't expect any dramatic victory. The Hunger March had a big impact on me personally because, apart frae the Spanish War – which was and still remains the central experience o' ma life

– the Hunger Marches were the main involvement on the broad political front.[229] The Hunger Marches gave us a sense o' understandin' what Marx meant when he talked aboot the proletariat being the main instrument for changin' capitalism intae a socialist society.

I didnae find any employment in Dundee after the 1934 March. As I've told you, our dole money could only give us one meal a week – and a pretty miserable meal at that. Quite frankly we starved. But we tried to do jobs, little jobs here and there, on the fly, for tae get an odd bob or two. Johnny O'Brien left and went back tae Glasgow and that left Danny Kelly, P. – Paddy Garris, alias Paddy or Peter Gilmour – and me. I was sellin' this clean-off powder. I couldnae do that job, it was something I couldnae take tae. But sometimes when I got so desperate I helped P. and that maybe eked us out a wee bit tae because P. was living purely on what he sold as cleaner. So I come home to Fife one weekend and P. packed a small suitcase wi' this stuff. It was ten shillings' worth at 4d a packet. When I went back tae Dundee, P. and Kelly had disappeared. I was left masel'. I never knew where they went. I think they were becomin' discouraged. Well, I immediately decided that was me finished with Dundee. So I come back almost immediately tae Fife. Years later, during the War, a miner who came to Fife from Cambuslang, where P. belonged, told me that P. had become the manager o' a workman's club there.

Well, I came back home and went immediately to the Michael pit. Apparently there were jobs opening up then. I went to the under-manager there, a very significant under-manager compared to the usual stupid, ignorant, blusterin' types, a man who I had a tremendous respect for and that even the Communists had a lot o' respect for – Stewart Bald. And he gave me a job. That was in January 1935 and I was still working in the Michael when I decided to go to Spain to fight wi' the International Brigade.

Tom Clarke

After leaving Harris Academy in Dundee when I was fourteen I had several different jobs. I worked in a butcher's, then in the shipyard, then with John Menzies the wholesale newsagents, then in the jute works, and finally I was portering for J. K. Mearns. In December 1924, not long before I was seventeen, I had a row with my boss. So I enlisted in the army, in the Cameron Highlanders. I served in this country, at Inverness and Edinburgh, but also in Germany at Cologne and Wiesbaden, then I did four years in Burma and two in India.

I'd been a Regular in the Camerons for eight years when I came out the army in January '33. I came back home to Dundee. There was no work, there was nothing doing. I couldn't get a job and you had the threat o' the Means Test. I was the eldest in our family. I had six brothers and two sisters. The two sisters were working and one brother. My father was a french polisher.

After I came home in January I got money for about six months, 15/3d a week or 76 new pence. That was for a single person. Then I was Means Tested and got nothing. Actually, I was really intending to leave home again and go away. But my mother said, 'No, no,' she says, 'we're a'right, you know, we'll manage.' But I did go away for a while.

I was becoming politically involved. I was still on the army reserve, but that didn't make any difference, I still became politically involved. One of the occasions I was on the City Square in Dundee and became involved. I was well-dressed, I had a fifty-bob suit on. There was a fellow standing beside me and he was criticising the speaker. Well, I was fairly naive at that time politically. But ah says, 'The bloke's telling the truth.' We got into discussion and shortly after I noticed there was a huge crowd standing round us. The meeting had finished. But then the next thing I saw, a couple of policemen came over and they told me, 'Get a move on.' I said, 'But what …?' 'Get a move on.' 'But,' I says, 'what about him?' 'Get a move on.' So I heard a voice saying, 'Ye'll hae tae get a move on, Tam. These bastards would swing for their mother.' I found out later who had spoken. I also found out that the fellow who had been in discussion with me was a detective. He was well-dressed too.

Well, these sorts of things led on – no opportunity of work nor such like – and I had been on demonstrations against the Means Test, on unemployed demonstrations in the town and such like. I eventually joined the Communist Party in '33, '34, round about then, in Dundee. Jimmy Hodgson was the secretary at that time. I never joined the National Unemployed Workers' Movement. Then when there was noise of a Hunger March coming off, I says, 'Well, I'll join that. I'll go on the Hunger March.'

The purpose of the March was marching against the Means Test. This was the whole thing because at that time, well, you had the Means Test operating. And if you were living in a household where there was somebody working, well, they had to keep you. This was the whole sum and substance of the thing.

This March was to come off in January 1934 to London. When I was in the army I was in the military band, and we were given first-aid training, stretcher bearing, and this sort of thing. So I had this wee bit skill of first-aid and such like which I didn't think at that time would be much use. But I was anxious to do something so I decided I would volunteer for the March. There would be about forty of us from Dundee and we went by motor lorry or closed van to Glasgow. Everybody collected there from Scotland.[230]

We slept in Glasgow that night. I think we were in a place in the Gorbals. They asked us if any of us knew anything about first-aid and there were about six of us. We were put in there. And we always marched at the rear of the column, just in case there was anybody dropped out. I remember there was one Aberdeen lad along with me and this other Glasgow fellow but he eventually fell out. He was crippling them with his ideas! He knew nothing of first-aid: he burst blisters with his hands

On the following day – it was the Monday – we left Glasgow. And I think all Glasgow turned out to see us off. I remember we were going through Glasgow and the Chief Constable came up to Harry McShane and asked him if he would split the March up to allow the traffic to get on. But McShane told him, 'Glasgow's ours today.' And he just carried on. I heard there would be about 50,000 marched along with us on the first day.[231]

We marched out of Glasgow. The weather was miserable, everybody's spirits was high. And after a bit we got on to a bus and they took us in buses to Kilmarnock. We stayed there the night.

In the first-aid section we really didn't have any work for the first day or two after that. We were going through the Burns' country. At Cumnock I remember sleeping in a masonic hall with Burns round about me and all the rest of it.[232] And the weather was fairly miserable. It was sleety, raining and such like.

I was fortunate in the sense that having come out the army and was reasonably fit and such like and had half-decent clothes, I didn't have to depend on anything at that time. But the feet of some of the Marchers were bad to start with, I'll admit, because you had fellows who had never done any walking at all. They had new boots. They'd got all these ammunition boots, army boots out of Millet's, I think it was. It was cruel on the feet for anybody who had never walked before. And they were coming with all sorts of blistered feet, stone bruises, and what not. Eventually some of them were even wanting massaged. We drew the line at that!

When we got over the Borders into Carlisle we went into the workhouse and they tried to impose workhouse conditions. But the leaders of the March – McShane, Kerrigan, Middleton and such like – wouldn't have anything like that.'No, no, we're coming in here, we're just sleeping in here. We're no' gaun tae be used as casuals.' We were allowed to go in and out. I went up to the hospital section and met some of the nurses and asked them if they could give us bandages and such like. The nurses were very kind. We got loaded up with bandages, different little medical things we asked for, first-aid. We also got a drink o' cocoa and such like.

I met a Catholic priest in Carlisle. He was a young lad and he had brought out the village to cheer us on the way.There weren't many in the village. But he'd come into Carlisle then to see us and ask us all about it. He was an Irishman. He was telling us about unemployment and the effect it had on the village where he was padre. He wished us the best of luck. That was the first experience I had had of the church actually coming in and expressing themselves in such a way.

Things weren't too bad by that time. We got on ultimately down to about Shap. I had to fall out because I had developed a touch o' colic. We'd been working on a stone floor and I think that was one o' the reasons. And the next day because o' the colic I was sent on by bus and missed marching over Shap Fells. That was usually the worst part of the March, I'd heard. But the weather wasn't too bad. It wasn't snowing at that time. And I remember that day when I was waiting on the Marchers coming in I met a couple of fellows who were on the tramp and they asked me where I was going. I told them, 'I'm going down to London.' 'Oh,' one of them says, 'go back. When you're on the road,' he says, 'never come into England. They put you in the spike and it's bloody awful. You've got to work breaking stones and all this sort of thing.' The spike was the English expression for the workhouse. If you were on the tramp you went in there and you were kept there for at least a day making up for your accommodation. And seemingly if you jumped the dyke the police were after you and you would get fourteen days or something like that. This was the gen I picked up from these fellows and they thought I was stupid. But when I told them I was going on the Hunger March they didn't have a clue. They were obviously professional tramps.

We got to Warrington and again we went up to the hospital there. It was an Irish doctor who was in charge. She would have given us the hospital if we'd asked for it. They were so friendly and offered us all the assistance. But we carried on.

One time when we were on the road this car drew up. I think it was a Rolls Royce – I'm not very good on cars. This woman and bloke got out. They were taking newsreels or films. Kerrigan said, 'That's Nancy Cunard.' I didn't know at the time who Nancy Cunard was.[233] To me here we were fighting capitalism and yet ye'd get these people coming along and dropping money, maybe a pound note or more, into a collection bag. I remember quizzing Kerrigan about this. I says, 'How the hell does this happen?' He says, 'Well, they're so accustomed to giving tips this doesn't mean a thing.'

They may have intended well, they may not, but they just gave tips.

A man who was the best dressed on the March often walked beside us in the rear. I asked whae he wis. He says, 'I'm the M.P., John McGovern.' He says, 'I'm comin' along wi' ye.' He says, 'I've been under lots of threats.' I says, 'What for?' He said he had lifted the mace or something in the House of Commons and his life was in danger. I remember going through the different towns people used to ask, 'Who's that bloke with the soft hat?' 'Well, that's McGovern.' 'Who is McGovern?' They didn't know who McGovern was until we told them.

In Birmingham we went into this school and it was full of policemen and warders from the workhouse. McShane was just a little fellow. He says, 'Come on, get all your men out o' here.' This Chief Constable was in charge. He looked a real swine. He was about eighteen stone and he hung with fat all over. He says, 'We're only here to help you.' McShane says, 'We don't need any help. We're organised.' And the Chief Constable says, 'All right.' So they all cleared out. A wee while later I was working away on some o' the fellows' feet and such like there was a lad came up to me and says, 'Here, doc, there's a roomful o' slops up there.' I says, 'What?' He says, 'A roomful of slops.' I says, 'No, they're all away.' He says, 'No, no.' He'd been scrounging around. So I went away along to where the March committee was meeting. It was Kerrigan, McShane, Middleton, and one or two others. McGovern the M.P. was a sort of spectator. I told McShane, 'This lad's after telling me there's a roomful of policemen up there.' He says, 'No, nonsense.' The lad says, 'I saw them.' McShane says, 'Come on then.' So Kerrigan, McShane, Middleton, myself and this laddie went away along. The laddie pointed to the door. McShane opened the door and the room was in darkness. He switched the light on and here was about twenty policemen sitting in the dark. McShane says, 'Come on, the whole bloody lot o' you, out o' here.' He was such a small fellow, hardly five foot, I think, and all these big fellows. So they all come slinking out. A wee while later I saw Kerrigan chasing one round the playground. Kerrigan had got him coming back in again and cornered him. The policeman says, 'Oh, don't,' he says, 'I'm only back for my piece.' There had obviously been some intentions of assault or something like that, because I had heard that on a previous Hunger March the same thing had happened in Rugby – when the Marchers were asleep during the night the police set about them. Whether they intended doing that or not to us in Birmingham I don't know, but it was rather suspicious they were there sitting in the dark.

But we got on very well. I mean we had no real trouble. We had demonstrations in all the different cities and such like and we got good receptions. Unfortunately, of course, the official Labour Party had nothing to do with it. But the local Labour Parties helped us, along with the Unemployed Workers' Movement. There were lots o' times when we went in where they had the women workers comin' in and supplying you with the food. We had sufficient to carry on. But I suppose some of them were getting better food then than at home. They were getting more of it anyway. I can't recall that the Dundee contingent was any worse than the average unemployed under-nourished worker. But the food they got on the road helped anyway. Everything was quite satisfactory – at least I was always quite satisfied.

There were some times we got some pocket money. We maybe got sixpence and you maybe either got into a cinema or the Co-op supplied cigarettes and tobacco. And this was a great asset. That was one of the other things that I think was very helpful – the Co-op did a great job in that respect.

We also had a one-legged shoe-repairer. He used to travel with the cook and the utensils and such like. We had this little lorry and it carried kitchen gear such as a boiler and such like and he travelled with that. Well, he only had the one leg and he was on the crutch. But he did a great job. He used to repair all the shoes and such like. It was rough and ready but he was able to keep you on the road. I always remember we thought about Long John Silver at times, seeing him. I don't know if he was a professional shoemaker or boot-repairer but the job he did was sufficient to keep the lads' shoes and boots together until they got down to London.

I can't recall anybody actually falling out from the March because of malnutrition or anything like that. Most of the trouble was bad feet, blistered feet, and such like. That was the only trouble. There were one or two, I think, left in hospital but they were sent home. I can't recall actually what was wrong with them. There was one fellow knocked over by a lorry coming along in the dark at night. That was round about Warrington. He was concussed and taken into hospital. We kept contact but eventually he was sent home after being in hospital for about ten days.

I think it was Coventry where we met some of the women Hunger Marchers. And there was a lot o' kidding went on there! At that time I was very naive. But we survived the kidding. And I think it was the same place where most of us had to go up to the workhouse and become deloused. I don't know where we had picked the lice up but there were plenty of them and we were all decontaminated.

Each town took over the head of the March in turn. But you always had the flute band in front and of course the banner 'Scotland to London' and such like. Each town had their banners from the N.U.W.M. But at the rear of the March the only time we heard the flute band was when we came into the finish and formed up. The leader of the flute band, at least what you might term the drum major, was killed later on in Spain. It was him who wrote the song *Jarama Valley*. He was a little fellow. I can't recall his name now. [234] The flute band was from Glasgow, we never had anything like that in Dundee. I think this just originated out of the Orange Lodge business or maybe the Roman Catholic thing. I can't say.

We sang songs on the March. One I remember – I think it was originally from the Soviet Union – was *From Scotland we are Marching*:

From Scotland we are marching,
From shipyard, mill and mine.
Our scarlet banners raised on high,
We toilers are in line.
We are a strong determined band,
Each with a weapon in his hand.
We are the Hunger Marchers of the proletariat,
We are the Hunger Marchers of the proletariat.

Actually they tried to stop that, because every time we sang 'Each with a weapon in his hand' the Marchers lifted up their sticks. And this might have been provocative. They tried to stop us doing that!

The songs helped us to march. There were groups started singing different songs. And this helped along a great deal. Sometimes it put you out o' step and sometimes it didn't. When I was playing in the Camerons' band we were 110 paces to the minute and I was more or less timed to that. But others again on the March were like light infantry. You were running along the bloody road! We always finished up with the flute band playing *The Internationale* when we marched into our final place at night. We always marched round. Oh, it was a great thing. Kerrigan was one of the great fellows at this. He had us all marched in in a close column.

The Dundee contingent on the March were members of the Communist Party, members of the N.U.W M. and people without any political affiliations – but at least they were demonstrating against the conditions under which we were living. I can't recall I.L.P. or Labour Party. The I.L.P. was very insignificant in Dundee and the Labour Party on the whole, because of the N.U.W.M. affiliation with the Communist Party – or at least the N.U.W.M. being started with the Communist Party and such like – frowned upon the Hunger Marchers. But I can't recall anybody from any of these parties, other than one or two in the Communist Party, some from the N.U.W.M., and others who just came along and who were vetted of course. It was the N.U.W.M. who vetted them.

We were able to carry on some days maybe about fifteen or twenty miles. There may have been longer marches but I can't recall. It took us approximately five weeks to go from Glasgow to London. Once or twice we had a day's rest. I can't recall very much about the weather. Coming down to Carlisle over the Borders it was snowing. And it rained occasionally. Most o' them had overcoats and such like. There were some Glasgow fellows who had been in a cycling club. They had cycling capes. I think most of them had a blanket. I don't think anything was supplied in that respect. I think everybody must have carried their own. I had a sleeping-bag. My brother was interested in climbing so I borrowed his sleeping-bag.

They used to have a break about every hour, depending often on the state of the Marchers and such like. We used to have that of course in the Regular army, ten minutes' break every hour. And I think they more or less followed that out. In the first-aid we didn't have much to do at the breaks: if they had bad feet, well, they just hirpled on. It didnae make any difference!

When we landed in London – I think it was Edmonton first of all – and we were coming down there at night on a Saturday, there was a huge crowd of Blackshirts began shouting insults. There were police there as well. In the first-aid we always marched at the rear of the column. And I turned round and started shoutin' back. Donald Renton from Edinburgh says, 'Oh, for Christ's sake, Tam,' he says, 'dinna say a word.' He says, 'The police'll set about you as well.' I says, 'But look …' He says, 'You've got to be very careful. The police back them up.' So we held our mouths shut.

We had a social evening that night with the people in Edmonton – I think the Communist Party run it. And then the following day we marched into Hyde Park. I remember we were going along Oxford Street. There was a couple o' mounted police right behind us and their horses were slavering down our backs. So I asked this policeman, I says, 'You might keep your horse back a wee bit.' He never paid any attention. I smoked an old pipe. I filled it up and blew the smoke in the horse's nostrils. The horse got off its mark! The policeman was a wee bit upset and told me to watch where I was blowing my smoke. I suggested he watch where he drove his horse.

In Hyde Park there was a tremendous reception. Again it was a grey day, real drizzly and dreich. I remember an Irishman coming over to me and he had a bottle of whiskey. I was speaking to Bob Stewart's wife at the time. Bob was a well-known Communist in Dundee but he was living down in London at that time. He was also a Prohibitionist or at least he had been before he became a member of the Communist Party. I remember Mrs Stewart saying to me about the whiskey, 'Oh, don't take it, Tom, don't take it.' I says, 'Oh, I'll hae tae tak it.'

We were in London for about a week. We demonstrated at the house of Commons and different places. But of course the Government refused to hear us. We were billeted in an old school in Deptford. I never saw such a dilapidated place. I noticed one of the women who looked after it, an old woman cleaner. Her hands were so deformed with arthritis and they were split open with hacks, wide hacks. I've never seen hacks like that in my life. This was just one of these things that brought me to realise how people lived. And I had to go up to St Olave's hospital in Deptford for dressings and stuff for the Marchers. I never saw such a dilapidated hospital. The paint was falling off the walls. Things were so bad I don't know how the staff were able to put up with it.

And then we were sent back home by rail. But again the authorities in London, instead of allowing us to have a mass demonstration in, say, Glasgow or Dundee when we landed, planned it so that it was midnight and nobody was on the street. However, when we arrived back in Dundee down at the Caledonian or West Station there were members of the Communist Party waiting to meet us. Then we marched up to the Unity Hall, where we had a cup o' tea and something to eat.

After I came back from the March I had a job for, oh, about a couple

of month workin' in a sort o' foondry. But that didn't last long and I was out
of a job again. You had to have so many weeks' stamps – I think, twenty-
six weeks' stamps – before you got back on the regular benefit again. And
I never had that. I just got now and then a job here and there and never
managed to accumulate sufficient at that time.

Then I went on the 1935 March from Dundee to Glasgow against the
Means Test. The Minister of Employment was to be in Glasgow.[235] Again
I was on the first-aid on that March. Well, there was a contingent came
down from Aberdeen and joined us in Dundee. And that night we slept in
the Dudhope Castle. I think that was the first and last time it had ever been
used since it was used during the First World War as a barracks. [236] It was
then I first met Bob Cooney, who was with the Aberdeen Marchers. Oh,
a wonderful character. I got to know him very well. he went out and
chalked the streets. Well, in Dundee that was against the law, the local
council had put a ban on that a year or two before. Bob was up at the court
the next day but he talked himself out of it.

We left Dundee by train over to Newport and then we marched from
Newport, right into Cupar Fife and all the way after that on to Glasgow. We
marched through Fife and then through Kinross.[237] There would be maybe
about the same number o' Marchers from Dundee as on the '34 March to
London, about forty. You had maybe the same from Aberdeen. I recall we
landed in Dunfermline and we were able to use the swimming pool there:
we had a bath that night and a swim.

When we were going through one of the Fife coalfields some of the
miners came along to walk with us. It was about the first time I ever met a
miner. I was talking to one of them. He was working. At that time I had a
great idea that I would like to have a sailing boat and I was talking about this.
And this miner says, 'But, man, ye could droon on that, your boat could
sink.' I says, 'But what about you fellows down the mines,' ah says, 'and the
mines come doon on the tap o' ye?' 'Ah,' he says, 'but yer mates'll aye come
for ye.' Now that was one of the finest thing ever I heard. And I cannae see
miners ever being beaten when they've got a spirit like that. Anybody who
has that faith in their people can never be beaten.

Then the next thing I remember we landed in to Glasgow. Coming
into Springburn there were about a policeman to every two Hunger
Marchers. This was the first time we had some sort of interference from the
police, well, not directly but in a snide sort of way. We'd left Kilsyth that
morning, we were getting into Glasgow and this policeman was walking
half-way between our row of four and the one in front and sort of breaking
the march up. So I asked this wee Glasgow bloke that was marching
alongside. I says, 'What do you do?' 'Oh,' he says, 'tap his heels.' So I tapped
the policeman's heels and he turned round. And I says, 'Look, if you want
to come in come in.' An inspector says, 'What's the trouble?' I says, 'Well,
your lad doesn't know whether he wants to march with us or not. But I'd
suggest he either come in or stay out.' He stayed out.

It was also on that March that I met Frank Pitcairn, who used to be the foreign correspondent for the *Daily Worker*. His actual name was Claud Cockburn. He was a great character, rather droll. He was with us right on the road to Glasgow. It wasn't a very momentous March but the people were very receptive. We had a tremendous reception again in Glasgow. We were to march to Glasgow Green that day. We were in Glasgow for a day or two but we weren't very successful with our March. There was a minister there from the Government but they didn't see us and we didn't gain much by this March either. It was just a question more or less of bringing it up and keeping the pot boiling, keeping it alive in people's minds that there were people suffering through this Government we had at that time. I always remember the Communist Party coined a phrase at that time: the National Government is a Government of Hunger and War. And there was nothing truer.

But it showed you also at that time the spirit of the people. All Glasgow turned out. This was the great thing at that time. You could depend at least on a great demonstration.[238] Whether it achieved anything or not is maybe debateable. But people were ready to demonstrate at that time and came out and demonstrated, although you had also the unemployed who stood on the sidewalk and jeered, 'What's this toff doin' on a March?' and such like, if you were half-decently dressed.

We stayed that night I think it was in one of the City Halls, because I remember there was a woman who was an epileptic. She threw a fit and I was the only one there who could do anything about it. And stupid bugger me, I had nothing to put in her mouth bar my finger. She nearly bit the finger off me! But that's all I can recall of the Glasgow March. I can't recall how long it took us. It couldn't have been any more than about a week or ten days. We came back to Dundee by train.

That was the last Hunger March I was on. I got a job in a shipyard after that, insulating for a refrigerator ship.

Well, looking back on Hunger Marches I was on I don't think we achieved any success. We still had this approach by Government; you were down and they were trying to keep you down. Lots of people who were working weren't prepared to be seen in such a way – they were hanging on to a job. And we've got practically the same thing at the present time. But the value of the Hunger Marches was it kept alive the spirit to keep fighting. If you don't keep fighting ye're going to be trodden on. There were some relaxations in some respects but on the whole nothing to what we wanted – the doing away with the Means Test.[239]

James Graham

It was the 1935 Hunger March I went on, from Ayr to Glasgow.

I was born here in the town of Ayr in December 1905. My father's occupation was professional soldier. He was in the Royal Scots Fusiliers. He would be a young man about twenty when he joined. He had finished his time as a baker wi' one o' the oldest firms in Ayr. For many years he served in the army in India. When the South African War broke out he transferred with the battalion to South Africa. He landed back home here and was employed at his trade as baker in one of the town shops. But having been in the outside world for so long it didn't suit him so he moved round about, working here and there, labouring. He finished up as a gas stoker.

When it came to 1914 he joined his old regiment and served right through to the end of the War. He never was overseas in the War: they said he was too old and that he wisnae fit. He didnae agree wi' them. He tried all manner o' tricks. He was sent over to Ireland. He had served in Ireland long before the War, when he was a young man. He'd probably be in Ireland in the 1916 Rebellion. Then he was in various places, all round. He was up at Kilwinning, he was up in the Grangemooth Docks. He was a bit harum scarum, my father. He had a hard life.

My mother belonged to Stirling. Her father was a wool sorter to trade. He was a well-educated man. There were a cousin or an uncle o' his was a provost o' Forfar and he was responsible for helping part of his education. Grandfather was a well-read man. And at one time he was a member of the great teetotal organisation, Good Templars. They had a meeting against drink and he was the chairman. The main speaker was one of the best known men in Britain at that time, Campbell Bannerman. He was a prime minister. As the chairman, my grandfather had to get up and do his introduction.[240]

Well, I was the eldest o' my family. I had two brothers and four sisters. When I'd be about twelve years of age I started as a message boy, delivering milk. I started about six o'clock in the morning, did the round, went to school, finished the school, went back and did another wee job, and received the magnificent sum of 1/6d a week. I was a proud wee laddie to get up wi' this 1/6d to gie to my mother. I was a man then.

I worked for some time with this firm. It was over a mile away from my home to my workplace. I left that firm to go to another milkman – an increase in wages: 1/10d a week.

I went to school in Ayr. I was there for nine years and left at fourteen. What a waste o' time! I didnae ken whether I was comin' or goin'. When I left school I was a message boy, deliverin' groceries. I had a bit o' experience wi' that firm travellin' round the countryside deliverin' messages. There was a lorry that was hired so I went up deliverin' messages wi' that. The first night I was out in it it was a Friday, and at half-past twelve midnight I was comin' ower the New Brig tae my home. My father was comin' to meet me. 'Whaur the hell have ye been?' Says I, 'At my work.' 'Oh, we'll hev tae alter this.' But I altered it afore I got any further because I refused to go wi' the barrow. I fell oot wi' the gaffer. He wanted me to go with a hand-barrow three miles up the road into the country. It was a great bit of a journey, up two braes, with this big barrow full of a week's messages for one household. When I knew where I had to go wi' this barrow, to push it and I was just a lump o' a boy and I wisnae a big boy either – I says, 'I don't think I'll bother gaun wi' that.' 'Oh, if you don't go you know what's goin' tae happen. Ye'll get your books.' I says, 'Right, I'll jist away the noo.' So I walked oot.

Then I got a job in Alexander's saw mill. I was supposed to learn the trade but it was a waste of years. I never learnt anything. I was there a couple o' years. I'd be about seventeen when I left that. I think I landed in the pits after that, Glenburn pit.

I started off at the coal but it never materialised. I couldnae make a wage at it. So that was the job finished. The gaffer says to me, 'Would you like a job as an oncost worker?' I says, 'Aye, I'll take any kind o' job as long as it's a job.' So I got a job workin' wi' the bricklayer doon the pit. So here I'm an apprentice bricklayer noo. I worked wi' this old fellow Matt Davies. We built stoppings, closing the air courses and diverting it. I had to go and get pails o' water , maybe along two or three roads where there was a dook. I carried pails o' water to him and mixed up some plaster . Then he took ill and they said, 'Do you think you could carry on?' So I became a fully fledged bricklayer. And when I wisnae buildin' stoppins I worked on the roads wi' the roadsman, puttin' in a new road intae the coalface. Then there were a wee bloke got a job tae clean up the pit and I was sent tae work wi' him. I got a powny tae drive, a pit powny. We filled in this hutch wi' whinstane and a' this and I pit too much in the hutch. When I pulled oot two snibbles in the hutch the weight pulled the powny back. It had to make a mad dive. It staggered and it hit me. So I had tae run past it tae get tae the other side o' him or I would ha' been crushed wi' the hutch. The powny got up on to the haulage and stuck on the wire. It was neighin' and it broke loose from the hutch. I was standin' there shakin' like a leaf. I thought I was gaun tae get killed. Then in 1926 the big strike come on and I never went back. I got a wee job part-time on the tramways system.

That was during the 1926 strike. So I worked away there on the tramways. I did the holiday period, the summer period when they put on extra trams. Then at the end o' the season they said, 'We'll send for ye if we need ye.' There were men taken ill so they sent for me tae work a fortnight or three weeks and gradually as time goes on I landed in the job. And I was there until the system broke up in 1931. That was me unemployed.

From that I did various jobs. I was a clerk. I was a motor driver and van salesman. I worked in a bakery and did all bloody kinds of jobs. I was a hod carrier. These were all temporary jobs.

When I got mairrit in 1932 I was on the buroo, unemployed. I was twenty-six when I got married. Then we had a child in 1933. At that time I got thirty-two bob a week. My wife gave up working when we got married. She'd been a housemaid in some of the big houses a' round about Ayr.

After I was married I became a member of the Independent Labour Party. By that time the I.L.P. had disaffiliated from the Labour Party. We used to chalk the streets – the knuckles were off ma fingers! We were a militant organisation. I was a proud man to have met the greatest of orators that's ever been in the House o' Commons: James Maxton. He was interested to know my name. They a' jist ca'ed each other 'Comrade' without ascertaining their names. He was intent on knowing my name. He says, 'What's your name?' 'Oh,' I says, 'I'm jist one o' your organisation.' 'And what is your name? I'm interested to know your name.' So I told him and I had a wee conversation wi' him. Mr John Pollock was there and was gaun tae offer me some books. I said, 'John, I've read them.' So that's how Maxton was interested in me.[241]

I was a member o' the Guild o' Youth and went up tae Irvine. There was a collection of agents and I was a senior person then. So I went there and became a consultant to the young ones. I taught one Sunday at their Sunday School. I gave them the gen, the precepts of this and that. I was in the I.L.P. right through the '30s more or less. It became jist a social organisation, because there were half o' them died oot. It was run by a lot o' auld women up there: 'There are too many Bolsheviks in this business.' So I drifted away from it.

There were several leading figures in the I.L.P. in Ayr. John Pollock was one. He was a Communist in Kilmarnock at one time, and a member of the Co-operative Society. But he drifted from the Communist Party to the I.L.P. And there were I.L.P. men in this town who were well-known characters. One was a woodwork teacher, and there was Peter Robb – I don't know what he did. There were several railwaymen and shilling-a-week men. They were members of the I.L.P. and the Scottish Socialist Party. Sanny Sloan, he was a shilling-a-week man. That was his occupation. It was quite common for miners who'd been victimised to become tally men, shilling-a-week men.[242]

When I became unemployed I joined the National Unemployed Workers' Movement. That was before I went into the I.L.P. Well, we were a' runnin' aboot unemployed. They started the N.U.W.M. but it never came tae anything, though we had quite a few members. There was a chap came from Glasgow – Stevenson – and he was a member of the Communist Party. He started up the N.U.W.M. in Ayr and we were contributin' the pennies or so much a week. There was a nucleus of whom I was one. We were members of the I.L.P. but we were taking part in this, holding meetings, sending for the likes of Harry McShane, a well-known Communist in Glasgow, to come and speak.

On one occasion Harry didnae turn up. So I was left there waitin' tae meet him. So I had to get up on my hind legs down at the lifeboat shed at the harbour, a weel-known meeting place, and explain the situation to them, the usual diatribe. Of course Ayr at that time had a fair quota o' unemployed. But when it came to demonstrations – my God! Of course it was then, and still is, a Tory stronghold. A mountebank, an ex-colonel of the British army, was our M.P. then: Colonel Thomas Moore. I believe he was a food controller during the Russian Revolution, when Churchill interceded on behalf of those poor people the Czars and Czarinas deposed for their generosity toward the starving masses in Russia. Britain went tae help out the White Russians. This Colonel Moore was out there and he was a food controller or something. I don't know who he was controlling food to. The Russians were starving and if they'd got a chance they'd maybe hae ate him. And it's a pity they didnae. He was M.P. for a long, long time, tae the shame and disgrace of the town of Ayr. He was a blot on the firmament.[243]

Well, the N.U.W.M. existed in Ayr, and then this Hunger March came along. Joe Stevenson says, 'Well, what are we gonnae dae?' So there were about eleven o' us went on the March to Glasgow from Ayr. There was big Tam Fisher, Mick Murphy, the Rodgers brothers – the brothers-in-law o' Mick Murphy – Erchie McBride, and myself and my brother. There were two or three Rodgers brothers on the Hunger March. Mick Murphy was one of the well-known fighting men about the town but he was a socialist like a lot o' Catholics. These Catholic chaps were agitators, they were a downtrodden section o' the community. If they're no' agitatin' they're fightin'. Ye can see where they come from – Ireland. Big Tam Fisher went tae Canada on one o' thae schemes. He wasna ta'en on wi' fermin' and he came back here. He thought he would be healthier on the buroo!

Bobby Blaikie went on the March too. But he didnae march oot the toon wi' us. He met us in Kilmarnock. I don't think he wanted tae walk oot the toon in case somebody seen him. So we walked frae here tae Kilmarnock, frae Kilmarnock tae Dunlop and up tae Barrhead, and frae Barrhead intae Glasgow. I think it took about three days. We stopped one night in Kilmarnock and in Dunlop. Then we stopped in Barrhead, Jimmy Maxton's town.

There was nothing but sair legs. Johnny Murphy – he was a Regular in the sojers – he became the doctor, the first-aid man and wis massaging their legs. Their legs were a' stiffening up and their muscles were gettin' sore. Johnny Murphy says, 'Oh, I'll sort these out.' So he was slappin' their legs and softenin' up their muscles. It was very funny.

I think the eleven from Ayr were all members of the N.U.W.M. Well, they were nominal members. They didnae weigh in. They hadnae pennies tae spare but they were there. They werenae a' active. The Rodgers boys, Joe Stevenson, my brother and I, we were always active. My brother was a great man for sellin' the *Daily Worker*. He wasn't in the Communist Party. He got these papers from I don't know where – I think it was Stevenson that organised it – but he used tae sell them.

Stevenson was the only member of the Communist Party on the March from Ayr. The Communist Party didn't exist at Ayr, no' that I know o'. But on the March, Joe, I suppose, was leadin' our contingent, the humble dozen of us. Stevensky was his real name. He was a Catholic, from Bellshill. His father was a Polish emigré miner. Later on Joe went to the Spanish Civil War and died wi' diptheria or cholera.[244]

When we left Ayr we had nothing. We jist marched out. I had a good stout pair o' boots. That was a' you needed. We had no sandwiches or food. We were waitin' tae get tae Kilmarnock. They met us wi' bags o' sandwiches and cups o' tea. Oh, they done us well, wherever we went. We were well enough fed. We had sandwiches and cups o' tea and biled eggs.

Kilmarnock's always been an active place in politics. It always re- turned a Labour member. The number o' Marchers was augmented at Kilmarnock considerably. We got quite a number there. Then we were meetin' them on the road, pickin' people up on the road. In the various villages we always met people. And of course you're moving into an industrial area when you go up through Ayrshire. Ayrshire's always been, well, minin' districts, iron and steel businesses. You were always meetin' people comin' from these areas. We had people like that.

I wouldnae like to say how many Marchers there were from Ayrshire. But they were increasing there. And then we had a band or a piper at some part o' the road. I never cairried sticks. But there were a lot o' them comin' from various parts – a Young Communist League frae the North, maybe Dundee or other industrial areas – some o' them had pilin' stabs or branches o' trees. I suppose they were used as walkin' sticks. But there was never trouble bar one time, goin' through Glasgow, wi' a lot o' agitators at the side o' the road. They were shoutin' the odds at big Tam Fisher. He was gaun tae jump oot the line. Of course the police were marchin' alongside us. They says, 'Get back in that line there.' He says, 'You should be checkin' them, no' us.' I don't know whether these agitators at the side o' the road would be Orangemen or no'. They'd be Tories.

The purpose o' the March we went on was to meet the Secretary of State for Scotland, a man called Godfrey Collins. And I don't think he countenanced it. He would have nothing to do with them. The Marchers were lookin' for work and better conditions, a bigger hand-out. Anyway I never seen halt nor hair o' Sir Godfrey Collins. You couldnae get intae the precincts o' the Town Chambers in Glasgow. Oh, these fellows, they're a' protected. Ye darenae look at them.

We went up North Frederick Street, one o' those streets roond aboot the Town Chambers. And there was some crowd. We had a big demon- stration on Glasgow Green and from one point it took about an hour and a quarter before they passed. So you see the numbers o' crowds that was there, the rag-tag and bobtail o' the working class, the puir souls. Maxton and Harry McShane and a' these boys were there as speakers, and McGovern. Yon's another scoundrel: McGovern feenished up in the Tory Party. [245]

I don't think it was a very successful March. I think we come back by bus.

After the March I got a job wi' a local firm for a wee while in aerated water manufacture. He was dealt in wi' the brewery at one time in the town and they were in the whisky busir.ess, distributors and that. I worked wi' them for a wee while, for a shillin' an hour. They had a forty-four-hour week. So that was the wage. I had learnt the drivin' when I come out the tramways and got drivin' instruction from the S.M.T. and passed a test. Anyway the chap I was with in the aerated water van, he broke a wrist one mornin' crankin' it up so I got the job tae drive the van. Then I got on to the buses, I was a bus driver, just for the summer months. I trailed back and forrit. Then I got a job wi' Turner, a brewer in the town. So I drove wi' him. In the summer months you were pittin' in your hours, of course. I went round about Troon and intae Kilmarnock and up the Irvine Valley, a' round about there. And the next day I went and did Troon, Irvine, Ardrossan. On Wednesdays and Fridays I went to Largs. So I was on that job for a wee while. Then I had a full-time job wi' a bricklayin' firm. I was out wi' them for a while as a hod-cairrier. I had one or two jobs wi' the Corporation, puttin' in water pipes. I worked as a navvy wi' the town on two or three occasions.

When the War came I went into the Air Force. And then after the War I was a postman, that was when I finished my career.

John Lochore

Darvel, Ayrshire, was where I was born, in March 1914. My father was a weaver and a specialist in his way: a dresser, he was called, and very proud of it. He was a socialist. One of my first recollections was his involvement in the weavers' strike just preceding the 1926 General Strike. He was a firm trade unionist. During the 1914 War, when there were scarcities of food he was a great poacher, out catching rabbits. And this was one of the defiant things about him: he didn't like landlords and gamekeepers at all. He was a great character: he loved the country, Darvel and Ayrshire, and he loved Burns and quoting his poems. He was also very anti-militarist. As a boy he had lost his right index finger in the factory. He was no good then to the British army in the 1914 War. He didn't need to be a conscientious objector – but if he had wanted to, he would have been.

1926, I think, was the period when his whole political stand showed – his complete support for the '26 strike, and his early support for the Russian Revolution. Whilst he didn't take part in any political activities as such, he was one of the first to buy the old *Sunday Worker*. My father was a great supporter of Johnny Burns, an Irishman, the only outstanding political figure in Darvel on the militant side. There were plenty of Labour Party supporters but Johnny Burns was one of the first Communists that I ever heard. My father supported his paper and his arguments. It was round about that period I first heard of Trotsky and the Red Army and things like that.[246] Johnny Burns was a weaver. It was the Morton family that developed the weaving industry in Darvel. Big San Morton, the kingpin of the business, was a distant cousin of my grandmother. He started rearing horses and had a stud farm in Ireland. and I think that was how Johnny Burns eventually came from Ireland to Darvel. He was one of the seeds that poor old San Morton brought back but didn't want to sow, because Johnny became a political agitator against the Mortons. He was a natural socialist, a natural militant or rebel. He was one of the first in Darvel to come out openly as a Communist and to take round the *Sunday Worker*.

One of the other influences on my father of course was my grandfather Lochore. He was one of the founders of the Scottish Labour Party.[247] He had helped create the Darvel Co-operative Society. He was a local bailie. He had been a policeman in his younger days in Glasgow but had got the sack for hitting a sergeant. That's when he came back to Darvel. When he helped to start the Co-op he was victimised and the only thing he could do over all these years – maybe twenty years – was become the cleaner and caretaker for the Co-op Hall. That was the only living he had. But he reared his family and was very respected in Darvel. He became the provost elect. He never became provost: he died in 1924 at the age of seventy-three, just before he was due to take office. There's a street in Darvel called after him. Though he was one of the founders of the Scottish Labour Party and there was a picture of Keir Hardie with big beard as you walked into his house, I think grandfather had a tendency still to be a bit Liberal-minded. But certainly Keir Hardie had had his tea in grandfather's house when he came to speak in Darvel. Oh, it was Hardie country, there's no question about it. Many working-class houses round about there had this photograph of Hardie.

Darvel of course had been Covenanters' country in earlier times. My father didn't become anti-religious but he softened on it. He used to say: 'If there is a God he must be bloody cruel.' He never encouraged us to go to Sunday School, although my mother did. She was English and very loyalist, more conventional than my father, and concerned about respectability. She had been born in Oxford and brought up in Truro, where her father was coachman to a clergyman. Uncle Jim, my mother's brother, was a cripple but became an apprentice photographer in Truro, then came to work as a photographer in Darvel. His first wife died and it was then my mother came up to Darvel to look after his child. And that was when she met my father. I had two brothers and three sisters. I was the youngest son, but two of my sisters were younger than me.

My eldest brother was a plumber who later on was unemployed for a number of years and then went to Corby, the Scottish town in Northamptonshire, before the 1939 War. He died there in 1986. He was a very cautious type, who tried to copy grandfather in maintaining he was Liberal and not Labour. My other brother Jimmy ran away to sea as a boy and was a ship's cook all his life. Jimmy is a great character, a great Scotchman who wouldn't speak English – everything's got to be in the vernacular – and a hard whisky drinker. My eldest sister Mary was a hard-working girl who wanted to look after her mother and the rest of the family. Helen, my middle sister, joined the Youth Co-op Circle. My youngest sister Betty went to Australia in 1950 and is still there with her family.

I was just four when I went to Mair's Free School in Darvel. It had been given by some philanthropist in the olden times. The teachers were all women. Well, these four teachers were spinsters who had lost their sweethearts in the 1914 War, every one of them: Miss Murdoch, Miss Craig, and the other two, whose names I forget. When later on I went to the junior school up the brae the woodwork teacher there had a leg off and had lost an eye in the War. Mr Stewart, who taught arithmetic and algebra, had a great big slice cut off his face when he had been in the Royal Flying Corps in the War. Another of our teachers William Wilson – we called him Wabbly Wilson – was shell-shocked in the War. He was the only teacher we liked to give us the strap: he couldn't steady himself and so never could hit us – hence 'Wabbly' Wilson. Another of the teachers, William Boyd, had been a conscientious objector. I don't know if his objection had been on religious or political grounds or both. He was Church of Scotland and when the minister collapsed one day in the pulpit, William Boyd went up and finished the sermon. This was the type of man he was, very religious. He came from a very middle-class family. His father, I think, was a banker. One of William Boyd's brothers was the local stonemason and the other was the burgh sanitary inspector. William Boyd eventually committed suicide. Another teacher, Mr. Bell, was too young to have gone to the War. He was very loyalist, very patriotic. They were great for recitation in our school: his poem, every verse of it, was 'The Burial of Sir John Moore'.[248] What I am trying to show is the reflection of the 1914-18 War on the teachers in the school. And it reflected in their teaching.

One other teacher, Miss Goldie, I should mention. She was the first to implant in my mind any feeling of politics, with the poem about 'Sceptre and Crown must tumble down/ And in the dust be equal made/ With the poor crooked scythe and spade.'[249] Oh, I enjoyed every part of my schooling. I loved every minute of it at Darvel.

Well, we then came to a very bad period immediately after the General Strike. My father got his job back after the strike but got what they called the rough edges. One of my memories is of the scabs, a man and woman who had scabbed, in Templeton Street, and seeing the strikers, the women weavers, getting hold of them and really pulling them physically from going into this factory. It was one of the moments of sadness that I can remember, the day the strike was called off. My father took us to hear A. J. Cook speaking in Galston. We walked over the moors right down to Galston. That was when Cook had to get olive oil to pour down his throat because of his being hoarse.

My aunties had started small home-baking businesses in Glasgow. And it was then, just after the strike, my father decided to take the whole family to Glasgow. So I spent the last six months of my schooling in Glasgow. This was a very strange period for me. It was quite a shock to be suddenly uprooted from Darvel, which I loved every part of.

My father set himself up in Bridgeton in a little dairy and home-baking business. My aunties were experienced and had been very successful in their business. But the shop my father had got was no good. He was beginning to worry. He was a country boy and had never been in the big city. He developed neurasthenia round about that period. That became quite a traumatic experience in my life, to witness my father being nervous even to cross the road. So that, plus the fact I wanted to get out and earn something to put into the kitty, made me leave school as soon as I could at fourteen.

My first job was in a place called Gordon House in the Trongate in Glasgow where they made umbrellas. It was a very rich family outfit, Gordon House. Well, I only lasted a week there. I had to open the door for customers coming out and in and this was against my whole character, so I left. I was still homesick for Darvel and all I wanted to do was get back into the country. So I went then to the cattlemarket in the Gallowgate in Glasgow and queued up for a job on a farm.

It was the Tuesday market and you went there to be fee'd, to queue to get hired. There were six of us stood in a row, and one girl. We all stood in a row and the big farmers came down in pairs. They had sticks and they came and poked our legs and our bottoms with their sticks, and they started laughing and guffawing, 'Aye, it's a guid bit o' meat.' Then they went over to the girl and referred to her tits and all that in their rough talk. We were treated like cattle. It was a very degrading experience. I can still see that girl shuffling about there with her little handbag and a little straw hat she wore. She was quite buxom. You can imagine how many of these maids in those days were hired away and then at the end of nine months came home with a child.

There was what they called a feeing fair held, but this where we were was only what they called the Tuesday market. It was just the normal weekly market and there was a part where anyone who had run away from their fee could go and get another fee. The six of us were just lads. Two were from Dr Barnardo's. They weren't the brightest of characters. Anyhow I got fee'd and went to this very rough farm out at Lennoxtown, for six shillings a week. It was a very old farm. My sleeping place was in a kind of bothy or chaumer, a loft with the bulls underneath. We were sleeping on hay mattresses full of little hay fleas. We weren't allowed into the farmhouse. You had to sit in the place where they did the dairying. You had a rough bag for a towel. The food was just porridge and bread and tatties. We started work at six o'clock in the morning and worked on and on and on. You got a little porridge maybe about eight o'clock, and some bread. And then about three or four o'clock you would get another snack. And then in the evening about six there would be potatoes. It was tatties all the time. Oh, Christ, we were starving mostly. In these days they had big bits of locust for the horses. And we used to go and pick it all out, pinch it and eat it!

There was another boy there, more experienced than me. His name was Dougie. He told me, 'I'm mair experienced than you. You'll be doin' the muckin' oot and I'll be doin' the mulkin'.' It was dairy and mixed farming. Dougie was so pleased that I was starting. He said his mother was an unmarried dairywoman in Mauchline, his faither had been a ploughman and he, Dougie, was goin' tae be a fermer. This was his talk. He was only a couple of years older than me but he felt I was very much his junior. So my first job was to muck the byres, get the muck into a barrow and wheel it down this narrow plank and tip it over into the midden. Every time I went to this plank I would go over with the barrow and fall right into the midden!

The farm was set amid beautiful scenery. One morning, four or five days after I arrived, I was out spreading muck in the fields. I could hear bagpipes and then coming up the hill I saw this covered wagon. They were gypsies or tramps. The piper was leading with the little horse. They had dogs tied to the back of the wagon and a coop of hens on the tailboard. They were marching away up there just like freedom itself. I was hungry and unhappy.

'Right,' I said, 'that's it. I'm off!' I threw away this big fork I'd been spreading the muck with and left. I walked all the way back to Glasgow.

I think it took me about a couple of days to walk home. It was a long walk for a laddie of fourteen. When I walked into my father's shop in Dale Street, off the main street in Brigton, he was making pancakes on the hotplate. He turned round and he says, 'Right. You've had enough?'

It was very bad unemployment round about that time, 1928, 1929. I worked around the shop for a time but was very restless. My older brother Jimmy had run away to sea and had been to Australia and in fact all over the world. I got it into my head that I would like to go to sea. So I then used to go down to the Glasgow docks. My eldest sister Mary was the gaffer then and told us what we should do. She used to give me threepence a day to go and find my job. I used to walk down to the docks and then carry on for miles and miles down to Clydebank, asking round the boats, looking for a job.

At that period the boats were lying there but they had watchmen on them for they weren't sailing at all. It was then I first encountered the Minority Movement, the seamen's Minority Movement. They were arguing against the official seamen's union, Havelock Wilson's Union.[250] There was a breakaway and they were trying to get it away from its policy. But this particular day I went into the offices of the Burns Laird Line in James Watt Street in Glasgow. I stood there three or four hours behind a glass panel. I could see the pursers coming in from the various ships, paying the money in, talking, and so forth. They would look round and through the glass at this boy standing there. I just stood there waiting and waiting, hoping that something might happen. And then suddenly it clicked. Willie Campbell, a purser, came and looked through the glass and I could see him speaking to another fellow. They beckoned me then with their forefinger. When I went in they said, 'H'mm, have you been to sea?' Well, I had been on a week's holiday trip on the *Dunara Castle* with my brother Jimmy. So I said, 'Yes, I've been to sea. I've been on the *Dunara Castle*.' And that white lie got me the job on the Burns Laird boats.

I was on them for about eighteen months. I was a cabin boy. We sailed from Glasgow to Belfast, Londonderry and Dublin – but mainly Belfast. We used to leave one night and then stay one night in Belfast and sail next night back again to Glasgow. I had one free day when we came back to Glasgow, one day I could go home. They were passenger and cattle boats. We always managed to get some tips from the passengers. And there were other little methods of making tea on our own and fiddling that. That was a bit extra. The wages were thirty shillings a week but eventually I managed to make quite good earnings – maybe £2 or £3 a week. It was a lot for a laddie of fourteen or fifteen.

It was quite a good experience. We sailed from Glasgow at nine o'clock at night. But we had to be on board and start work at six o'clock, getting food and everything ready for the cabin passengers. We worked till about eleven, half-past eleven or twelve midnight. By that time you were pretty well beyond Greenock and out into the ocean. Then at six or seven o'clock in the morning we would be getting into Whitehaven, just before coming into Belfast Lough. So we rose then and worked right through till after lunchtime. Then we had three hours down till six and then work again until midnight. Then you had one day off. Oh, by God, it was hard going!

The conditions on board were not too bad as conditions went then. All the stewards slept in the one cabin, which was in the poop. The fo'c'sle was for the black squad. There would be about eight stewards. We were all in bunks, like a prison. I always chose the one up above, 'cause I felt it was safest: there was a lot of hard drinking, though I didn't drink at all. The steward I was working for, Bob Shannon, drank a lot. He was the steerage steward, in charge of the steerage passengers. That was how I could always fiddle a little by making teas, because he got drunk and I had to put him to bed. It was then we had our little fiddle. But I learnt quite a lot – how to use myself, how to get around.

This was the period when they divided the streets in Belfast with corrugated-iron sheets, because of the sectarian business. We saw some of the effects of it on board. Some of the crew were Irish from Belfast. Two of the boys working as mess-room stewards were Irish Catholics, and of course the boys who had been recruited in Glasgow were Protestants. So this little bit of tension was in the ship too. It never affected me really but there was that friction then.

After about eighteen months on the Burns Laird boats I wanted to travel, go round the world. Little Tommy Stevens, who was the union man – I joined the seamen's union then – got me a berth on a boat called the *North Anglia* that was going to South America. The *North Anglia* had been a German ship and had been scuttled at the end of the War at Scapa Flow. It was a very, very old ship – metal decks. We found we were living with bugs and cockroaches and rats. Roberts of Newcastle was the company that owned it.

That was one of the really roughest periods in my life. I was only one voyage on the *North Anglia* – but that lasted for nine months! The first experience I had was the night I joined her at Clydebank about half-past eleven. She was sailing the next morning. It was a Geordie watchman that was on at the end of the gangplank. There were quite a number of Geordies in the crew. I can always remember him saying, 'Who's there?' I said, 'Cabin boy.' He said 'Well, ye're doon the poop wi' the chippie. Ye'll smell him doon there. And you'll hear him snorin'.' So I went down the poop – it was like a well deck – and then up and into what they call the poop-and-down. It's where the anchor goes down at the end of the boat, the chain locker. It stank of alcohol and paraffin when you went down there, and I could hear this snoring. It was this man lying in the bed, drunk as a lord. I then went into the other part, great big steel stanchions above, and there was the other bunk.

Some old dirty bedclothes had just been thrown over it. I sat on the side of the bed and then lay down for a bit. It was one of those sleeps that you weren't sleeping: I was half-dazed. The only light was the moon coming through the porthole. All of a sudden I felt something touching my legs. I got up. It was two rats, jumping over, playing leap frog over my feet. I dashed upstairs in a fright on to the deck itself. This would probably be about two or three in the morning. And, oh, it was cold. I had only a tiny thin jacket on. I walked about all night long, bashing my arms to try and get heat.

And then about six in the morning the chippie came up, the carpenter. He came up just to make his water over the side of the ship. That was a terrible experience too for I was only sixteen then and I had never been used to anything like that! And then this big man he turned round. He was all dishevelled and his eyes were all bloodshot and he says, 'Who the hell are you?' I says, 'Oh, I'm the cabin boy.' 'Och,' he says and then he just turned round and went down into the poop again and left me. He was the one that had been snoring and smelling of alcohol. He turned out to be a very nice fellow, very nice indeed.

Well, at about six in the morning I went down to see my boss, the steward. I'm now in my seventies and I've lived quite a full life. But this steward was the cruellest man I can remember. He was a Geordie, a little fat fellow. His hair was brushed with a middle parting and he had a little moustache. He told me what my duties were. I had to do lots of work, scrubbing and polishing and, oh, goodness knows what. He was just like a tyrant over us. He was a shyster, just taking advantage of a lad.

The skipper was an old Welshman from Aberaron. He had had his leg off during the First World War and had a pin leg. He had a very little squeaky North Welsh voice. He was a miserable bugger, too, very, very hard and would give you very little.

There would be about a couple of dozen in the crew. In the engine-room staff there was the chief, a second and a third, the donkeyman and then four firemen. The sailors were mainly Highlanders. They would be about six or eight – six and two apprentices. Then we had the carpenter or chippie – he was a Welshman – and the skipper, the mate, and second mate. Then there was the chief steward – my boss – a mess-room steward, the cook, and me as cabin boy. The cook was a heavy drinker. He was drunk from the time he left the Clyde until he came back to Newcastle nine months afterwards.

We went to South America, a thousand miles up the River Plate, to Paraguay and Bolivia. There was a war on at that time between them.[251] We were taking coal to the Bolivians and we bought linseed from the Paraguayans. One of the worst things that happened arose over a banjo mandolin I had brought with me. When we got to Concepción, to load on linseed, the mess-room steward arranged with a student to buy my banjo mandolin for a pound, so that we could go out and see the town. You weren't allowed to take musical instruments ashore – there was a tax on them. So I put it under my little raglan raincoat and we walked down and through the sheds where the linseed was lying. Two *marineros*, little marine policemen, rushed out while I was strumming my banjo mandolin. They got hold of it, ripped it open with a little knife they had. They thought I was smuggling tobacco in it. So I was put under arrest and taken away to the calaboose. The mess-room steward had gone scot free and went back to the ship to report I had been arrested.

I was put into this jail for three days and three nights. The bed was a stone slab. The window was just little slits. And all the urine, etc., from other cells ran down a gutter, trinkle, trinkle, trinkle, all the time. And they didn't feed you either. You were supposed to buy your own food. The relatives of the other prisoners used to bring them food. But of course I had no relatives there. And it was three days before the skipper of the *North Anglia*, Pin Leg Thomas, came and bailed me out.

The ship couldn't leave the port until I had been tried. I had to go and sit in a little room outside where they were trying my case. I think it was the Swedish consul who acted as interpreter. They fined me so many thousand *guaranies* – more than I had earned from the time I left Glasgow until I got back again. And as I was still a juvenile the company had to pay my fine. I got a hell of a dressing-down from Pin Leg Thomas. As I say, the ship couldn't leave and we were there for sixteen days.

During these sixteen days they were loading the raw linseed into the ship. Each morning the *marineros* used to walk from their station down the docks, pick up one of their policemen and drop one, like the changing of the guard. It was each morning this took place at eight o'clock. And of course the seamen and the others used to pull my leg and frighten me: 'They're coming for ye now.' I thought I'd be arrested again. I used to run and dive into the linseed in the holds and make two little holes to watch out until the policemen had passed again. Raw linseed is sticky stuff and it was sticking in my hair and eyelashes – everywhere. Sixteen days I was doing this. I looked as if I had some disease. It was a very, very nerve-wracking period for me.

In mid-ocean I became a very great friend of the wireless officer. The first time I ran across him I was going along and could hear a woman singing, a beautiful voice. I thought, 'Well, there's no woman on board ship.' The voice came from the wireless officer's room so I knocked on the door and opened it. He was playing a saw and it was just like a woman's voice.

He and I became great friends. I used to spend hours with him during my time off. He came from Leicester. He was a young man and he was a committed socialist. He was the first to tell me all about Karl Marx and Lenin and the theoretical side. He was a very educated fellow altogether. Through him I learned that the cargo we had picked up at Concepción – the linseed – had been sold three times whilst we were at sea, and each time the company had made a profit on it.

We arrived in Amsterdam to unload the cargo and sailed from there across to South Shields. While were were in Amsterdam there was a big whaler recruiting crew for a trip away down to the Falklands for six months. I made application to become a cabin boy on this whaler. I got the berth all right but Pin Leg Thomas my skipper wouldn't allow it because I owed so much money! So I arrived back in South Shields and all I got was my fare back to Glasgow – nothing else, no wages for my nine months on the *North Anglia*, nothing. Everything was taken off to pay my fine. By law they had to give you your fare back to your home port, so all I got was my single ticket back to St Enoch Station in Glasgow. And it was the cruellest nine months of my life, under this despot steward.

Unemployment was really bad then, in 1930, '31. I used to look for work. It was absolutely hopeless trying to find it. So from 1931 on I had periods of spasmodic jobs, such as working in a bakery, or various little jobs, nothing substantial. That was the position until about the beginning of 1935 I got a job with the *Sunday Express*.

It was in those years between about 1931 and 1936 that I became more and more politically active. One of the influences was the discussion with my friend the wireless officer on the *North Anglia*. But much earlier than that there had been the influence of my father, Johnny Burns, and my grand-father, then Miss Goldie at school and William Boyd. You could see the roots growing.

I joined the I.L.P. Guild of Youth when I was on the Burns Laird Irish boats. I had a night off, and it was always midweek. At that period I had no mates. I never have had any mates. That's the funny thing about it. Like most lads I had mates when I was at school but never since I left school. I've always been a loner. So on my nights off from the Irish boats in Glasgow I would go to the Metropole Theatre and enjoy that. Then I got a feeling I wanted to express myself. I wanted to go on the stage. I saw an advert for a pierrot troup. I went to see about this troup. That was when I got the banjo mandolin. But around that time I had connected with the I.L.P., through a family friend, Geordie Carmichael. His brother was Jimmy Carmichael, later M.P. for Bridgeton, and his nephew was Neil Carmichael, much later on Secretary for Transport in the Wilson Labour Government.[252]

I joined the Bridgeton I.L.P. Guild of Youth. And then I took to the platform and was speaking with Maxton and McGovern and Fenner Brockway, Campbell Stephen and other I.L.P. leaders.[253] I spoke all over the place – at the Olympia in London, the City Hall in Glasgow, the Mound in Edinburgh. I became the Scottish organiser of the Guild of Youth. I used to work from Carmichael's office, up in the north side of Glasgow. I was unemployed but was working full-time on I.L.P. Guild of Youth business. I travelled all over Scotland.

I followed Tom Taylor as Scottish organiser of the Guild of Youth about 1933 or into 1934. He's Lord Taylor of Gryfe now. He was a good speaker then but you could detect his careerism.[254]

This of course was when the Nazis had got into power in Germany, Dollfuss was assassinated in Austria, the Meerut prisoners had just come back, and there was the trial of the Scottsboro Boys.[255] Then there were two lads from Glasgow went to visit Germany and had been arrested by the Nazis and there were tremendous demonstrations.

It was during this period of my unemployment that I frequented the library at Bridgeton Cross and read everything I could lay my hands on. And it was here that I was introduced to the works of Upton Sinclair, Jack London, Pat McGill and maybe above all *The Ragged Trousered Philanthropists* by Robert Tressell. In that library I travelled to the frozen north, the paths and trails of the gold rush, Klondyke with Jack London, to the sleazy streets and to the warehouse with Sinclair, and the *Rat Pit* with Pat McGill.[256] This was a new world opened for me, new characters and above all new social ideas. And I was also travelling to Glasgow Green to hear the debates on religion, atheism, agnosticism, and to listen to the banter and agitational voices of Guy Aldred and Colin Blair McIntyre. McIntyre, who had his own party, was an admirer of John Maclean. Eventually he became a Glasgow councillor. It was there too I continually heard of John Maclean, the Scottish revolutionary schoolteacher.

In 1932 of course the I.L.P. had disaffiliated from the Labour Party. By 1934 some of us in the Guild of Youth decided to work for what we called Youth Unity. We saw the future as lying in joining up with the Young Communist League. There was Eddie Clark, later a Glasgow councillor, and there was the Guild of Youth treasurer for Glasgow – I forget his name now. We won over Louis Povey, the secretary of the Guild, and Horace Green, chairman, who came from Newcastle. There were several young women involved in it too. One of them was Margaret Paterson, who later on became the mother of Fred Reid, the labour historian.[257] And there was Annie MacDougall from Bridgeton. Her family was virtually part of the Maxtons, they were so close to one another. Annie was a brilliant woman. And then there was Marion Robertson who became active in the printworkers' union later on. There was quite a group of us in Glasgow.

I started to edit a little paper called *Youth Unity*.[258] It was first duplicated then eventually printed in the cellar of the I.L.P. at London Road, Bridgeton. *Youth Unity* was advocating movement away from the Fourth International.[259] We wanted to link up with the Young Communist League. That was the battle then that took place, that was when the split took place. Brockway was our main target. He was the one that supported the Fourth International. He supported Trotsky and was against anything that came through the Comintern. Brockway was the one we attacked from the Youth Unity point of view.

It was at a meeting in 1934, a debate between John Gollan and Hector McNeill in the Unitarian Church in Lamb's Pass in Glasgow, that I took the decision to declare openly that I was joining the Young Communist League.[260] There were two points in my life that I can remember debating with myself for weeks. One was the question of God – that was a private thing that I debated with myself when I was eighteen. But the question of joining the Young Communist League was one of the things I debated with myself for a long time. It was quite a deliberate decision but it wasn't any easy decision, because of this feeling that once I had committed myself to it there was no turning back.

And I had a high personal regard for Maxton. He was one of the nicest men you could ever meet. You couldn't be offended by him. If you had any opposition he could destroy it right away by his friendliness. He would look at you with his blue eyes. When I went on the Hunger March and each of us in London went to see his constituency M.P., Maxton was my M.P. I went with the other Marchers from Bridgeton to see him. He knew I had left the I.L.P. by then and joined the Young Communist League. I felt a bit awkward because he had been such a friend. But it melted as soon as he came over to me. He was warm and friendly as ever, no question of any opposition or animosity. I had been really close to him when I had been in the I.L.P. He had been the first to take me round the House of Commons and it was he who made me come and speak at Olympia and took me to Ayr and other places to speak on his platform. And that was from the time when we first had gone to these little weekly socials and whist drives they held in the I.L.P. Rooms in London Road in Brigton.

There was a lot of socialising in the I.L.P. This was one of the great advantages of the I.L.P., because it was really in the roots of the people, very close to them indeed. The I.L.P.used to organise such things as a day-out on the sewerage boat. This was what they called the boat that used to go down from the Broomielaw and empty the sewerage out. Well, the I.L.P. used to take advantage of this and all the old women from Brigton Cross would go and have their day out down the river on the boat. And then there was the other period when the I.L.P. would take the people round the various houses in the Highlands where boys from Glasgow had been put out to the crofters. The Town Council had done that because they were under-privileged children or boys who had got into trouble. It was the councillors' job to go round these various places and see that these boys weren't being put on to, exploited. They could organise the visits so that so many people could go round. It was done really from the socialist point of view. This was one of the things I advocated when I did eventually join the Communist Party. In the Communist Party we didnae have branches at one time. It was purely groups or fractions. We started working for setting up branches so that the Party could get in local people and make it more of a family, homely type of thing, like the I.L.P.

Davie Burke was the organiser of the Young Communist League for Scotland. Later on he became the Tobacco Workers' Union organiser. He died some years ago.[261] And then of course John Gollan had just come out of prison then or before that. He had been in Moscow and he had come back into this country. He was the most brilliant young orator I had ever heard, with his clarity and reasoning, and he was so nice about it. He looked like a dying character when I saw him! Then another young fellow I associate with my activity in the Y.C.L. was Hamish Fraser. I think he was just a student, I don't think he was actually in the Y.C.L. But I got arrested with him at the Mound in Edinburgh.[262]

Well, round about that period my brother Jimmy, the sea cook, and my eldest sister Mary were agitating for me to get a job and forget all about this politics. My brother came home from a voyage on a little boat called *Busiris* and said he had a job for me on this boat. I had had a kipper to eat that night that had upset my stomach and I was feeling rather ill. But I was determined I had got to go to the *Busiris*. So I had to hire a taxi to take me down to the Broomielaw.

We went down on the Mediterranean run, right round to Almeria, Alicante, and Barcelona. It was in Almeria I met a lad who came aboard and told me all about the trouble in the Asturias. Franco had come and operated the iron fist against the miners there. This lad's relatives had been in the uprising. What he told me had a very big influence on my opinion then, having it from the horse's mouth.[263]

I did that one trip on the *Busiris* and then I went back on another ship, again just for one trip. Barney Colquhoun, who had been a fireman on the *North Anglia* when I'd gone on it to South America, was on this other little boat. He knew all about Spain, went round to the bull-fights and was in the cafés and so on. It was through him I made contact with people in Catalonia and Barcelona itself, though I was never in Asturias myself. Though I can't remember the date exactly, I must have made these two trips to Spain sometime around the end of 1934 and the beginning of 1935.

Soon after I came back from that second trip to Spain I became a canvasser for the *Sunday Express*. It was a Y.C.L.-er who introduced me into this job. It was a wonderful experience. I canvassed every town and village in Scotland from Aberdeen to Gretna Green, to bump up the sales. The wage was £3 a week and you got lodging allowance. But you had to get thirteen new orders every day. And the day you didn't get thirteen was the day you got the sack. There was no question about it. You had to get thirteen orders every day.

We didn't have a car. We used to travel by train or bus. We would be at maybe Castle Douglas and the various places in Kirkcudbrightshire for a week, then over to Peebles and go round the various villages there. It was a very skilful job. If you went to a house and could see some nappies on the line you knew you were going to get a mother coming to the door. Otherwise when you rang the bell or knocked on the door you never knew who was coming to answer it. So you had to calculate as best you could, by looking at the clothes line or something like that, who was coming from behind that door. And then of course you had to start the work. We had several dodges. Very often you would see the chinks of the curtains moving when you were outside the gate. You'd work in pairs then and get a measuring tape and start measuring the front of the gate, the path, and so on. The householders were so curious to know what it was all about they would come to the door. Then of course you would give them some story about how you were surveying – then start working in the *Sunday Express*.

The mischievous tricks and fanciful tales to sell Beaverbrook papers came from youthful devilment. The only annoyance in the end was the local newsagent got angry when he had to cancel orders for other papers and change to the *Sunday Express*.

In the evenings another Y.C.L.-er, Malcolm, and I made a point of having a private canvass for the *Daily Worker*, and it could be said that the circulation war of the press barons had a side-effect advantageous to the workers' press. The Scottish *Daily Worker* was pleased with the results.

Then £3 a week was a wonderful wage, plus travelling expenses. I worked five days a week and it gave me quite some time to organise and quite a few recruits were made. I remember when I lodged at a temperance hotel at Cumnock I converted the landlord's daughter to becoming a reader of the *Daily Worker*. Some weeks later when we were on the Hunger March and marching through there on our way south, a banner outside the hotel proclaimed 'Good Luck!' and the daughter and her father were leaning out of the window throwing money to our collectors. There was almost the same story at Gretna, where I had canvassed along with Malcolm almost every resident in the R.A.F. quarters for the *Express*. Later when we passed on the Hunger March not only was the collection healthy but the *Daily Worker* man who travelled on foot with us sold out his quota. I don't think Lord Beaverbrook would have put me on his pension list.

But Edinburgh was the city where I got the sack from the *Sunday Express*. The streets I was allocated to were tenements and before a door was opened a bell had to be rung. A voice from an upstairs window would shout down, 'No' the day.' So I got the sack because I couldn't get thirteen new orders a day. To the delight of David Burke I landed back in Glasgow, ready for the Hunger March of October-November 1936 on London.

My mother was having it quite hard then. My father had died by this time. My brother Jimmy was away at sea and had got married. My other brother was unemployed and on the Means Test. I had only one young sister still at home, so I was the sole support. I was the one who had to draw any Labour Exchange money. It was then that Davie Burke, the Scottish organiser of the Young Communist League, who had been asked by the National Unemployed Workers' Movement to form the Youth section in the Hunger March, approached me to go on the March. It was quite a big decision. You couldn't draw your dole money when you were on the March, and it meant that my mother would have to go without it. I don't think I discussed it with her. I think I told her a lie, that I was going out of town, or something like that. I just decided I was going on the Hunger March. I went with Davie Burke and quite a number of others of whom we became the leadership.

I had joined the National Unemployed Workers' Movement in the days when I was unemployed and in the I.L.P., round about 1933-34. I joined before I went into the Y.C.L.

The I.L.P. of course didn't like the N.U.W.M. then. They knew that it was closely allied with the Communist Party. I joined the N.U.W.M at the Brigton Labour Exchange – they used to recruit there – some day when I was signing on. People like McShane and Middleton and Aitken Ferguson and Kerrigan used all to come round to the Labour Exchanges when the people were going to have their money and then have meetings.

I wasn't a very active member of the N.U.W.M. before I went on the Hunger March. It was a very loose organisation. I don't think they had branch meetings in Brigton: I can't say I was being organised. I was away a lot when I was on the boats.

The N.U.W.M. was a loose, non-party organisation and had members of all political parties in its ranks. Indeed, we had a number of Scottish Nationalists. It did collect many tough characters who were prepared to have a go. Many had personal problems and, in fact, fought rent problems in the Glasgow courts. A number had experienced the rougher side of poverty and were deficient of the law, but then class loyalty was always evident.

I have many friends whom I became acquainted with during my days in the East End. There was an N.U.W.M. club above Collet's Bookshop in High Street and it was there that many fierce discussions took place. I remember one day in the club meeting James Barke, the renowned Scottish writer. He wasn't unemployed but was researching for his writings.[264] Margaret Paterson's mother made tea. She was a very popular figure. The bookshop below the club – although books were out of reach of their pockets – was visited regularly by the unemployed. Douglas Brody, an Aberdonian, was the manager.

Some of the younger members of the N.U.W.M were politically affiliated and on occasion it was a day-out when David Burke and a number of us would adjourn at dinner-time to a working men's soup kitchen for a bowl at one penny. On those occasions we discussed the reorganisation of the world and with Davie's Leninist leadership we could see the end to capitalism. Of course the N.U.W.M. was led by activists but not all were politically affiliated.

There was still the influence of John Maclean's marches of the unemployed to the West End big houses and the Glasgow City Council on the day of its meetings, when deputations would enter the Chambers. John, of course, was long dead by this time, but his memory lingered on and his influence was still felt. Paddy Dollan, who was on the Council, was the bogey-man then. His ears must have burned day and night.

One thing, the unemployed movement broke the religious barriers of the community and prevented it becoming divided. The highly intellectual discussions that took place on almost every subject were astonishing. Names like Plato, Einstein, Ingersoll, William Morris, and others, were commonplace in these discussions.[265] One young man who frequented the club at High Street was Tommy Flynn. He was a superb athlete and a keen cyclist. His parents intended him to become a Catholic priest. He was the only person of that background that I heard speaking at Bridgeton Cross – for the Young Communist League, of course. But he was dragged off the box and punched. It took courage for him to speak there. Tommy eventually died as a machine-gunner in the Thaelmann Battalion in the Spanish War.

When the 1936 Hunger March was being organised, I remember attending a meeting at Crown Street where all the details and organisation was discussed. Present were Kerrigan, McShane, Middleton, and Aitken

Ferguson. The job of organising the Youth fell to Davie Burke and myself. The Socialist Sunday School and the hikers from Balmaha and Loch Lomond provided many recruits.

At that period the Spanish War of course had just broken out. Spain, Spain, was filling my thoughts even before I went on the Hunger March. Phil Gillan, a character from Polmadie in Glasgow, was one of the first to go to Spain to fight. He was an inspiration for all us others.

I made a speech at a mass unemployed meeting against the Unemployment Assistance Board. The demonstration was in Hanover Street in Glasgow and there were thousands there – you've never seen such a gathering in your life. George Middleton, along with Aitken Ferguson, was the main speaker. As such they never impressed me. They spoke in short pithy sentences and would finish each telling point with a stab of their fingers. Nevertheless they got their points across. Then I was invited from the Youth movement, and having quite oratorical abilities I carried the meeting. But I only spoke about the Spanish conflict – not about the unemployed. I got quite a severe telling-off afterwards. Middleton and McShane reported me: it was purely a demonstration against the U.A.B. and here was I talking about recruiting for the International column in Spain. The two issues, for me, were connected. A few months later I was in Spain myself and I can remember when we were all wounded after the battle of Jarama, Jimmy Campbell lying in his hospital bed in Murcia, he says, 'Ye ken, Johnny, I knew ye were comin' oot here!' He had been one of the audience at the Hanover Street unemployed demonstration.

The ticking-off I got didn't prevent me from continuing to recruit for Spain as well as for the Hunger March. About this period the *Daily Worker* wanted somebody to make early deliveries of the paper round the shops. The driver of the van was a fellow called Alex Donaldson, and I was asked through Bob McElhone to assist him. In the meantime I had decided that I was going to join the International Brigade and I encouraged Alex Donaldson to do so, too. Later on he became the press man in Spain and when he came back I think he turned against the Communist Party somehow. Anyway I shouldn't have encouraged him to join the International Brigade, because he was performing a very important job for the *Worker.* So I got hauled up about that too.

Even on the Hunger March there were complete discussions about Spain all the time. This was when the news came through about Phil Gillan, when we were marching down. And there were another two or three – their names escape me now – who were recruited on to the International Brigade.

Before we set out on the Hunger March there were some boots provided. The N.U.W.M. managed to collect them from well-wishers. And there were old puttees and raincoats and things like that that helped out. I got an old raincoat which buttoned on the wrong side from an aunt of mine – it was a woman's coat! Many people bought clothing from paddy's market and so on. The Socialist Sunday School helped a lot too with, I think, goods and equipment. And many of them were taking part in the March. I remember old Rab Chambers, the chairman of the Socialist Sunday School, was still working at the carriage works as we were leaving Glasgow. And he was out right in front of all the workers, cheering us on. And the S.C.W.S. and the Co-ops were very helpful. There was a wonderful outdoor movement that had developed around Loch Lomond. The boots that I had were my hiking boots for the weekends. And underneath my right foot I've still got a bad corn from that Hunger March.

The March was against the Unemployment Assistance Board. This was the new regulation that was brought out. It was going to curtail benefit and also extend the Means Test. On the March the majority of the Marchers lost no benefit since they were already affected by the Means Test. And where relatives and dependants were affected by being cut off, the N.U.W.M. had a fund from public collections to help hardship cases. My own mother didn't get anything from that fund. This was the sort of Scottish Calvinistic type of thing: they wouldn't accept. In the Spanish conflict she had a pound sent through to her every week. But she couldn't do anything else but accept it. We never knew where it came from. But accepting money from the Movement was not the done thing.

In the Youth contingent on the Hunger March there were about thirty or forty. They marched in the mainstream of the March but as a separate group. They were right nearly at the top of the column. As I had been asked by the N.U.W.M. to take part in organising the Youth section I was one of its leadership on the March. Davie Burke, who was the big kingpin politically, had this leadership round him. There was myself and John Connolly.

The main March was led by Peter Kerrigan. Among the leadership was Councillor John Heenan. He was an I.L.P. councillor. Politically I can never remember him siding with the militant side. But he was very earthy, very willing to look after the coppers of the unemployed and that type of thing. And it didn't matter to him whom he associated with in order to do this. Then there was Eddie Laughlin. He was a councillor in Lanarkshire somewhere. I couldn't say if he was a member of the Communist Party but I think he could be. And Willie Keegan, from round about Lesmahagow, was on the leadership too and he was a Communist. There was quite a big contingent from Lesmahagow.

I came to know Kerrigan very well. I worked quite closely with him. He was a very, very hard man. He was very, very firm and very Party-lineish – no deviation and so forth. But as far as honesty and integrity went he was the model for that. There was no question. There was a story put about that when the working class went on these Hunger Marches people like Kerrigan would stay in a hotel at night. This of course was a lot of lies. They just shared everything the same as everyone else on the March.

Kerrigan was very loud in his voice. But he could be very shy, too. You could make him blush in certain things. I can remember one incident later on when we were in Spain. In Madrigueras, on the 27th of January

1937, the Irish Battalion of the International Brigade had found out that
George Nathan had done something against somebody in County Cork
during The Troubles there in the early 1920s. So the Irish Battalion were
protesting against it.[266] And André Marty the Frenchman, a very big tall man
who had led the Black Sea Mutiny of the French Navy during the Russian
Revolutionary wars, came down. Kerrigan was there. And Marty made a
speech. It was like balls of fire coming out the man's mouth! Marty said he
would shoot them and so forth if they didn't behave. And Kerrigan got up
to protest. Marty of course gave a blast against him. Well, the Scotsmen
present that knew Kerrigan couldn't believe it, because he was just like a
little boy – he was six feet three or four tall – who shrank down then with
this blast. That was the only time I ever saw him being put in his place. But
this Marty came and I can hear his voice now. And it was all in French – but
we got the message![267]

     I was a member of the March Council. There was a daily meeting for
everything, within reason. It met I think in the evening. Oh, it dealt with
discipline, food, finance – everything. Kerrigan of course would give the
leadership, and if some problem was raised it would be raised by one of the
other members. But it was more or less on the question never of policy but
only of organisation. There was never any question of needing to disagree.

     When we set out from Glasgow there was quite a big contingent from
Bridgeton that I knew personally. Nolan, Mooney and another lad who
eventually went to Spain – I just can't recollect his name – were on it. I
should think from Brigton there would be something like twenty on the
Hunger March, quite a big contingent. I remember when we were leaving
Glasgow we were given a lot of support. It was all money throwing. That
was a hazard – pennies hitting you on the head. You had to have something
on your head because a penny coming down could give a big bump. It was
the pennies coming from the tenements.

     Now the first part of the March was marred by the expulsion of a
young Marcher. He had stolen a pair of his mate's boots. And this was a
cardinal sin. After a long deliberation the March Council decided he had to
be expelled in the interests of general morale. The ceremony of expulsion
took place in a field outside Thornhill. We were guided into this big field
by Kerrigan. And then the March Council, who had already met to hear
about the lad stealing the pair of boots, went in the middle of this great big
circle of Marchers and pronounced the judgement: this lad had to be
expelled because of the crime he had committed. And you could feel in that
field the feeling of shock against the sentence. You could feel there was
something going to happen there. There were a few voices raised and
shouted in protest against his being expelled, being so roughly treated. You
can imagine – two days after marching away down to the south of Scotland
somebody being told he's being expelled. It was quite harsh treatment. It
meant he had to walk all the way back to Lanarkshire or wherever he came
from. And the disgrace of it. The Marchers felt it was a bit too heavy. One
or two shouted. And you could feel it. You could feel there was something

happening. I remember feeling that it was a bit too harsh. I was of course a member of the March Council myself. It had been decided he should be punished in some way but not that he should be so harshly treated.

Anyhow that lad was expelled. And I can see him yet walking out of this big circle of Marchers, out of the field and through the farm gate. He climbed over the gate and out on to the road. He was quite a young lad, he'd be about twenty or twenty-one. It was very upsetting. But nothing happened, no revolt took place. It was a near thing.

When we got to the actual Border between Scotland and England I was voted to do the oration. Traditionally what happened on these Marches was they'd go into a field and hold a meeting: 'We're entering England and we're carrying the message'. Being voted to do the oration was evidently some great privilege. So I made this oration. I finished, saying: 'This is our own native heath. Now is the time to take it over!' It was this feeling that we were marching for the Revolution. It was of course a bit exaggerated at that period.

When we got over the Border we went down through to Kendal. That was where there was another near-revolt. As we trod over the Borders through the villages the going was hard and it was on one of the longest stretches between Penrith and Kendal that our strength and grit were challenged. The route took us over Shap Fells, a distance of some twenty miles. The food lorry used to be at a point for us to meet it and they would then dish up the lunch. But this particular day the food lorry broke down and the usual midday meal of stew was missing. This was a calamity In addition to missing the meal a very special service of attention to foot problems by a one-legged cobbler, who travelled on the food lorry, was also absent. He had a last and a hammer on the lorry and he was also an expert on sore feet. Understandably there was nearly a revolt among the Marchers. That evening it was a band of tired and angry men who arrived in Kendal. And it was only the homely reception we got there that compensated for the loss of the vital meal.

Our progress through Lancashire was warm: the population waved and cheered us on our way along the stretches of dark, dismal streets lined with idle weavers. The March was getting bigger and longer, with recruits joining on the way. But the next thing was in Manchester. I don't know whether we met the others in Manchester. But when we got there it was drizzling. Usually when we got into a place there were church halls, Labour halls, or schools to go into. The exception was in Manchester. Everything had been filled up. Part of the Scottish contingent had been housed somewhere, but there was nothing for our part. And the decision was taken by someone – I think it would be the local reception committee – that the only place we could go to was the workhouse. We completely refused. We would not enter a workhouse. Accepting such charity was repugnant and it was the intention of the majority to sleep on the pavement rather than enter the cold clammy confines of that building. During the arguments the rain pelted down and it was getting dark. Grudgingly we entered the workhouse. One of the conditions of our entering was that no chores such as stick chopping would be undertaken. It was a custom for inmates to perform some duty in repayment for their night's accommodation. I can still taste the water, cold tea and the doughy chunks of bread spread or smeared with cheap, greasy margarine. The miserable superintendent, who resembled a character from Dickens, was more than glad to be rid of the Hunger Marchers. We certainly missed the reception of Co-op Guilds and trade unions on that occasion.

From Lancashire our route took us through the Potteries. Our reception through the Five Towns reflected the people there. They gave us a wonderful reception. But they had really been hard hit in the Hungry Thirties. That was where you felt it. You could see the starvation in their pinched thin faces.

But then through the Midlands we by-passed Birmingham, and coming out at the centre of England – Merriden, the famous cyclists' memorial – we came to Coventry. There were two reasons for the by-pass. The first was that we were getting behind our timetable, and the second was that on a previous March the Birmingham police had fixed the route so that it almost broke the whole thing up. And our leaders weren't going to allow that to happen this time.

As we approached Coventry we were met by the Lord Mayor of that city – a Labour mayor. He was accompanied by councillors and trade unionists who had taken a day off work for the occasion. It was a nice gesture but we paid dearly for it footwise. The welcoming committee had planned to use the March to rally the populace of that great engineering city and march through the streets in order to boost their election campaign at that time. But it meant we had walked round Birmingham, through Merriden, and then when we got into Coventry we had to march round all the cobbled streets. You can imagine the condition we were in when we finished up.

Now it was in Coventry that Wal Hannington, the national organiser of the N.U.W.M. came to address us. And he possessed the most powerful voice I have ever heard. He knew how to use it. He finished by singing *MacGregor's Gathering*. I can hear it now from over fifty years ago:

> Gather, gather, gather,
> Give the roofs to the flames
> And their flesh to the eagle.

And how appropriate the song was to the March. It did our hearts good. It was after that, from Rugby, that I left by train with Kerrigan to go to London to meet the March Council there, to prepare for the reception.

But before I come to that there are one or two other things I remember about the March on the way down toward London. First, the attitude of local Labour Parties, unions and Co-ops was absolutely friendly. Never from the moment that we left Glasgow was there one word of anyone saying, 'Go back!', or anything like that. When we went down through Annan, the more non-industrial rural parts, you had staring – no hostility – but staring, seeing these men walking through. But when you went through Gretna itself, which housed R.A.F. personnel, then you got a good reception, the young R.A.F. wives – working-class people – coming out with food and money. It was all very, very friendly. Only once – in Manchester – did we have to go into the workhouse. When we got into Kendal, for instance – that was when the lorry broke down and it was a very, very big thing for men who were just depending on that – it wasn't a strong labour movement there, it was more of a church organisation and Co-op.[268]

We found churches, Labour Parties, I.L.P.s, Communist Parties and trade unions receiving us. In Coventry we had that reception from the Lord Mayor, Councillor George Hodgkins. There was a Transport and General Workers' Union shop steward there who hailed from Lanarkshire, Jock Ferguson. Jock had a reputation as a militant and he was in the forefront of our reception.

There was strict discipline on collections. No collector was allowed in a pub and any habit of friendly folk taking the Marchers out to have a drink was discouraged. Kerrigan was a strict disciplinarian. There were never any excesses reported. If a collector on duty went into a pub he was taken off the job right away if he was found there.

Well, Kerrigan and I went down from Rugby to London by train but the others carried on marching and we met them in London. In London Aneurin Bevan, Jennie Lee, Hannen Swaffer, Wal Hannington, Tom Mann, Ben Tillett and Willie Gallacher were on the March Council.[269] During the week in London I went and spoke at a number of public meetings, along with Tom Mann. And he was the greatest jovial character. I remember one meeting with him at Battersea Town Hall. He had on an old-fashioned coat, not like a swallow-tail coat but a long, Victorian type of coat, and he had his big flowing moustache. When he got up to speak he said, 'Good Evening.' Then he says, 'Excuse me one moment.' He turned round and took out his false teeth, top and bottom, wrapped them in a hanky, put them in his pocket, turned round again to face his audience, and says, 'Right, we shall proceed!' And then he gives this oration that raised them to the heights.

I was elected by the March Council to speak. And at Trafalgar Square I spoke with Hannen Swaffer, Aneurin Bevan and Harry Pollitt on the big plinth. That was the only picture the *Daily Herald* published of the Hunger March. Hannen Swaffer was a weak speaker. When I finished he came up and said, 'And where are you from?' Of course he was referring to my Scotch voice. I says, 'I'm from the Y.C.L.' Now this was objectionable. This was what the general Labour movement did object to: that the Communists were taking over these things. And of course this sort of defiant, rebellious answer wasn't the correct thing. These were the sort of stupid sectarian actions that we did on occasions do in these times. Hannen Swaffer turned away in disgust.

As I have already said, I met Maxton at the House of Commons as my M.P., along with other Marchers. We stayed in London a few days and then all the others went straight home. I was asked to go to the North-East of England to do a bit of organising for the Young Communist League. But I had decided I was going to join the International Brigade, and that was when I went back to Glasgow. I don't think I'd been in touch with home since I left on the March. I can't remember writing to my family.

Only a few weeks passed between the Hunger March and my going to Spain in November 1936. Along with about fifty other volunteers I set off from a back street in the centre of Glasgow. It was supposed to be a secret departure but just as the two rather old and worn-looking buses were ready to leave, some dozens of well-wishers emerged from the closes to say their farewells. I can still see and hear one of the girls who had come to say goodbye to her young sweetheart. She was Isa Alexander, a beautiful brown-eyed girl from Arcadia Street. He was John Connolly from the Gorbals, who had been on the Hunger March with me. With tears in her eyes she cried to him, 'Don't forget, John, to come back – I'll be waiting for you.' No one came to wave to me. I had told no one of my departure, although I had come back to Glasgow especially to have some last hours with my mother. She had great faith in me and had never stood in my way in anything I had ever done.

My experiences in Spain are another story. I was wounded in the arm at the battle of Jarama in February 1937. After some time in hospital and then working as a courier and assisting Peter Kerrigan in visiting the wounded and in welfare work among them, I was put in charge of a group of volunteers being sent back to Britain because they were wounded or sick. I arrived back in May 1937 and then plunged into a speaking tour campaigning for goods and volunteers for Spain that took me from Land's End to John O'Groats.

To register the number who went from the Hunger March to Spain would be interesting. Beyond my immediate circle from Glasgow and district I can think of numbers going into dozens. Out of that half dozen of us from the Youth contingent on the Hunger March who decided to go to Spain, I'm the only one alive. The others were killed. It's a sorrow I've carried in my mind all these years. Often I sit in my thoughts and think, 'And I'm the only one here.' If it hadn't been for my influence would it have been different?

Some commentators on the Hunger Marches have had a callous attitude in picking out any misdemeanours by individuals, giving the impression that the Marchers were lumpen-class fodder. This is far from the truth and a distortion. The men I marched with from Glasgow to London were poor in worldly things but rich in mind. Their nightly discussions on the daily march were of the highest aesthetic quality. To picture them as the roughs and toughs from the Gorbals out for a kick – forget it. Mind you, if it came to a confrontation their ranks would be solid.

Whilst their language conveyed the quick-witted, wise-cracking, short pithy sentences of Glaswegians, seldom did you ever hear vulgarities or gutter language.

Looking back on the Hunger March now, more than half a century later, I believe I would do exactly the same and would choose the same mates. There were certain bits of artificiality about it in the sense that I wasn't one of the starving masses, though I was unemployed at the time I went on the March. I was simply an organiser. The March was well conducted from beginning to end.

The campaign for Spain which developed during our period on the road sapped some energy from the support for the March. The trade unionists, Co-operators, church people who provided us with food, clothing and shelter on our March were the same people who led the campaign for food for Spain. For me it is hard to separate Spain and the March. I see them as one.

The Jarrow March which took place at the same time as ours equally was of significance, but over the years the media and the establishment have put it to the fore and have virtually ignored the N.U.W.M. March.

So be it. Years and years afterward I have met people in London, Coventry and in Wales who talked of the influence the March had on them and for some it was their first step to the Labour movement. I can remember when sharing a meeting with him many years afterward, old George Hodgkins, ex-mayor of Coventry, talking about the effect of the unemployed March of 1936. If ever I have an epitaph I hope it says: He was a Hunger Marcher.

Guy Bolton

I was born in Lesmahagow on the 15th of January 1907 but I wasna a good boy. I wouldnae go to the school, sometimes three weeks at a time, I wouldnae go. In fact, the whipper-in come to my mother's hoose to see why I wasn't at the school. She says, 'He's at the school.' He says, 'Mrs Bolton, he's no' at the school. And I'll tell ye more than that, he hasnae been at the school for three weeks.' And she was gaun tae splash him wi' the girdle for darin' tae say that I wisnae at the school.

For a number o' years up tae I left the school I played cowboys masel', gallopin' ower the place, stealin' a turnip – that was my dinner. I got on well enough wi' the teacher that I had. But when I come to the age o' about thirteen he says, 'It seems, Bolton, I cannae learn ye any more. I think ye'd as weel go home and jist don't come back.' And that was my exit frae the school.

When I left school I couldnae get a job in the pits till I was fourteen. So again I got playin' cowboys masel'. Well, I was jist turnin' intae a man then, in my ain estimation. And I got a job in Bellfield colliery, Coalburn, about three miles frae Lesmahagow. I was gaun tae start on the Monday but the 1921 strike come on. So that was thirteen weeks of holidays to start wi'. And that was the fun and games – out stealin' hens' eggs, stealin' tatties and turnips. In fact, that's a' ye got tae eat efter the first couple o' weeks. But your mother went in debt in the Store and she got the basics, jist the rough basics. Ye got a piece on jeely and maybe ye got a pair o' troosers frae the minister tae weer cut doon. And if ye got a new jersey and a pair o' troosers it looked good. You wis dressed, you wis Tommy the Toff. You got a pair o' boots, tackety boots, aboot the month o' October. And when thae boots was run done – and that wasnae too long – that was the summer started. It wis your bare feet then till October again, no matter the weather. That was the position then: a' the bairns went wi' their bare feet.

Well, eventually the strike finished and my faither had a wee job, a wee bit o' contract in No. 9 pit in Coalburn. And he asked the under-manager if he could bring me oot some Saturday morning for a shift, jist tae see the pit, to see if I'd like it. So I went oot on a Saturday mornin' and it was me that shovelled the shot, I did the shovellin'. I was jist startin' tae grow then, I was a big boy. I could shovel wi' two hands, that way or that way. So I got a job in the pit, where ye worked wi' a pit powny. I wisnae awfy long in that tae ma faither went tae the under-manager and says, 'That yins been long enough at the powny noo. He'll need tae be at the powny for hissel'.' So I had tae go and work wi' him at fillin' the tubs and hand-drawin' them oot tae the sidin'.

Things went on quite quietly. I worked wi' ma faither. He got the pey and I got ma pocket money. But I wanted a pey for masel' so me and another boy went tae the under-manager and asked for a job on the coal face. We asked tae tak a place at the coal, six feet high and twelve feet wide and cut wi' a six feet bar, undercut. We wis young and strong, we kenned we could murder it. It wis hard work and I wis lookin' for flaws and faults. But I wis a wee bit mouthy. I wis talkin' aboot conditions even as a boy. And somebody must have heard me because at a branch meetin' of the old Lanarkshire County Miners' Union – it wis the first branch meetin' ever I was at – I got nominated to go and represent the Youth Committee. And that same week when this other lad and me wis fillin' the tubs they picked oot one o' our tubs on the pitheid and cowped it up. And here was maybe aboot eight or ten pund o' this stour, jist coal coom. That wis foreign material. So we baith got the sack. But strangely the other boy got his job back in jist a week's time. I never got ma job back.

I'd maybe be aboot seventeen. We could maybe earn, say, fifteen shillings a shift, which was an awfy money, a helluva money. So I had tae go tae Motherwell and defend masel' at the buroo. The Auchlochan Coal Company didnae want nothin' tae dae wi' me. And I don't know why for I had never even attended a committee meetin' – I never got the chance. I was out the pit, I was sacked. Somebody must ha' been talkin' aboot me bein' too big in the mooth or something like that. It must ha' been that. Well, in these times it wis quite hard times.

It couldnae ha' been on account of ma faither that I got the sack. He was a very quiet livin' man. Ma faither went doon the pit when he was nine year auld. I think it was in Springburn. It was the ironstone mines then. His father was killed there. And there were ten sons and one daughter in the family. Ma faither was the second auldest. His auldest brother was workin' doon the pit. Ma faither went doon the pit in the mornin' for half a day then he come back up and went tae the school. Well, naturally he fell asleep. He couldnae keep his eyes open. He was fifty-six year auld afore he could write his ain name. He had tae learn tae write it to go on the buroo.

He must ha' been born about 1880 and he went doon the pit afore he was ten year auld. [270] It wasnae illegal to go down at that time. Of coorse whit he was doin' there was jist sittin' at what they ca' the trap door – a trap door tae divert the air current in a different direction. So when a powny come oot, he opened the trap door, put the powny through and let it shut. That wis his job. Well, up at six o'clock in the mornin', ye can understand what the boy was like at midday, a wee laddie, nine year auld. He couldnae keep his eyes open at the school. So he was illiterate. He couldnae read the paper. My mother aye had tae read the papers tae him. He couldnae dae things like that.

As I say, ma grandfaither Bolton was killed in the ironstone in

Springburn. He came from Ireland actually, but what part I don't know. My mother's side o' the family were a' miners tae. One of my mother's brothers was a big fightin' man, Jack Ritchie. He won the amateur championship o' Britain three times and got a cup for it. He went and fought in Spain in the Civil War. He was a rebel, a great John Maclean man, John Maclean daft. My mother herself was in ferm service, maistly indoor work, in the byres, cleanin' out, milkin', wheelbarryin' and a' that cairry-on. I was the third in our family. There were nine o' us, but only three boys and one o' them died. And I had a sister died in infancy an' a'. One was I think two year and ten month and the other yin was one year and eight month. And they took the fever – scarlet and diphtheria, I think. One o' them was ta'en tae Lanark hospital, and one o' them was left in the hoose. And the polis come to the door at six o'clock in the mornin'. The doctor was there in the hoose where the wee boy had died jist at that, at six o'clock. And the polis landed at the door tae tell my mother that the wee girl had died in the hospital. Two dead at the same time.

Ma faither's plans wis to go to America. He had friends in Philadelphia and they said to him tae take us a' tae America. That would be before the 1914 War. He was savin' a' these years maybe twa or three shillins a week. It took a long, long time. I think his plans were comin' near fruition when these deaths happened wi' the two wee bairns. And ma mother had said to him: 'Geordie, I'm no' gaun tae America. Ah'm no' leavin' a faimly lyin' oot there in the kirkyaird, I'm no' daein' it.' That was it cancelled.

When I got the sack frae the pit that would be about 1923 or 1924. I cannae recall jist how long I was unemployed. But I never got back into the Coalburn pits. But I got a job up in what they ca'ed the Hagshaw mines up in Coalburn and I was there until the '26 strike. And of course it was the same then as it was in the '21 strike. Ye had tae go oot and look for your food, because there were nothing, nothing. And we went and we got bolder. It was rabbits and hens. We always kept dogs for the poachin', no' racin' dugs but poachin' dugs that could kill a hare or rabbits. We thought we'd take a change tae mutton and the smell, the smell o' mutton cookin'! But unfortunately we filled too many pots, and so many o' us got arrested an ta'en away to Lanark. There were three or fower teams o' brothers: brother, brother, brother, brother, brother, brother. So they took a decision that the aulder brothers would take the punishment and the younger brothers would get off. And I mind the judge tellin' them: 'Ye know, I could sentence ye to death, to be hung by the neck until ye're dead for this offence. That's the law of the land for stealin' sheep.' And they got three month in the jail. My aulder brother Jock he was one. He said that I never was there. Well, the other brothers: Tam Broon said Jock Broon never was there, and Alex Summers said that Alan Summers never was there. When they come oot the jail the silver band met them at the station. There was a welcome home party. They were seen as martyrs.

It was before the '26 strike that I joined the Communist Party. It was in 1924, after I got the sack, and I was only about seventeen at the time. I was mixin' wi' the unemployed. And a gentleman o' the name o' Sam Henderson come oot frae Glasgow and held meetins. He was a shop steward I think wi' the Glesgae Corporation buses. I went to listen to his meetins and decided to join the 'Party. Then of course jist efter the '26 strike, when they picked a' the boys out – 'Ye're no' gaun back, and you're no' gaun back' – two or three of us, Jock Pirie and masel' and Jimmy Hunter, formed the Lesmahagow branch of the National Unemployed Workers' Movement.

I got back into the Hagshaw mines after the '26 strike. I wisnae victimised. You see, thir were cheap mines. They couldnae get men tae work in them. It was too far away. Ye'd tae walk miles. So much so that the ton rates – it was a' ton rates in these days – in the Hagshaw mines was double the ton rates in Coalburn. But if you was on the backshift and up wi' the two o'clock train and you missed the half-past seven train back home, ye'd twelve mile tae walk. So you'd tae lay in tae it tae get your wage oot. But ye could dae it wi' the double ton-rates, ye see.

In fact, we used tae go intae what they ca'ed the machine-cut places and tak a hutch oot o' this yin, a hutch oot o' that yin and a hutch oot o' the other yin, and yer neebour was gettin' the place ready at the time, tae hae a richt blast tae have plenty o' coal the next nicht. Aw, ye wis stealin' the coal but ye were stealin' it aff the coal company. Ye wisnae stealin' it frae your fellow miners. It wis the Arden Coal Company, a small company. I think that's the only coal they had and it was a gold mine. It was a big valley and they could tear the sod off and there was the coal right along the valley, both sides. There were no brushers in the pit, only a handfu' o' oncost boys at switches or pownies or what have you. It wis total profit. They gave us double ton rates – so they could afford it!

But we werenae really well off. If you earned twelve shillins a day you wouldnae tell naebody. That was a big wage. In fact, efter the '26 strike this double ton rate come off. It come off because we wis beat, smashed. And ye come back to normal ton rates. Men couldnae make a wage – impossible. A shift was to fill I think twelve tubs. They werena big tubs. That might be five and a half ton for a pair o' men. But ye'd to fill that every day. It was hand-hewn coal, hand hewn and explosives – no machines. And I come home this day. My wage for six shifts, once you peyed your railway tickets and your insurance, etc., etc. – and I can never forget it – was £2.5/10d. So that's how well off we was. So I came hame this day and, oh, I was sick. I telt my mother, 'Here, mother, there's a pound. I'm gaun for a walk'. 'Oh? Where ye gaun for a walk tae?' Says I, 'I'll tell ye later on.' So I went away tae Fort William. Me and another boy, Gerry Broon, we walked tae Fort William, tae the tunnellin'.

Tae Fort William from Lesmahagow, oh, it took us a day or twa tae dae it – we didnae dae it in a nicht! It would be '28 or '29, nearer '28 when oo went up there. It was a hydro-electric scheme they were building. Anyway we walked a' the way tae Fort William. We steyed in Perth one night, in a shed full o' horses. It must ha' been a Co-operative stable, where there were big cairts and lorries and bundles o' hey in the corner. We jist dossed doon there for the night. Then we slept again at Kinlochrannoch, in jist like a meetin' place for folk, a wee kind o' auld hoose. And they're a' sittin' wi' their pipes havin' a smoke and bletherin' when the twa o' us come in and we went for a sait. And oo said 'Aye,' and we started tellin' them jist whae we wis. They asked if oo wis hungry. 'Oh,' we said, 'we're hungry.' So they took and got us some sandwiches. And then a fellow spoke up. He says, 'Yer name's Gavin Bolton, isn't it?' I jist aboot collapsed. He was a schoolteacher in Lesmahagow skule. I jist forget his name but he was up there havin' a holiday. He was a big nice fellow. He gie'd us half-a-croon each, which was a lot o' money.

So eventually we landed at Fort William and it was late in the day. So we seen this local fellow and asked him if he could gie us ony idea where the big tunnel wis so we could be there in the mornin'. He says, 'An' where are ye gaun the nicht?' I said, 'We've nae idea at a'. We'll need tae get a place tae sleep.' 'Well,' he says, 'ken what I'd dae if I was you ? Go up tae the convent and ask the nuns for somethin' tae eat.' He says, 'Come back doon and' – he showed us this street, 'just in there there's an auld buildin' that's condemned. And that's where a' the boys pits in their nicht when they're waitin' tae gaun up tae the job in the mornin'.'

So we went up first tae the convent and as long as I live I'll never forget it: 'Aw, certainly. Jist stand there and we'll bring ye oot a piece.' And I got nearly a loaf – spread wi' lard. I ate it and I was chokin' on every bite, chokin' at every bite! We slept in the condemned place that night on the auld flair. There were wee fires gaun in the fireplaces, sticks and that. So we went up tae the tunnel in the mornin'. And I was a wee bit mair brash than my butty. I went in first. Ye'd tae strip off tae see there were nae lice on ye or nothin' tae start wi'. Well, of course ye could ha' refused and walked oot but ye was wantin' a job. You could see the point in it because they knew you was lyin' rough. And I got a job. He asked me if I knew anythin' aboot blast borin'. 'Oh,' I says, 'I havenae handled it but I've seen it and I know I could handle it.' 'Well,' he says, 'you're big enough. A'right,' he says, 'jist get the train at one o'clock.' It would take us where we were gaun tae.

But here my neebour, Gerry Broon, had made a mistake: he didnae get a job. So he kind o' panicked. And he come up the next day. He had twa mile to come up the wee railway up the side o' Ben Nevis. And I had tae go tae the shift boss and from him tae the heid man, tae see if I could get somebody on that shift tae help ma neebour. He says, 'Where is your neebour?' I says, 'He's oot at the door.' He says, 'Bring him in.' Gerry Broon was as big as me and strong like me. The heid man says, 'And how did you no' get a job?' I says, 'He made a mistake. He said he had never worked wi' blast borers. And I know that he could work wi' a blast borer as well as anybody if he just seen how he was gaun tae handle it.' He says, 'I believe ye.' And he gave him a chit and ten bob. And the ten bob was gaun tae be kept aff me. So Gerry Broon was tae go back doon tae the base camp and start the next day. But he didnae start beside me. He got away miles further up at a different camp. There were adits intae the hill. They burst intae a certain distance – we ca'ed it an adit – then they started traivillin' east and west. Then maybe six mile further up, the same again. So that they a' met. But there were ten different camps. So ye could say there were twenty faces a' gaun at the one time, two at each camp, east and west. It was a huge scheme, twenty-one mile long. The tunnel was well under way when we landed, but it had still a long way to go. It was twenty feet wide and twenty feet high. But it was concreted roond and roond and it was reduced tae fourteen feet in diameter for the actual water runnin'. I think the work took about three or fower year. It had started before the '26 strike. The price of that contract – I can remember it well – was £10,000,000 to drive that tunnel, Balfour and Beattie.

I was there aboot nine month. Ye could earn roughly about twelve shillins a shift on an average. But then some weeks ye'd maybe need tae work a ten-hoor shift. A lot depended on the weather, for the water tae drive the turbines. On a lean spell ye maybe jist had an eight-hoor shift, 1/6d an hoor. And it cost ye, I think, twenty-one shillins for your food a week. We lived in big bung huts, maybe wi' aboot thirty men in a hut. Political activities were nil up in a place like that. There wis jist caird playin' and drinkin'. There wis no union there. There might be men still payin' their union dues at home or wherever they were. But it was a complete turn-roond a' the time. There were very few who could say they were there for more than nine month tae a year. There wis an awfy lot o' Irishmen there. They saved up tae get back tae Ireland tae buy a sheep or a coo. They never drank a' their life and three or fower quid a week was a fortune tae them. They could save up maybe twa or three hunder pound in nine month and away they go. It wis jist a complete turn-roond. And the employment office doon at the valve shaft – almost at Fort William, where the big aluminium works is – wis constant every day, men comin' and men gaun. In fact, a lot o' folk went missin' that was never heard tell o', maybe robbed and flung doon one o' the big ravines.

It wis quite rough. But then I was a young man and I was as strong as a horse and I could shovel either way. Ye got shovellin' tae start wi', then ye went frae shovellin' on tae second man on the blast borer, then frae that on tae the borer. But what chased me oot o' it was at this particular time there were aboot eight weeks o' dry weather and a' the hillsides wis dry. And a' ye got daein' was borin' the face and blastin' it. Ye was firin' aboot thirty shots, wi' ten pund in each hole – and there's a lot o' explosives. And ye only got ten minutes tae the blast. Oh, the smoke, the fumes – yellow! Ye couldnae see. Ye had tae go in and waft it. Ye were supposed tae keep the shovels goin' tae turn it ower. I said, 'Oh, this is no' for me!' That finished me wi' that, ye couldnae stick it. So I came hame tae Lesmahagow, came hame in style wi' the train. The Sunday fare was 6/8d tae Glesgae.

Efter that I got a job in Uddingston in Viewpark pit and I worked there for a very short period. When I got my first pay it was thirty-eight shillins, for a week on the coal face. Ah says tae the contractor, 'In the name o' Christ, what's this?' 'Oh,' he says, 'it's eight bob a shift. That's a' I can pey

ye, eight bob a shift.' 'Oh, well, sir, ' says I, 'ye can jist stop peyin' me.' And
I finished wi' him. I worked a fortnight tae get my first pey. I got my two
weeks' pey and I had under fower poond.

Then I got a job in Ferniegair pit, about a couple o' miles south o'
Hamilton Cross, just aside the Carlisle road. I got lodgings wi' an old lady
at Uddingston Cross, jist doon the road gaun tae Bellshill, on the left-hand
side. I can see the cottage yet and the auld woman, a fine auld woman she
was. Well, Ferniegair was a hell of a pit for black damp. We wis preparatory
workers, brushin' and leavin' everythin' ready for the coal-cuttin' machine
for the next colliers in the mornin'. We went doon to oor work this night
– we were in ahint the face – and the lamps wouldnae burn. So there were
a sister pit jist doon the rail tracks aboot three or fower hunder yairds. They
sent the pony driver away doon to the other pit and get x amount o' safety
lamps. So the boy brung up oil-burnin' lamps. They wouldnae burn either.
So they sent him back for electric Glennies. Ah says, 'Oh, no, no, no. Tell
the contractors tae make up my time and I'll come in the mornin' and see
ye at the pit. Will ye dae that?' He says, 'What wey?' I says, 'Christ, yer
licht'll no' burn in there. A moose'll no' live in it. Ah want tae live a wee
while.'

I wis in Ferniegair jist nine month. So I come back tae the dole again
in Lesmahagow. And masel' and two pals we got a chance o' jobs in
Kirkcudbrightshire – quarry work. So away we went: New Galloway. In
the first quarry, Aichie quarry, it wis a Dunfermline firm that had the
contract. I see their lorries gaun aboot yet. They were buildin' a new road
atween Newton Stewart and New Galloway. It was an eighteen-mile road.
They jist burst intae the side o' the hills and started away a quarry. When it
was too far tae cairry the stuff they jist started another quarry. We worked
in two o' them, Clatterin'shaws was the other one. They put us on to a
contract, fourpence a ton for shovellin' nine-inch metal intae lorries. We
had tae delve it wi' big graips. Ye had tae make yer ain flair wi' the graip and
load it up into lorries at fourpence a ton. It was hard, hard work. I mean ye
couldnae earn wages at it. It was the winter because ye got a lot o' snow but
the snow never lay doon there. It was six inches deep at night and nothing
in the morning. That's hoo it went. And it was the same there: ye was
poachin' for rabbits tae feed yoursel'. None o' us spent money on food. We
lived jist in a hut, fower men in a hut. Ye had jist the one pot and the one
frying pan! I wisnae politically active there, there were nae way o' bein' that.
Ye wis too busy lookin' for food. So that was that. I come back hame after
nae mair than about eight or nine month. I come back hame and got started
then on the National Unemployed Workers' Movement.

I had joined the N.U.W.M. earlier on. In fact, we had formed a
branch, a first-class branch, in Lesmahagow. It had at least 300 members.
They werenae a' frae Lesmahagow. The wee villages roond aboot –
Blackwood, Kirkmuirhill, Auchenheath, Boghead – they a' come and
signed the dole there. They were a' minin' villages. There were nothing else
there. There were nae mines where we lived, Coalburn was the nearest. But

they traivelled on the workmen's train, or you went on bikes or walked. If I could pit it this way: if I knew the population of Lesmahagow at that time I could tell you hoo many were unemployed. Because at the very maist there were two grave-diggers, there were a saw mill that employed maybe two men and three apprentices: of coorse whenever they reached their time they had to go oot. Then there were a blacksmith's shop, jist the faither and a son. Then of coorse there wis shopkeepers. There wis nae industry – nothing.

Well, in the N.U.W.M. we had local marches, local meetings, maybe a march tae Larkha' and a meeting there. In fact, we once had Alex Moffat and Tom Mann through at Larkhall. And we marched frae Lesmhagow doon tae the meetin'. We met the usual crowd, Labour Party, under the banner o' the Clarion Cycling Club. As we were marchin' in they were fleein' away for a run on their bikes. And they knew Tom Mann was comin' and Alex Moffat. So that's how much interest the Labour Party had in the unemployed.

We didnae have any women in the Lesmahagow N.U.W.M. Well, there might be maybe one young woman, but it was very, very rare. There were nae women on the buroo at that time.

I couldnae tell ye how many o' the N.U.W.M. members were in the Communist Party. There was a goodly number. But I can safely say they were to a man behind the Party leadership. Ye took their penny but that was the amount o' work o' an awful lot o' them. We had a good solid core and that was the main thing. If you ca'ed a meetin' ye could get hundreds in. If you ca'ed a march ye got plenty to go marchin'. In fact we could ha' got fifty volunteers to go on a march tae London. A' the leaders were in the Communist Party, a' the heid yins, and a good lot o' the other boys an' a'. But ye could say they were maistly jist dues-payin' members – but game tae go oot and sell a paper or spare a penny for the *Daily Worker* or for penny pamphlets. We got fowerpence for a bus tae go tae Coalburn and we walked frae Coalburn across the Douglas Moor intae Douglas and ye had a full day sellin' maybe Harry Pollitt's pamphlets or Unemployed Movement pamphlets or Wal Hannington or what have you. It was a combination o' the N.U.W.M. and the Communist Party that did that. The N.U.W.M. committee was the same committee as the Communist Party, pit it that wey. Under the N.U.W.M. or the Communist Party – we wisnae fussy, 'cause it was popular.

I would say the majority o' the N.U.W.M. members had nae affiliations tae nane o' the political parties, they were jist socialists in their minds, no' actually members. I cannae recall any o' the N.U.W.M. bein' in the I.L.P. There were I.L.P.-ers in Lesmahagow but there was nae branch. There would be only a wee core in the toon. In fact when young Smillie – Alex Smillie – stood for Parliament, a' the I.L.P. was on the platform, half-a-dozen o' them. And I don't think any o' the N.U.W.M. wis in the Labour Party. It was the same as the I.L.P.: a wee core o' chancers. 'Cause we knew them a' as chancers. In fact, an incident during the General Strike when the

Russians sent ower about £1¹/₂ million o' money for the miners: these were
the people that handled it, the Labour leaders who were also the union men.
We seen them comin' tae Lesmahagow frae Coalburn in taxis on a Sunday
night intae the Commercial Hotel, bonafyin' at the Commercial Hotel, and
away back hame at midnight wi' taxis. [271] They were the local leaders o' the
Lanarkshire Miners' Union that were in the Labour Party.

The N.U.W.M. was a penny for the funds, a penny for the doctor, and
a penny for the ambulance fund. The ambulance fund was so that if maybe
a child needed tae go to the hospital in Glesgae ye got the expenses for an
ambulance or that, bus fare, jist whatever was required. So it was thruppence
a week. Well, my buroo money at that time for my wife and our laddie and
lassie was £1.9/3d a week. Well, the thruppence went for the subscription
so we had £1.9/-- that's like £1.45 the day -- for the fower o' us. I had got
married in 1933 and I was settled doon on the buroo then! But I was active
in the N.U.W.M. and the Communist Party. I had rejoined both o' them
when I came back frae the quarries. It was the first thing I done.

I was unemployed frae then, about 1931, '32, up tae the spring o' '37.
We got two shillins for each child. My wife was never allowed to work. If
she had had a job I would ha' had nae buroo money. In fact, I think a matter
that's interestin' but it would be hard to understand by present-day young
folk: ye had to look for work -- and prove it. Ye got a green card in yer haund
and wherever you asked for work had tae sign it that they hadnae a job for
ye. And ye'd go maybe up tae the pits in the mornin', maybe ye'd have
twelve standin' roond aboot ye waitin' on the under-manager comin' oot
tae see if there were ony work. And he would walk straight past ye. And
he'd be in his office for maybe an hoor. And he'd come oot and ye'd say,
'Ony chance o' ye needin' ony men? Ony starts?' 'Nothin' daein'. And ye'd
ask him tae sign the green caird: 'I've nae time for that,' and he'd bang on.
So you'd walked three mile tae the pit, stood an hoor and a haulf, and ye
walked back three mile. It was Coalburn pit ye walked tae, No. 9, or No.
6, or No. 10, or whatever -- one you knew had a gaffer in the mornin'. But
because he didnae sign yer green caird ye couldnae prove ye were lookin'
for work, ye had nothin' tae prove it.

It was very near daily ye went lookin' for work. But it kind o'
slackened off, fell away, the green caird from the Labour Exchange. It was
jist impossible, impossible. In fact, we got well left one time. We had a green
caird, we wis gaun away tae Ayrshire tae look for work by oor way o' it,
away on the bikes, two o' us. We did look for a job. They were sinkin' the
Barony pit at this time. We did go up and we asked for a job. But there was nae
chance o' a job there either. So we landed in Kilwinning. We went in tae check
oor cairds at the buroo, an', oh, the bloke was awfy affable and nice. He says, 'I
suppose ye'll jist hae been tryin' tae kill yer time?' Simple: 'Aye.' We went hame
-- and there were nae buroo money for us! They said we wisnae lookin' for
work. The Kilwinning bloke had reported us back tae the Labour Exchange in
Lesmahagow. We lost money for twenty weeks, I just cannae mind how much
it was. That's what happened. That wis how they treated ye.

Oh, the poverty was bad at Lesmahagow! Well, it was a regular habit that the men was oot on the nicht shift, either stealin' coal at the coal bings and bringin' it hame in a barry, or oot stealin' turnips or tatties, or oot at the big ferm hooses stealin' hens or things like that. There was poachin' for rabbits, poachin' for hares. In fact, we had dugs. We kept half o' a buildin' gaun, by Christ, wi' hares and rabbits.

When we first got married oor hoose wis jist a single-end. Oor rent was 2/5d a week. There was neither gas nor electric in it, but a great big coal fire. The hoose was an auld, auld hoose. Lesmahagow church was built 1100 and something and I think oors had been the church warden's house. It could ha' been. The wa's were right thickness, and there were jist wee windaes. There wis an outside toilet and outside washhouse. Well, it wisnae too hot bringin' up children in that hoose. Of coorse, the point is ye kent nothing else. My wife's mother's hoose was gas right enough but jist a water spiggot in the hoose. And the hoose we lived in before I was merrit we had nae water in it. Ye had tae cairry water frae half-way doon the street. And when your mother was washin' ye had tae carry water frae the street tap aboot, say, sixty or seeventy yairds intae the washhouse. My job on a Thursday was tae fill thae tubs. And, oh, I grudged it!

When we got married it was a struggle tae make ends meet. Ye got twenty-nine shillins frae the buroo on a Friday. There was a Peart's Stores in Lesmahagow. My wife remembers that eggs were 9d a dozen, ham was a shillin' a pund, sugar was 2d a pund, milk was 2d a pint, a loaf was 2¹/₂d. She could go doon tae Peart's Stores and get a week's messages, plus ten Capstan for me, for about 12/6d. And that was green cheese, ham, eggs, matches, cigarettes, green beans, barley, beans, whatever you were needin'. That was the basics. But we wis gettin' that tight. I was awfy friendly wi' Councillor Barney McCourt, a Welsh fellow. He was a fine man, a grand old Communist councillor in Bellshill for a long while up tae he died.[272] We used tae get a visit frae him quite often. I said, 'Look here, Barney, you're a councillor. Now we're sittin' here, and it's no' a heavy rent, but we jist can't afford to pey it. There's no' a copper.' He says, 'I ken there's no', Guy. But,' he says, 'a' ye need tae dae is write in tae Hamilton and send a shillin' postal order and ask for a sanitary inspector's report on your house. They'll send out an inspector, and he'll copy oot a' the things that's wrong in the hoose and ye'll hand one o' the copies tae the landlord and keep one.' He said we would need jist tae pay half-rent. However, we kept payin' our 2/5d a week and this went on for six months, and then the landlord began to bother us. So we went back tae the lawyer in Hamilton and he said, 'Oh, ye shouldnae have been payin' that full rent.' And he counted it up and he says, 'Now you can sit for six months and pay no rent.' So we sat for six months and we paid no rent. And every time we met the landlord he would say, 'Away and pey your rent!' And we said, 'Away and sort the hoose!' And when the six months was up we got another hoose! Ah, but wait till I tell you: the rent was 4/6d!

Oh, it wis hard goin'. We had twenty-nine shillins a week and we spent 12/6d a week on food. But then we had oor milk and bread and insurance tae pey, and the paraffin. And you had your coal tae buy – coal frae the Doozie pit was ninepence a bag. The Doozie pit belonged tae the Arden Coal Company. We got three bags at ninepence a bag. And then I needed half-a-croon for ma pocket: I was a smoker then – Capstan. And as time went on and ye were needin' a new pair o' shoes, which were about ten shillins, we jist couldnae afford it. So ye had tae look aboot ye for a shillin'-a-week man tae get a pair o' shoes tae pey up, because that wis a' ye could dae. The wife's mother lived in the next village frae us, two and a half mile away, and if the wife wanted tae see her mother through the week – it was only 2¹/₂d. in the bus – she had tae put one bairn in the pram and the other walked wi' her and hoped her mother would gie her a shillin' when she was there. She was a wee bit better off than us! So the wife was walkin' five miles tae see her mother and back, and sometimes she propped the older bairn up on the end o' the pram comin' back the road. Oh, we never had any holidays! We never had a holiday till efter oor third bairn was born – that was durin' the War, in 1941, and we went tae Portybelly.

Well, the march by the N.U.W.M. tae Larkha', that was only keepin' everybody alive to the fact that there were an Unemployed Movement that tried tae battle for whatever wis on the go at the particular time. It wisnae a Hunger March. But it was good trainin' for the big yin. I got involved on the 1936 Hunger March tae London through the central committees o' the N.U.W.M. and that. We had meetins every weekend at the street corner, while ye had maybe Barney McCourt or Eddie McLachlan frae Blantyre or Matt McNaught frae Blantyre or whiles a wee boy frae Glesgae. And we had Bill Ross, the organiser o' the N.U.W.M. frae Bellshill. He was a nice fellow. I think he's dead noo tae. He wisnae strong. And we had Peter Cregan, who was the Lanarkshire secretary of the Party and of the area committee of the N.U.W.M. and who did all the organising of the contingent from Lanarkshire. Well, we had meetins practically every pey-day in the buroo – a Friday. Well, the 1936 March was organised along these lines. The last meetin' I attended afore it Peter Kerrigan and Bill Pearson o'the Lanarkshire Miners' Union wis there.[273] That's the two that sticks in my mind. They were discussin' the Hunger March and how many we should take frae each place. I think that meetin' was in Lesmahagow. That's when Bill Pearson said there were one man in Scotland he knew could be the quartermaster for the March when they decided the March was gaun ahead. And I said, 'Christ, Bill, steady up!' He says, 'Ye'll dae it. Ye've done it for years and ye'll dae it.' 'Well,' I says, 'I'll have a go at it, Peter.' He says, 'A' right, we'll help you in any way we can.'

The purpose of the '36 March was tae draw the attention of the public, especially in the South, that they were demandin' the right tae work. That was really what it was all about. Fower o' us went frae Lesmahagow. They were a' unemployed miners: Andrew Hillan, Willie Hamilton, Jock McEwan, and masel'. We got the bus fares tae Hamilton and we got five shillins, I think, oot the funds o' the N.U.W.M. That wis oor pocket money for gaun tae London! When we got tae Hamilton we didnae know the position there. There were a Movement in Hamilton tae, jist the same. But we jist fund wer ain way across tae Bellshill. Ah kent where we was gaun tae in Bellshill. I knew a' the Bellshill people. I cannae really remember if we steyed in Bellshill but I think we marched frae Bellshill intae Glesgae. I remember oo stayed in a kind o' Christian Brethren place at Duke Street, almost at Parkheid Cross. I mind we got a big basin o' biled eggs in the mornin' and they were biled as hard as bricks! And we jist wis young so we wired intae them. This was for oor breakfast afore we set oot. But I jist cannae remember where we set oot frae. I know that the first stop was Barrhead.

Them in Barrheid knew that we wis comin'. They were prepared for us. So everythin' was plain' sailin'. But, oh, I was a lost laddie the first day or two. But I was well takin' by the haund in Kilmarnock, wi' the Campbells. I think they were cobblers, shoemakers. Tom Campbell says, 'Ye're no' very healthy lookin' claes-wise.' 'No,' I says, 'Tom, I'm sorry, but it's the best I've got.' A' I had was my jaicket and jersey and troosers and heavy bits, and your normal underwear, but no change o' clothin' – jist what you went away wi'. 'Well,' Tom Campbell says, 'ye're no gaun aboot like that.' So he gied me a set o' claes. Later on I took it up tae big Peter Kerrigan. Says I, 'Here I've got a new set o'claes, Peter. I got it gien me.' 'Well, it's no' yours, it's no' yours. That belongs tae the March.' Of course I expected that sort of thing. 'I'm no' needin' onythin', I'm no' needin' claes,' ye ken! So I didnae get the claes. But Tom Campbell was a fine man. He went along wi' me a' the time and he did the talkin' for me, he talked for me at Kilmarnock. That gied me a grand start, listenin' tae his talk, and explainin' the position how these boys were and what they were daein' – 'They're no' only marchin' for theirsel', they're marchin' for the rest o' the unemployed that's in the whole country.' There were three million at that time.[274]

That night at Kilmarnock big Peter Kerrigan got me and he says, 'Now you'll need tae get away in the mornin'.' 'Cause there was nothin' waitin' for us. It wis Catrine in Ayrshire. He says, 'Try the Co-operatives and ony shops ye can get haud o'. If ye can get haud o' onybody that's sympathetic they'll gie ye a haund tae guide ye where tae go and look today.' So by good luck I went away in the mornin'. We had a wee motor van. It cost £14. And when the Marchers landed in Catrine we had a ton o' grub. It was fifty pund o' this and fifty pund o' that, and fifty punds o' everythin' else and about three or fower bags o' tatties. And my final plea wis: 'Now these are a' ordinary fellaes and they like a smoke. If ye jist could gie us Woodbine, a packet atween each two.' That meant aboot three boxes o' Woodbine, aboot 750 fags. And I got it every day.

That wis at Catrine and the next place was Dumfries. And I almost lost my nerve there. One o' the March Council come tae me and says, 'Look here, Guy, look at thir.' This boy needed a pair o' boots. He was walkin' on his bare feet. So we bought him a pair o' boots and it was £3 for a good pair. Wee Bobby McLellan was the treasurer o' the March and anything and everything I got it was a' accoonted for. There were never nae money involved. That wis the only money that wis spent – £3 for thae boots. And I got a helluva row. Big Peter says, 'Jesus Christ! Who are ye supplyin' the boots for? The Duke o' Hamilton? £3 for a pair o' bits?!' Course it wis mair a joke. 'Well,' he says, 'I wouldnae dae the same again, Guy, withoot a lot o' consideration.' 'Well,' I says, 'you go and look at Matt McNaught's boots!' And that was that. That was the only money that I handled, that £3 for the pair o' boots. That's the only money ah spent all the way down to London.

Well, as I've said when I left Lesmahagow masel' a' I had was my jaicket and jersey and troosers and, well, I had nae boots. So I went to the Parish Chambers and I got a pair o' boots for nothing. They were big heavy boots. They were boots that had been worn by somebody else. They were thick soles, loaded wi' tackets. But the leather was as hard as hard. When I got ma feet intae them I thought I would never get them back oot. I said tae the wife, 'Jesus Christ, Grace, what'll I do wi' thir?' She says, 'Ah ken what tae do wi' them.' And she away and bought castor ile and saftened them for twa or three days wi' castor ile and made them like sponges. So that was them till I was back hame. They took me a' the road. Well, as I say, I wasnae walkin' much. A' ma walkin' was in the villages or toons where we were gaun tae look for directions tae a Co-operative or a big firm.

I jist had a bunnet, I always did. But I had nae pack, nothin', I jist set away wi' nothin'. I didnae have a stick. I cannae recall any instructions aboot sticks. I suppose plenty had walkin' sticks but I didnae have one and neither had the boys alang wi' me. The fower o' us frae Lesmahagow had the five shillins frae the N.U.W.M. branch funds – that was it till we come back! Well, the odd yin on the March was maybe luckier than some o' us. They whiles maybe got a half-croon postal order sent tae them, maybe through their brothers or maybe somebody that was workin'. I mean I don't know much aboot it but I could see an odd yin wi' a half-croon postal order. But we never wis lucky enough. We never had nae chance o' gettin' half-a-croon. Because they'd tae go tae the parish tae get the starvation-level scale, ye ken, when they couldnae get the buroo money. The wife had tae go tae the parish. We got no money frae the buroo when we were on the March. We knew that before we went. Of course I wasnae bein' fed at hame. I reckon my wife would get roughly a pound for the three of them frae the parish council. But I never had a penny till I came back hame.

There were maybe about 150 on the March frae Glesgae. But we joined up wi' another team frae Aberdeen and Dundee and some frae Edinburgh tae, that came right doon that coast. So when we landed in London there were aboot 300 o' us.[275] Where we met up wi' the others noo I cannae recall. I never got in a position where I could really get to know the Marchers, bar them that was aboot the kitchen. We went ahead, masel' and a young fellow who was the driver o' the wee van. We set off each mornin' ahead o' the Marchers. First thing in the mornin' we wis away, even afore they had the bilers on the lorry. We went direct to the place we were stayin' that night. We had to go to the big places, the Co-operatives, the big shops. The first place oo went tae were the Co-ops. And we made it quite plain that onythin' less than fifty pund o' stuff wasnae any use, and three bags o' tatties and what have ye. And I always minded the Woodbine. A' that was given freely by the shops. The only money that I handled, as I say, was that £3 for a pair o' boots in Dumfries. We got good support frae the shops. Ah cannae recall ever havin' much trouble at a' o' gettin' what I asked for right the way down. We went tae the Co-ops first but we tried other shops tae. It a' depended on the time available for us. We'd go roond a' the wee shops, maybe get somethin' here, or twa or three tins o' stuff there, or maybe three or four pund o' veal – anythin at a'.

They asked ye what was required. So I jist explained to them, says I, 'It's a' big biler work. It's a great big biler o' soup and a big biler o' mince and tatties.' It was maybe soup in the one biler and tatties and maybe biled turnip. There were nothing special. Maybe fifty pund o' sausage, fifty pund o' mince, or fifty pund o' veal. That was the minimum I asked for and I cannae recall bein' refused. And maybe askin' for three boxes o' Woodbine. At that time they were tuppence for five. I explained: says I, 'We're no' askin' for much. These fellows are roond fightin' for the unemployed. What applies to you here,' says I, 'ye're losin' your trade because they cannae spend money: they've got no money tae spend. And we're fightin' for tae get increased allowances, or for work. And,' says I, 'I think the least ye could dae for them is gie them a fag each. And a' I'm askin' is a five-packet atween every two men. And one'll get three the day and the other'll get two the morn and what have ye.' I never failed. We were never short o' that fag. It wasnae mony fags, mind ye, three fags a day. But they were never short till the day they come back hame. Of course, I could gether up mair; on the wee-er shops I could maybe get a box o' Woodbine. And very often I could ha' got a surplus o' cigarettes. But they were a' kept in the kitchen.

Wi' the food ye couldnae really build up a surplus because there were nae fridges nor nothin', and nae room in the van. So we didnae really have any wee bit extra that we could keep in the van for the next stage. What we gethered was for that night and for the next mornin', gettin' it for their breakfast.

The Labour Party was awfy absent, awfy absent. I don't mean tae say individual Labour Party members. I don't know aboot that. But officially they were very, very absent. I never got nae cuttins at a', never. I might ha' been talkin' tae somebody and no' know who they were. But they would gie me nice instructions where tae go and how to approach. I always tried tae dae that, tae catch somebody. If I met somebody that looked a local I'd talk tae them and ask them if they could gie me a wee bit idea o' somebody I could talk tae. I explained who I wis. He might jist say, 'I'm yer man.' I mind o' one case, in Macclesfield I think it wis, this bloke says, 'I'm yer man. I've been waitin' for yez.' So I telt him what I wanted.

There were reception committees at some places who were expectin' us, but no' everywhere. We never got names and addresses in advance –

there were nae wey o' knowin' that. They werena that well organised ahead. I jist had tae introduce masel', find somebody tae help me, tae guide me whaur tae go first, the Co-operative first.

I hadnae anythin' tae dae wi' beddin' or sleepin' arrangements. The leaders must ha' been in contact wi' the local people in each place, arrangin' for a place tae sleep. But there were nothing, jist the boards, ye slept down on the boards, nae beddin'. And I didnae have anythin' tae dae wi' the cookin' o' the food. I got the stuff and they had a wee lorry forby the van and they had two big bilers on it. Well, they got the bilers off on tae wherever they were gaun tae dae the cookin'. It wis a' ootside. And it wis a' eaten ootside. They got the bilers down and they came on behind us. They dropped off whenever they got the place where they were gaun tae have their cookin'. They didnae need tae go roond, of course – me and this other boy wi' the motor did that. This other boy drove the motor and whiles put a word in if he thought it jist would help. I'm no' boastin' that I was good at it. I was satisfied that I did a first-class job. We took the stuff back tae the bilers when oo thought we had got a' we could get. And there'd be mair often a surplus o' some things that could keep, maybe cheese – ye didnae need tae throw it oot. Maybe a dozen eggs that ye didnae need tae throw oot. In fact we ance got, oh, dozens o' eggs, and every man got a biled egg for his breakfast! A biler fu' o' biled eggs!

I cannae recall anythin' difficult aboot gettin' particular kinds o'food. Well, truthfully, I cannae recall ever gettin' milk. I think they a' had tae dae withoot milk, bar odd yins that maybe had half-a-croon that got sent them, maybe bocht a pint o' milk for theirsel', although it was only maybe coppers. Well, I mean how could ye supply milk for 150 men? How could ye land in a village and ask for seventy-five pints o' milk? Naebody had that kind o' stuff in stock.

Well, the March went frae Kilmarnock tae Catrine, tae Dumfries and then frae there tae Carlisle. Then we got buses. I don't know whae paid for them, but we got buses ower the Shap intae Kendal. And we got a nice reception in Kendal. But that's as far as I can remember the stoppin' places. I could name ye the places but I couldnae gie ye them in rotation. But I remember in Preston. Pat Devine was there. Well, he was a first-class speaker, a great orator. And he demanded that I go up and speak on the platform. Ah says, 'D'ye no' think I'm daein' plenty?' He says, 'Jist go up and tell them aboot the hardship, hoo ye was livin'!' Ah says, 'Christ, we wis livin' aff the fields, stealin' tatties.' He says, 'That's what tae tell them.' Well, I'd maybe chaired meetins and that but I was never a public speaker. And at that time I had a wee bit impediment. I could come on a word that I couldna say, no' stammer, but I jist couldnae say it. I have it yet in fact, ye jist cannae help these things. But I was fluent enough on that occasion. It wis easy tae talk aboot poachin', stealin', and a' the rest o' it, and that's how ye'd tae live.

The Marchers were maistly young, well, young tae middled aged. There were nae wey o' kennin' what sort o' workers they were bar ye got havin' a wee bit talk wi' somebody. They could tell ye they come frae

Dundee and they worked in so-and-so or they did this or did that – when they were working! Wi' some o' them it wis that long ye forgot what ye wis! Anyway the first hiccough was when we got tae Warwick. When they landed in Warwick we'd everything set up. And we were a' sittin' aboot wi' our meals and Peter Kerrigan come roond and he says, 'Boys, I want ye tae jist pause for a wee minute.' And that day they had marched eighteen mile. 'Now,' he says, 'in 1934 in this same town there were a helluva battle. The polis attacked and we have got the whisper it's gaun tae happen again.[276] Noo we either staund and fight them and a' land in the jile and burst up the March. Or we decide that Banbury is eighteen mile ahead. Now,' he says, 'ah know what youse wid want tae dae is tae staund and have a go. But,' he says, 'boys' – and he explained the position, 'we've walked here and we're makin' for Westminster, the Houses o' Parliament in London. Now,' he says, 'if we have a battle here, that's the end o' the March. So,' he says,'let every man be honest tae hissel'. Pit his hand up whether we stand and fight – or march.' So the vote went to march. And they carried on frae there other eighteen mile, right in through the nicht. And I'll never forget: one o' the boys in the kitchen staff was a Welsh boy and he was sittin' on the edge o' the lorry. I was on the lorry by this time, the same lorry as them, I dinnae mind the reason for it. But when the lorry was passin' the boys, Taffy, wi' the tears runnin' doon his cheeks, shouts: 'Stick it, boys! Stick it, boys! Stick it!' And big Peter says, 'Yes, Taffy, it's a' right for you!' Taffy's sittin' on the lorry! Sittin' on the lorry! But Peter said it in a joke. It was some tackle: thirty-six mile. They jist had a rest for their food and then went on again, went away singin'. Oh, it was good, really good.

I dinnae remember any trouble on the March, wi' police or Blackshirts, no' even in London. I think masel' there might be one or two or maybe three o' the Marchers sent home for misconductin' theirsel', misconduct. Then I think there might be fower or five that had been havin' a walk efter we landed in places and they got a chance o' jobs and never jined the March again. So let's say a maximum, between bein' sent hame and desertin' the March, there might be ten. But I would say not one more – maybe less. I mean, I'm no' minimisin' it. It wis roond aboot ten oot o' aboot 300 by the time we got tae London.

We arrived in Watford – I'm gaun doon fast noo – we landed in Watford, and March Council meeting. So big Peter Kerrigan says, 'Now look here, Guy. I've got a job for ye.' He says, 'I want you tae gaun intae London and ye ken how much is in the fund?' I didnae ken how much was in the fund but I kent there must have been a few pound, because they were collectin' tins a' the wey. And I never asked Bobby McLellan, the treasurer, for a penny, not one penny did I ever ask him for. Peter says, 'We're needin' at least 150 jaickets and 150 pair o' troosers. So,' he says, 'you and your young friend here'll go in advance intae London and find your way tae Shadwell.' I'd never been in London. Says I, 'I'll need tae find ma wey tae London first!' Peter says, 'Christ, you'll manage. Get tae Shadwell anyway, where a' the Jew shops are and ye ken what tae tell them: we're the anti-

Fascist boys.'

So away we went. And we got 150 jaickets and 150 pair o' troosers. And it was either a shillin' for the jaickets and 1/6d for the troosers or vicey verse. And the bloke that served us gied us twa pund back, says, 'That'll help yer funds.' That was in yin shop. I telt him who oo wis: anti-Fascists. Well, that's when the trouble was startin' in London, in 1936 – Cable Street and that.

Well, there were some o' the Marchers gey poor lookin', they really were. They were poor tae start wi'. I was poor masel'. In fact, I had tae get a jaicket masel'. I got a light kind o' flannel double-briested jaicket. I needed it or I wouldna ha' gotten it. It wasnae a jaicket I fancied! I had jist been wearin' the claes I left Lesmahagow wi' till I got a chinge at Watford: I had different jaickets.

Washin' on the March was jist spiggots or taps, jist a wash. Oh, we was a' ready for the bath tub! Ye jist washed yer face and haunds. But I got a bath – I think it wis at Berkhamstead. This man and wife – they were quite weel pit on – and they were among us, sympathisin' and a' the rest o' it. And they spoke tae me. They says, 'You seem to be daein' a job.' So I explained whae I wis and what I was daein' an' that. And I says, 'I'll tell ye the truth. I don't feel too happy, I don't feel too clean.' The wife says, 'Well, I'll tell ye what you'll do. My husband and I will jist take you with us.' And they took me tae their hoose and showed me the bathroom. She says, 'And jist you have a smoke.' She filled the bath up and went ben wi' a' this scent. She must ha' put somethin' in the bath – big bubbles were floatin' in it. That was the first bath ever I had my feet in in my life, where ye could fill the bath wi' runnin' water and lie doon in it. It was the first time I'd ever sat doon in a bath. I was twenty-nine year old and I had this bubble bath. I thought I was in the right set. At hame we had tae go doon intae the wash-house and fill a tub there, pit a bit patchie up in the window, lock the door, and that wis that. Oh, that was life at that time. But maist o' the Marchers jist washed their faces and their necks on the March. That's a' ye could dae. Well, ye might get the odd brave yin, because it wis cauld ootside, it was cauld at times. But they were a' shaved. They were telt that, tae keep theirsel' clean, so they were a' shaved. They were telt that tae start wi', that we were respectable. That wis the policy, we were well disciplined, respectable, and clean.

The leaders o' the March were Peter Kerrigan, wee Bobby McLellan frae Bellshill, a wee nice man, wi' sandy hair, and smart, aye clean and tidy. And Matt McNaught frae Blantyre. They were the leaders, well, there one or two mair. Big Peter Kerrigan walked tae London twice on that March – at the front one meenit, the back the next, then back tae the front. Oh, he was a big, powerful man. And he had a pack on his back. I think he had a sleepin'-bag in it, in fact I think he had everythin' in it! I was on the March Council masel' but I cannae recall if it met every day. I was at very few meetins. They might have a discussion at one o' their rests on the road, and maybe a meetin' at night. I was at very few meetins, bar they wanted something special done – I was sent for then! I was always ahead on the road.

But there would be about half a dozen on the March Council, the leaders o' each contingent. Maist o' them were Communist Party. There might be odd boys that wisnae attached tae the Party that was popular in their ain area that wis on the March Committee – possibly. But you could say it was a Communist March.

I would really think a' the Marchers theirsels would be in the N.U.W.M. Because they were the organisations and it was oot o' these bodies that the volunteers came frae. It wisnae a case o' pickin' somebody because they were popular. It was if they werenae in there, well, they werenae involved. I would say they were a' N.U.W.M., and a lot o' Communist members.

I'm no' jist sure how mony days I wis in London. I missed a lot o' the best in London tae. There were big meetins and marches in Trafalgar Square and tae Westminster. Well, I missed the Westminster yin. The cook had turned no weel and I had tae help in the cookhouse. I remember tae, that big Peter Kerrigan's guid brother turned no' weel. He was jist lyin' on the flair and I was lyin' next tae him. And when I wakened up Peter says, 'By Christ, you can sleep, sir.' I says, 'What's wrang? Is something wrang?' 'Aye,' he says, 'Mo is gey no weel.' He was ta'en away tae the hospital. And he didnae last long efter that. Efter the March he died. He'd ta'en ill jist suddenly durin' the night and I was lyin' sound asleep, never knew a thing. He wis jist a bit o' a laddie, maybe early twenties, Peter's wife's brother, Morris Glasgow.

So, as I say, I'm jist no' sure how mony days I wis in London. But I wis a day longer than the rest. Peter gied us wir orders. 'Now,' he says, 'that van cost £14 an' ye're no' sellin' it ablow £14.' So oo was left. A' the others came hame on the train. We got I think it was seeven or eight shillins for tae buy wir meat. Well, ye could get fish suppers at that time for a tanner. It was plenty for the occasion. And there were a laugh at the end o' it. Oo went tae this place for tae get a sale for the motor. It wis jist a private place, jist wi' twa or three motors aboot it. And we got £28 for the motor: double the price! We telt him we wis goin' somewhere and we needed twa or three pound. And says I, 'We'd like £40 for it.' 'Oh,' he says, 'away and get lost.' He says, 'I'll gie ye £20.' 'Oh,' says I, 'surely, surely.' It went frae £25 tae £28. Ah says, 'I'd better stop or he micht no' take it at a'.' So we got £28 for it. Big Peter laughed when we told him. He said, 'Ye said ye couldnae be a quartermaster!' He says tae me, 'Ye're a Jew, man, ye're a Jew, man.'

We had got a ticket to come hame on the train. This boy and me had two tins o' peaches, that wis wir meat for tae take hame wi' us. We had nae money – the money, twa or three shillins, was away. Says I tae him, 'What do you say if we eat up oor peaches and I'll take the twa tins doon tae the cook's place on the train an' see if they'll gie us twa mugs o' tea?' The boy says, 'It's a Pullman first-class dinin' car. Ye'll no' get in there.' Ah says, 'I can try it.' So away I walked doon through the dinin' car, richt doon tae where the kitchen wis. And I telt the boy there and asked if we could get tea – 'Certainly.' And he gied us twa sandwiches as weel. And as I went back up, the train must ha' been on a bit o' a bend, for I shook and some o' the tea threw up on tae this woman's dress. 'Oh,' I says, 'I'm sorry, I'm awfy sorry.' It come oot that we had been on the Hunger March. Then it was the best laugh o' the whole March. 'Well, sit doon and tell us aboot it,' says she. And she bought the two o' us wir dinner on the train!

Well, ye must go back again in history to that period before ye can say the March was successful. And I couldnae tell ye whether the unemployed was reduced. The March was successful in so far as it was organised and carried out. And at the end o' the story, when they coonted the money oot in the boxes and the treasurer's fund back in Glasgow, they had over £300. So I don't know if ye ca' that a success or a failure! I say I was a success! The response was good. There is nae question. There were a lot o' sympathy undoubtedly.

That was the last Hunger March. The Spanish War was on then. And a' the battles then was tae get foodstuffs for Spain – clothing, scarves, jerseys and foodstuffs. That was the next involvement. Well, three o' us – Hillan, Hamilton and masel' – from Lesmahagow we went doon tae Bellshill tae put oor name forward tae go tae Spain. But that wis the verra mornin', when we wis on the road tae Bellshill, the word had come oot apparently that the Government was stoppin' all volunteers. In future no person was allowed tae leave Great Britain. So we jist had tae gaun back hame.[277]

It wisnae long efter that till I got a job in Douglas Water colliery. That wis in 1937. And it meant cyclin' eight mile there and eight mile back on the maist open road in Britain – the Carlisle road, between Lesmahagow and Douglas. It wis a' the same how ye went – whether ye were gaun up the wey or back the wey – the wind was in your face. Says I, 'I'm gaun tae treat masel' tae one o' these capes for the bike.' And I bocht it at Young's in Sauchiehall Street in Glesgae for 3/6d. It had a velvet collar on it. I couldnae really afford it. I tied it on the back o' the bike. And I thought I'd never get yaisin' it, it would never come rain. Then one night, oh, oh, it was a storm. Ye could hardly move ony wey. And I put on my cape. In the middle o' Douglas Moor I landed on the bank side o' the road, blown off. And I never saw my cape again. A' that was left was the velvet collar!

I was in Douglas Water colliery about seven or eight year, till the end o' the 1945 War. Then I came through frae there tae Fishcross here in Clackmannanshire and worked in the Devon colliery. A small group of Party men including myself managed through political and hard work within three years to control the pit. We made it one of the best pits in Scotland both wage-wise and in conditions. When the Devon closed I went to Glenochil mine, between Fishcross and Tullibody, till that closed. Then I went to Stoke-on-Trent for a year or so, then I came home and went to Bogside mine in Fife. I retired from work in 1971 from Castlehill mine, part of the Longannet project in Fife. My son George has become president of the Scottish Area of the National Union of Mineworkers and chairman of the Communist Party of Great Britain.

Hugh Duffy

I was born in Bannockburn in January 1918. My father was a miner, born in Blantyre, and he went to Bannockburn to work in the pits. He'd been away at the War – I imagine it was somewhere round about 1915 he'd volunteered. They had all volunteered from Blantyre – there was, oh, a dozen or so all in the same age, knew each other, had all volunteered. He'd be in his early twenties then. They were all together at Bulford Camp. They got up to a lot o' antics, as you can well imagine. One o' them got the Military Medal; he was a postman in Blantyre.

My father never spoke much about the War. He was in the Artillery and he was in the horses, pullin' up the guns and that. Well, he came home on leave from France and didn't go back. That would be 1917. He was absent without leave – deserted – probably about a year and a half, and then the hostilities ceased. My father was a man that read a lot and studied a lot and was politically minded. Before that, he was religiously-minded, because many's the one who's told me that he was gaun tae study for the priesthood. Well, that fell by the way. But he was a very serious man. He neither drank nor smoked. He'd back a horse but that was as far as he would go. So he just came home on leave and decided he wasn't going back again. And then he went away to Bannockburn to get a job. That was to avoid the police. He worked in Fallin pit. I think there was some enquiries made, which was covered up by the neebours: they had wonderful people that lived at Fallin. And there was a cover-up at Blantyre as well: they would say no to everything here. So he was never arrested. He jist come back to Blantyre shortly after I'd be a year old. I think everyone got an amnesty at that time. As I say, he didn't speak much about the War at all, because it was distasteful to him. Later on, if he saw something on the T.V. and it was horses, he would mention, 'That's the kind o' horses we had.' They a' came frae Canada and he could tell ye then one or two things.

My father was a member o' the Labour Party, frae I was a tiny tot he was a Labour man. And he was active in arranging dances and all that for funds for the Communist Party in the church hall in Blantyre. He wasn't a member o' the Communist Party. He was a Roman Catholic but he left the church for a long period when his mother died o' Bright's disease or something when she was fifty-six. I think he lost his faith then, and stayed away for twenty-five years. I remember him going back when we were a' grown-up.

347

My grandfather Duffy was a miner too. His mother had come over here from Ireland in the potato famine. I remember my grandfather well. He was of the old school. He could take a pint and he would be first doon the pit – early. He worked in Dixon's pit, they were nearly a' Dixon's. He was a man's man. He liked his drink and he was a very outdoor man. He lived till he was eighty-six. He took all his four sons down the pit.

Also my gran adopted a boy of maybe thirteen from Smillie's Home in Lanark.[278] She had eleven in the house – a room and kitchen – and yet she went and took another one! And he wis a darkie. When you went for a child tae Smillie's Home you got a male or female but you never got the colour. And that's who she got. And he was a by-word here in Blantyre because he wouldnae work in the pit. He did go down the pit but my grandfather couldnae dae nothin' wi' him. He jist didnae want tae work and he ran away. Then he come back and he went roond the streets sellin' laces and matches. One o' ma aunties used tae take him in. And when we were goin' tae the school we used tae say, 'Oh, there's Jimmy the Darkie.' And I never thought for a minute that I was talkin' about my uncle. He would sing, 'Jimmy the Darkie's here today and he won't be here tomorrow.' Eventually he got married and he come back. But it's a' died oot noo. I only remember him when I was a schoolboy.

My mother was an orphan and she came from Shettleston. She was illegitimate. My father went down with her on several occasions to the registrar and the parish priest but never found any trace o' her parents. As a young woman she worked on the tables at the Priory pit picking the brass out, or pickin' the stones. They used tae say 'brass' 'cause there wis some brass in the coal, ye could see the brass. Well, she was picked out to go down tae clean the office, so that was her out o' the muck and cleanin' the office. Then the manager asked her to go up to his house to become a servant. So she worked there right up tae she was married. She was adopted out to a family in Blantyre during that time.

I have no memories whatsoever of Bannockburn or Fallin. We came back to Blantyre when I was about a year old. We came back to Dixon's Rows. I can remember everythin' as clear as a bell about Dixon's Rows. It was minin' rows – you're talkin' about thirteen streets – with dirt roads, dirt pavements, and a gutter along in front o' the house. Most o' the blocks – like a terraced block – would be at least four houses, maybe six, and there'd be the one toilet and a washhouse round the back for the whole block. We had taps in the house but before that there were a communal tap. I don't remember that, it would be back before the First War. It was a flush toilet but it was communal use. And it was a bit ropey to say the least, unless ye caught it efter whosever turn it wis tae brush it oot. They'd throw in some water and use an old brush, that wis a'. But let one day elapse and that was it – there was shit everywhere. Oh, it was horrible to go in. And then they would cut newspapers in squares for toilet paper. Oh, I hated that!

The first house we had was a single-end. I remember that distinctly. There was two built-in beds, wi' the bedboards holdin' the mattress. They generally kept coal underneath because ye had nothing outside other than that toilet. Although we had the gas in, we still had oil lamps survivin', no electricity. We had a fireplace with about four or five bars, big thick vertical bars. I can remember tryin' tae make toast at it and ye generally finished up wi' pittin' four big marks on the bread.

The second house we had in Dixon's Rows was a room and kitchen. I don't think there were a bigger hoose than a room and kitchen: single-ends, and room and kitchens. One particular time in the room and kitchen, the room was uninhabitable 'cause there were a green at the back and it wis flooded. And at the corner o' the room wall ye could see the daylight. Actually, I got a frog in the room one mornin'. The back grass, jist behind the raw, never wis yaised. As kids we said it wis haunted wi' the kilty, a Highlander. So it got tae the stage that if anybody opened that room door at night we were terrified.

Now the sleepin' arrangement, as far as I remember it: there were four o' us, ma two sisters and the youngest boy, and me. Now me bein' the oldest I had a single iron bed in the middle o' the floor. And ma mither and father's in that set-in bed, and ma two sisters and the youngest boy was in the other set-in bed: three beds in one room, and the six o' us in them. And some folk yaised tae squeeze a lodger in tae.

Most o' the floors was flagstaines, though the room was widden. And, oh, clocks! Cockroaches! There were a street next to the street we were in. Well, they took a' the kids away frae that street, except one or two. I was one that escaped. The rest a' got scarlet fever, which was frae the drains, open drains – a shuch, as we cried it. Well, if they were washin' up and that they would maybe take the bucket oot and empty it oot – waste water an' that. They put red ashes down for the road. And then Dixon's pit would send a scraper and scrape the mud. The scraper was a machine frae the ferm. And they would scrape the mud or scratch it, tae shove by for the winter-time. But it wisnae a pavement – jist mud. But, oh, scarlet fever was very common. They used tae shave their heids, cut a' their hair off. If ye look at the infant mortality rate – very high.

And tuberculosis: my aunty and uncle took it, two o' them, one at sixteen and one at eighteen. And later on, my girlfriend suffered wi' it. She was ta'en tae a sanatorium at Bridge o' Weir. But she survived, wi' one lung.

I can also remember when I was about six year old and there was three of us – the fourth wasn't born – and my father had went back up tae Stirlingshire and got fixed up wi' a job. But there was no money. There was three slice o' bread left in the house. And my mother toasted it, put the margarine on it, gave the three of us a slice each – and sat down and cried. And I looked at her and my wee brains worked. Ye were old for your age, just like thae kids in Africa just now – they're old and they're only babies. And ah says, 'Well, I'll do somethin' about that.' I was only six year old but I realised all that. And then what you saw round about you impressed ma brain, impressed on me a great deal. And that's one o' them, when she cried. But there wis a postal order in the post the next mornin' that he'd sent her. This was the depression, 1924.

Then my father got a job back again in Loanend, another pit at Blantyre, on the borders to Cambuslang, up above Halfway. He was there during the time of the General Strike. That's when we got fed wi' rolls and sausage oot o' a great big claes basket at school. And they used the wash-houses in Dixon's Rows as soup kitchens. My father was out for six or seven month. Oh, I remember that well. One story was they hijacked the baker's van. This was the Co-operative baker, horse and cart. And the driver says, 'Do what you like, but leave ma drawins' – you know, the leather bag round his neck. So they emptied the van and distributed the bread and the loaves, the miners in Dixon's Rows. There was another case where they broke into Gibson's store and again the stuff was taken out and shared. Cheeses were hidden under floorboards. And one bloke was marched down to the police station wi' his fryin' pan and the bacon still in it!

I remember some o' the older characters. One was Aggie Armstrong. She had a pair o' feet! It was said she could walk over broken glass, the soles of her feet were so hard. You'd think it was leather soles she had on. It was her natural soles because she never wore shoes. But we got boots. The parish gave ye boots. And there were some o' them would pawn them. So you know what they done? They sunk three holes in them and the pawn wouldnae take them. And ye went up there tae the parish and they would gie ye clothin' an' a'. I remember gaun up and it wis a grey semmit. And ma young brother couldnae wear it 'cause he scratched hissel'. Ah wore them a'right. Oh, the pawnshops were busy. Well, your whole street was full o' shops. They were a' doin' a trade.

You had a certain person, a character who would run to the pawn for everyone. He run the cutter, that was the phrase they used. The man we had up there was wee Danny Kelly, up and doon tae the pawn. When you saw him he would have a barrow and he was comin' back wi' the money. I went mysel' an odd time. But he went, he'd get thruppence 'cause he would have the reputation o' bein' able tae get five shillins and we might get only four shillins. He'd get thruppence each round, he was notorious. Remember, these people would be pawnin' their Sunday suit. They'd only be in on Friday and it would be lifted back oot Wednesday or Tuesday. People would come to your door, 'Would you gie's a len o' a shillin tae Monday?' She'd get that shillin, pey it back on the Monday and on Friday she'd get a len o' the shillin again. It fitted in wi' their dole money or whatever. One kind o' sad thing: ma Auntie Maggie wis a very vain person, and wi' them a' bein' lassies in her hoose she wouldnae let naebody touch her dresses or nothin'. And they a' had a shawl, a Paisley shawl. This was for their first wean. It was the done thing. So here didn't her mother, ma granny, take the Paisley shawl and go doon tae the pawn. And Maggie comes in and she wants the shawl – oh, they took it tae dances for their shou'der – couldnae get the shawl and kicked up an awfy din. Well, ma gran got somebody tae run doon in a panic tae the pawn, brought it back up and she says tae

Maggie: 'There yer shawl, ye bastard. Ye'll never need it.' Well, Maggie married but she never had a child. Oh, Dixon's Raws was somethin'!

I liked the school. I wis good at the school. Things came easy to me. I enjoyed mostly everything. I would have liked to stay on. I did sit an exam for the Higher Grade but I don't know what happened there. But I had to leave school as soon as I was fourteen. I went straight doon the Stepps pit, Cardowan colliery. From here in Blantyre to Cardowan you're talkin' about fifteen miles away at least. I worked there for a month. But I didn't like it. The manager's name was Peacock and he had a nickname. He had steel-blue eyes, cold eyes. And at the bottom, where I was, you had to put on hutches, push them on. And there was a can o' water tae slake your thirst. There were two o' us boys, and the other young fellow was takin' a drink. This Peacock shouted ower and swore at him; 'I don't bloody pey you for drinkin' water.' So the day came of course when Peacock caught me drinkin' water. Well, he shouted the same things at me but I jist carried on and drank ma fill. But I didnae answer back 'cause I knew I'd get the sack.

The wages were 3/6d a day. It was a five-and-a-half-day week, wi' Saturday mornin. And I had tae work a quarter shift one or two nights, which really sickened me, because the special bus tae Blantyre was not available. So wi' workin' the overtime I had tae get an ordinary bus intae Glasgow and then another bus from Glasgow tae Blantyre. And of course ye were black. There were nae pit baths. And I was wearin' ma pit clothes. And of course you were affronted goin' on tae the bus and sittin' wi' people. In fact, it wis quite a common thing tae get a suit wasted wi' a miner comin' on a bus or a tramcar. Some thoughtful miners had a raincoat they put over their pit claes. So I remember feeling very embarrassed about that, and it happened several times in the month I was at Cardowan colliery. And of course it was costin' extra fares tae dae that.

Well, Peacock the manager he come down to the bottom o' the pit and it was a' whitewashed. And it looked quite good. I was oncost, jist guidin' the cages on. So as the rakes o' bogies come doon ye'd two went that way and two went straight on. So for tae turn them ye had tae push, and of course ye had tae uncouple them. My father always told me, 'Never put your head between the hutches.' So you put your left hand on the bogie and you swung down, hand under, uncoupled the chain tae let the two go forward that wis gaun on tae the cage. Well, I'll tell ye, it made ye fit. Ye were like a monkey. But ye'd tae push it tae make it swerve tae the right. So I got the idea, which was a great idea, tae put my back tae the whitewashed wall, put ma feet up, and pushed it quite easily. The only trouble was I'd rubbed a' the whitewash off the wall. And the manager come down and roared at me because I was usin' this leverage. It wis just a simple thing but it halved ma physical output in that job. It was easy then but to do it without that was murder.

I loathed the pit completely. I had tae start work at seven or seven-thirty in the mornin', after a lot o' journeyin' frae Blantyre and got home again roughly about tea-time. I went doon tae the pictures at night and never saw the film – sound asleep, jist sound asleep. Efter a month or so I loathed the job that much I jist gave it up even though I didnae have another job. My father of course agreed wi' me. He wouldnae let anybody work anywhere they didnae want to. Well, when I'd first gone down the pit the only advice he did give me was, he says, 'You're handy. You're good wi' your head. Learn somethin' about it – fireman or maybe electrician – because there is some good jobs in the pit, but not as a miner.' That was the advice he gave me.

After I left the pit I done a lot o' casual work. Even as a laddie o' ten I'd had a wee job sellin' coal off the Spittal bing. We a' went tae the bing. I sold half-a-dozen bags every week, a shillin' a bag. I had my regular customers. I was caught twice wi' the police and fined. And I was in school when I started wi' radio. It was a hobby o' mine. I had the first wireless wi' a loudspeaker in our street. I had learned it from a crippled chap who built his own. We bought the wire and wound the coils and went to the barrows and bought a valve and earphones. When we lived in Dixon's Rows – and we moved frae there intae a council house when I was about fourteen – I connected the wires tae the single iron bed I slept in as an aerial for ma crystal set wi' earphones. I had built that when I was at school. I bought the earphones for haulf a croon at the barras. I remember I put the earphones over to ma mother in bed but she wouldnae touch them. Ah says, 'Well, jist put your ear jist near it.' And I turned the earphones in such a way she could hear Henry Hall and his Dance Orchestra. As soon as she heard it then I gradually put them on her ears. So the next time she had a pound menage wi' the Great Universal Stores, she says, 'D'ye want tae yaise that tae buy stuff, Hughie, to build a two-valve set?' And I built that. And as I said, Hugh Hailes, the cripple had a wireless set wi' a loudspeaker and we a' gathered roond aboot him at Ascot, Derby Day and that.

So after I left the pit I worked for a chap who opened a wireless shop. I was repairin' radios, chargin' batteries and everythin'. And I was doin' quite a bit o' private work on my own account. I had many jobs and it became more or less full-time. So the shop was becomin' part-time. I jist sort o' travelled about. I was quite happy if I got a pound or two. And I was still doin' that almost up to the time I went on the Hunger March.

I was never politically active. I never joined any political party. The Young Communist League had a wee shop down on the main street at Blantyre and we used tae get books oot o' it. But I never actually joined the Young Communist League. I was familiar with it and I knew most of them. So when the Hunger March come up I was unemployed at that time and I went down to the Y.C.L. bookshop and put my name in for the March. For some reason or other I was taken but not because of any allegiance to the Y.C.L. That was in 1936. It was a purely individual thing. I didn't even know that one o' my pals, John Carroll, was goin' until he turned up tae. The National Unemployed Workers' Movement had a branch in Blantyre but I wasnae a member o' that either. The reason I volunteered to go on the March was it was a protest because we were on the buroo and I think we had

about nine bob a week. It was pretty hard goin' and the Means Test made
it really bad. In ma case I didnae have a brother that was workin'. Ma sisters
were workin' in the laundry, but it wis one o' thon poor-paid jobs, eight or
nine shillins a week. And ma father was on the buroo or parish at that time
tae. All o' us were still at home at that time. They recommended that tae
keep a person alive wis a halfpenny short o' five shillins: 4/11¹/₂d was their
standard for sufficient food to keep a person. So that was my reason for goin'
on the March – a protest.

I think we were supplied wi' boots from the N.U.W.M., but not
clothes. The N.U.W.M. jist bought the boots from their funds. They sold
wee football tickets and things, anything to raise funds. So they must ha'
bought the boots from them. I had a haversack but I jist went in ma ordinary
clothes – shirt, jersey and trousers. I can mind o' cairryin' separate white
collars and I washed them regular. So I always had a white collar and a tie.
I never had a raincoat or coat o' any kind. I had a Mexican hat, a sombrero,
wi' a chinstrap and a wee button thing ye could tighten it up. I marched oot
o' Glasgow wi' that and my cousin saw me and his eyes popped oot his heid
'cause he didnae know I was goin' on the March. I don't know where I got
the sombrero. I think somebody stuck it in ma hand.

But first of all we assembled down here on the main road in Blantyre.
I think there would be twenty-eight of us, that was the Blantyre contingent.
We had a good turn-oot, the streets was lined doon there. We walked across
tae Uddingston, then we all loaded intae a tramcar intae Glasgow, where all
the contingents met to form the March as a whole. We spent the night in
some o' the public halls in, I think, Kinning Park. Then up in the mornin'
and we set off as a Hunger March, headin' for Kilmarnock.

Most o' the men frae Blantyre were miners. They were all older than
me and John Carroll. John and I was the youngest – eighteen. We knew
each other, we went to school together. The leaders of our contingent frae
Blantyre were Matthew McNaught and Ned Laughlin. That wis the two
main men. They were very, very active in the N.U.W.M. and the
Communist Party. They were figureheads in Blantyre. But none o' the rest.
They were jist common five-eights, wi' no political thingmy. I don't think
there were many in the Communist Party and nobody in the Labour Party.
Willie Marshall was active in the I.L.P. Others I can remember were John
Maclean and big Ned McGuire, both miners. But McNaught and Laughlin,
they held the public meetins and a' that sort o' thing.

I didnae wear ma sombrero a' the way to London. In actual fact, I fell
out the March because o' ma feet. I had flat feet. I began to feel the pressure
on them pretty quickly the first couple o' days. But I carried on. Actually,
I fell oot and fell in once or twice during the March. The police car generally
picked ye up. There wis always a police car away at the back and they'd see
me sittin' at the side o' the road. Of course when ye're like that ye're no'
really botherin' whether the goin' would suit ye or no'. You were jist tramp
royal.

Nobody had asked when I volunteered for the March, they didnae know I had flat feet. The first doctor I saw was at Kirkconnel. 'You know,' he says, 'this is a very serious thing. This could ruin you for your life.' And I thought, 'Well, they're a bit sore. But they're hale, they're a' in the one piece.' Well, it wis jist past Carlisle, I think, that I come off the March permanently on to the chuck wagon. Most that couldnae keep marchin' were sent back home wi' a train ticket and a few bob. But they retained me because I was good as a salesman. I sold the *Daily Worker* and collected all their drawins on the March goin' down. I collected all the money in tins.

So I travelled on the chuck wagon in advance o' the marchers. I chalked the streets and shouted through the loudspeaker, 'The Hunger Marchers are comin! They'll be here at six o'clock! Turn out and support them in their cause!' And then the lads come marchin' in. We had done wir spiel, chalked the streets – that was me free. I washed and had my collar and tie back on again. So frae Carlisle I travelled on the chuck wagon, maybe jumpin' off and tryin' my legs oot again. But when I came tae Aylesbury they were so bad that I couldnae walk. It was more a kind o' tiredness, pullin' of ligaments and a' that. So I went intae the workhouse hospital along wi' another chap, Mick McComisky. He had a poisoned leg – one o' the brass studs comin' up through the boot in the soles o' his feet. He was very ill, they nearly took his leg off. Mick was a Blantyre man. I was in the workhouse hospital and missed the Marchers' turn-out at the Cenotaph in London. And Mick was o' course kept in even after that.

I remember Guy Bolton, the quartermaster, and the cobbler wi' the one leg. And there was an older man, Taffy the Welshman, he was the cook. I remember him at the big portable boilers: a layer o' sliced potatoes, a layer o' sausage, a layer o' onions, and another layer o' potatoes. It jist went right up till it reached the top. And he kindled a fire underneath it. They used tae watch for that smoke on the road: 'A mile tae go'.

We got good support, great support, right down through England. We sold a lot o' copies o' the *Daily Worker* as we went. But they laid a trap – I would say it was a trap – at Warwick. They had police in the cellars armed wi' batons. Well, they come oot and told us that. And we had tae march on again, which meant another march all night. But here the leaders – Peter Kerrigan and them – got some buses and we all piled in the bus and on to the next town. So we avoided that but it could ha' been that they were gaun tae stop us.

But generally it was support that was being given. Some people I would say were surprised. 'Whit, are yez hungry? Whit are Hunger Marchers?' They'd not taken the real reason behind it was lack of work. It was a protest, definitely a protest.

Well, I missed the turn-out in London but they took me up to London prior to returnin' back home. That wis the closin' stages so I wis only in London a matter o' four or five days. We were in a school in Poplar, that's where there were a hole in the flair and I got a cauld in the eye and it swelled up thon height – very unpleasant. So when we come back tae Glasgow I asked Peter Kerrigan could I go home instead o' goin' to the City Halls tae stay the night and have a rally the next day? 'Aye, away you go, Hughie,' he says. So I went straight home here. But we had a reception here in Blantyre in the Co-operative Hall. They had tables set apart for us, wi' a meal, and I do remember sittin' down to the white table-cloth. And McNaught and them made a few speeches and there was probably a concert or somethin' after it.

Lookin' back on the Hunger March I think it showed somethin' that's lackin' today. And it was peaceful. That's the important thing. There was no trouble, not from us, no trouble whatsoever. And yet we had made a protest and we put wir heart and soul intae it every way, every man. I felt it had been a success. It was a lesson of life, one o' the many things that comes up that ye never forget and I would say ye learned by it. It broadened my mind, definitely. And of course it kind o' hardened you off for goin' intae the army because ye got better beds in the army than what we had on the Hunger March!

After the Hunger March I went back down to Birmingham and worked for a year or two there in a bathroom fittins factory, thirty shillins a week. Then I come back up to Blantyre in 1938, comin' up for 1939. I reported to the Labour Exchange and put in for a course in bricklayin' and was sent to Wallsend, Newcastle. I worked as a bricklayer in London until they called me up in the War. Of course I was a conscientious objector: 'I'm no' gaun – on humanitarian grounds.' There was five judges or whatever you call them on the bench. One who was a Roman Catholic says, 'The Roman Catholic Church does not condemn this War.' Ah says, 'Neither do they condone it.' It was to no avail: I was turned down – 'Fit for service'. But I just got my tools together and away I went tae Wigan to work. Then it wis munitions and they caught up wi' me there. Well, 1942 I went over to the police station and says, 'You've got call-up papers for me', 'cause I knew they had come through. So I got a travel warrant and everything to go to Bradford, I reported in and they gave me a uniform: 'Put that on.' Then the next day they arrested me! Ah says, 'What are ye daein'?' 'Field-general court-martial.' Actually it was quite a common thing for many non-reporters. So I got put up in front o' the court-martial and got a year's imprisonment – Chorley detention, very strict of course. I done about six or seven weeks there and got a special release because I smuggled a letter out about the conditions. One o' the conditions that ah was subject tae was – wi' me havin' the bad feet, I was excused the marchin' and drillin' – I was workin' a treadle sewin' machine in the industrial shed. I was in a communal cell – sixty men in each cell – and I think there were four big thirty-gallon buckets for urine. And they were brimmin' over. If they'd ha' made it five it'd ha' been a'right. But they made it four. So I got the letter smuggled out tae Chapman. He was our M.P. for Rutherglen and he was also Under-Secretary for War.[279] And we had a local councillor here in Blantyre, Beecroft. So they all started work on my behalf. It was printed in the local paper: 'Young Blantyre man spends Christmas and New Year in the clink'. So I got special release. So I stayed in the army, R.E.M.E., till the end o' the

War. Then I got a special release, bein' a bricklayer. I got a bit fed up wi' bricklayin' so in 1955 I got a job servicin' washin' machines in Glasgow, then in 1962 I started wi' Johnny Bloom, the millionaire, in Rolls Electromatic and I finally became manager for Scotland until he went bankrupt.[280] Then up to 1970 I had a shop wi' a partner and when he died I jist went freelancin' right up to the present-day. I'm jist part-time because I'm pensionable age.

John Carroll

Dixon's Raws, miners' raws in Blantyre, that's where I was reared. My father was a miner a' his days. He worked in several pits. Craighead and Udston were the two main ones. Another pit they worked in, him and his father, was Earnock, Burnbank. My father had three brothers and they were all miners.

I cannae mind o' my grandfather Carroll and I don't know anything about where he was born. But my other grandfather, my mother's father, came frae Ireland, County Cavan and he landed in Durham. He came over to the pits in Durham somewhere about the 1870s, then he came up to Blantyre. I remember him. He had a big white beard that grew down to his chest, Auld Jimmy. He died when I was at school.

My mother was born in Durham. As a girl she worked as a domestic servant round here in Blantyre. She died when she was ninety past, over twenty years ago. I had three brothers and three sisters. I was the youngest o' the family. I was born in January 1918.

I went to St Joseph's School in Blantyre. I didnae like the school. I wisnae interested. I'll tell ye how ye werenae interested, because ye were gaun tae school and ye had yer bare feet and ye were sittin' in that classroom, ye were cold and ye were hungry. A' ye wanted tae do was tae get out o' the school and go and do somethin' tae get coppers for your mother – wee jobs. Well, the wee jobs I did was gaun tae the bing, gettin' coal, sellin' it maybe for three pennies a bag round the doors. Sometimes we carried it – wi' the barrow. The police wid come and they would smash the barras a' in. That happened to me, jist a wee lad. I've seen us trawlin' frae the bing and some o' the young lassies had prams wi' the coal in them and we had barras. And the police would come with their batons and they'd smash the barras. Oh, they raided ye. That was during the 1926 strike and after, in the '30s. They thought that ye widnae go tae the tip then if ye hadnae a barra. They were gettin' reports frae the pit, frae the manager. It was theft, oh, it was theft. But we used tae carry it.

In fact, I was in the court, in Hamilton court, and I'll tell ye how it was. Ah wisnae at the bing that day. It was Neilie McLachlan that got caught and he gave ma name. Neilie was one o' ma school pals. His father and his mother come ower – I remember it – and he says, 'Well, if you go to the court we'll pay the fine.' I went tae court. I think it wis ten shillins I got fined. That was a lot o' money then. I'd be about ten or eleven at the time.

We always went tae the one bing – the Priory. We never went tae
Spittal bing because that wis too open. The Spittal bing was on the road and
the police could watch you there. But the Priory bing ye'd always a chance
o' gettin' off down the Clyde, you could escape more easily. So that's what
ye did after school.

My brothers were all up, they were all up. They worked doon the pits.
I had a brother died. He lost a leg through an accident in the pit which he
never reported and he got nothin'. About a year after he lost his leg he died
– gangrene. He was twenty-four. I would be about twelve year old when
he died. He was my brother next above me.

I left school when I was fifteen. And do you know why? You left the
school at fourteen but if I left at fourteen I was gettin' nothin'. So ma fither
says, 'You stey on tae you're fifteen. I'll get that two shillins.' He was gettin'
two shillins for me at the school. That was the parish. And then when I left
the school when I was fifteen do you know where I went to? The parish. I
got half-a-croon, right up tae I was seventeen or eighteen.

I didnae have a job. There were nowt. I didnae go round askin' for
jobs. It was a waste of time. I didnae try tae get a job in the pit. My mother
didnae want me to go to the pit. So from fifteen till I was nearly eighteen I
never had a job at all.

When I was fifteen and unemployed I went on the 1933 March tae
Edinburgh. We left down there at Hastie's, the wee hut in the middle o'
Blantyre, and we went frae there tae Shotts. I cannae remember the
numbers on the March frae Blantyre but, oh, there were maybe thirty or
forty. That's about sixteen maybe seventeen miles tae Shotts. We steyed
there overnight. Then we went tae West Calder and frae there tae
Edinburgh.[281] We gathered in folk on the way. I'll never forget that, I'll
never forget that in ma life. We marched roond aboot Princes Street for
aboot eight hours. And they wouldnae let us sit doon and they widnae gie
us any place tae sleep. So we all bedded down in Princes Street, right alang
– the Castle lights blazin'. And we got an issue o' bananas. And efter we ate
the bananas we pit a' the skins on the railins. I can always remember sleepin'
beside a fellah in Princes Street and he came frae Bellshill. I cannae mind his
first name but his second name was Ross. That fellah, I believe, was a
principal either in the Labour Party or the Communist Party. I think he kind
o' come up a bit. Anyway I slept like a log. I had jist a blanket and had my
head on the pack. So that was not long efter I left school. I jist went masel'
on the March.

Well, when I was seventeen or eighteen I was gettin' 4/6d aff the
parish. Here I got a job carrying coal – coalman. I went tae Glasgow and
carried coal up there. The coal merchant was a Blantyre man – Devanney.
Well, they come oot the pits and started a wee business. They were father
and – I cannae mind, but there were a lot o' sons. At that time, when I
started, they had jist the one lorry. But they finished up wi' several. There
were another fellah worked for Devanney as well as me ootside the family.

The job wisnae hard. You were young. Ah, it wisnae hard once ye got used tae it. Ye thought nothin' of it. There wis a knack in carryin' it right. I was gettin' about twenty-five shillins a week. Oh, that was a lot o' money at that time. But I was workin' for it. Och, we were away at seven o'clock in the mornin'. We didnae come back tae aboot eight at night. It wis twelve or thirteen hours a day, Monday tae Saturday, six days a week. So it wis seventy to eighty hours a week for twenty-five bob. I stuck it for about a year and a half. Then I gave it up.

I remember I wis only a young fellah tae – I wis on the pairish at the time – and I marched up wi' them a' tae the Pairish Chambers. Big Jock Richardson, he was the chairman o' the Council, the Barrel King, they ca'ed him. He was the garage proprietor. He dealt in barrels frae Paisley. He had a big belly. So he says, 'I've been twenty years a councillor,' he says, 'and I never heard tell o' this.' Big Alan Hughes says, 'Have ye no'?' – BOWFF! A big black eye! So there were two – what will we say, volunteered tae let a' the rest go. They went tae the court and it wis Mat McNaught and Jimmy Beecroft. Jimmy got forty days and Matt got thirty days in Barlinnie. Oh, I remember that.

We got boots, I mind the pairish boots – they stamped them, stamped them. And a grey suit. It came efter the War, there were a style! They knew that ye were a pairish. But there used tae be three or four pawns in Blantyre, quite flourishing, oh!

Oh, housing conditions they were bad, oh! There were nine o' us in a room and kitchen in Dixon's Raws. And my mother had a lodger, big Willie Cables. At that time my older sister had went tae Australia. And there were one away workin' at East Fortune. I was the youngest and when I was a laddie sometimes I used tae sleep wi' ma sisters. My mother and fither were in the kitchen, three brothers they were in the room. Ye see in the paper now about this topless thing, and 'Oh, it's terrible.' Christ, when I was a youngster, God Almighty that was a' we seen. That was a' we seen.

But another thing. I used tae come in frae the dancin' maybe about two or three in the mornin'. And I used tae light the gas mantle jist above the fireplace. And whenever ye got a light there were a thousand clocks – cockroaches. And I used tae get a shovel and they would a' rise tae the shovel. I pit them in the fire and, oh, the bangs! Ma mother used tae say, 'Is that the clocks?' Ah says, 'Aye, maw, that's the clocks.' See, they were only wee flagstones on the tap o' the ground. That wis a'. Ye took that and ye were on the ground.

There wis nae disinfectant. In the summer-time the fire wis on and the fleas they'd crawl in below the bed. See the fleas – we used tae go tae the pictures and ye'd catch them in the pictures and bring them intae the hoose. Ma mother used tae have a big pail o' sheep's dirt and she used tae throw that in below the bed tae kill them off. Usually in the mornin' ye'd be a' bites. That wis daily. And even lice. When ye went tae the pictures ye got a dose o' lice. I've seen us at the fire, pickin' off the lice.

Mice and rats we never seen very much o' them. There were a lot o' dogs an' that. The raws was a'thegither – there'd be 300 houses anyway in

Dixon's Raws – and the dogs, oh, there were nae rats. They were a' coal company houses. I lived there till I got married in 1938.

When I was a wean I took diphtheria. That wis death at that time, that wis death. I was the first tae get the hole in the throat tae breathe. And I survived that. It wis death! See the diphtheria at that time – that was you finished. And scarlet fever was common. They cut a' my hair off. And, och, there were hundreds died of tuberculosis.

And when ye went tae that toilet, see, a' the bowl, it was a' shit. Ye couldnae sit doon, ye couldnae dae nothin'. I went away ower the parks, farmland. That's where the houses is built noo in Blantyre. There were pails in the hoose at night for the lassies. They couldnae go out through the night. They used tae empty the pails in the mornin'. Oh, a terrible smell and stench a' the time. And the reason why the lassies didnae go tae the toilets at any time was that there was a wee hole cut out o' the door and it went right tae that pan, right tae that bowl. And that's how they didnae go. One fellah got the blame o' that. Oh, there wis nae privacy. The women used tae go away ben the room and shut the door. But it was still the pail.

I remember when a' ye had was a wee gas-ring. That was what a' the cookin' was done on, that wee gas-ring. Nae hot water. I'll tell ye another thing ye'll never see noo and it wis very common at that time: blackheids. Ye know the reason why? There were nae hot water. It was a' cold water. We ca'ed it the jawbox. When ye'd to go tae the school ye'd wash your face in the jawbox – cold water. Ye don't see many blackheids now.

And see tryin' tae get paper on thae wa's? Oh, Christ! Ye'd pit the paper on and the next thing it wid be hingin' aff. Ach, the hooses were a' single brick, single brick. But we had always plenty coal. That was one thing we had – plenty coal. But see the miners at that time: when they a' got a ton o' coal it was aff their wages. Oh, so there werenae many tons ordered – it was always the bing, we went tae the bing. Some kind o' weel aff ones got tons but they used tae say, 'Oh, I've a ton o' coal aff me this week.' They used tae get a len o' coal checks.

There wis a Blantyre Co-operative Society. It wis a great thing. They stuck by the miners, oh, they did. In '26, oh, they stuck by the miners. Then the herrin' merchants used tae come frae Glescae, wi' boxes o' herrins. Oh, they were Loch Fyne. They were that size, great big herrins. And they'd go up and doon the raws shoutin', 'Thruppence a pund, herrin'!' But naebody'd buy any during the day. They waited till aboot night. Well, they couldnae take them back tae Glescae. 'Penny a pund, herrin'!' And they got rid o' a' their herrin'!

It wisnae long efter I gave up the coal carryin' job I heard about the Hunger March in 1936. And I says, 'I'll go tae London.' See, the thing was I wanted tae go tae London tae get a job. I wisnae interested in the March. It was experience tae go on the road and tae go and get a job. I wasnae in any party but I did work for the Communists. Oh, they were strong in the Blantyre area. In fact, I think they had a Communist councillor at that time.[282] I wisnae a member of the National Unemployed Workers' Movement either. They had a branch in Blantyre. It had a lot o' members, oh, hundreds. They met wi' the Communist Party in the wooden hut at Hastie's Farm jist doon the road there, in the middle o' Blantyre. Actually the N.U.W.M. was the Communist Party – the same leaders, Eddie Laughlin and Matt McNaught. They were active in both the Communist Party and the N.U.W.M. Before the hut they had the Y.M.C.A. Hall. That was a great place. But they had to move out o' that because they couldnae pey the rent. They got tossed out and they got the wee hut at Hastie's Farm. That's where they met, that was their base. But I was no' actually political. I would chalk the streets jist for a meetin'. The Young Communist League used tae go campin'. I went with them but I never joined the Y.C.L. I wisnae interested in politics. It was social, gettin' about, I liked the outdoor life, dancin' and one thing and another.

So when I heard about the March I jist went down to the hut and I asked them if I could go. They gave ye a pair o' boots, leather tackety boots. Put the boots on and away wi' what ye had! I jist went wi' ma ordinary clothes on, a jacket and a jersey, shirt and trousers. I had one set o' underwear and one pair o' socks. I didnae have a bunnet or a hat, nor a walkin' stick. We had jist a blanket. It was rolled up and we had it on our back. They gave us a haversack and we got a mug and a plate and a knife, a spoon and a fork, a' in the haversack.

There were aboot a couple o' dozen o' us left on the March frae Blantyre. I remember Willie Marshall was one. He was a miner. And there was John Flynn – Galley was his nickname. Oh, he wisnae a cook, jist happened tae get that nickname. And of course Hughie Duffy. Ned McGuire and Jimmy Maclean – they're dead – were there, and Baldy Shearer – Archibald Shearer – and Mick McComisky. There's other three I remember was killed in Spain: Tommy Brannan, Willie Fleck and Fox. They went tae Spain frae London. Tommy Brannan was in the Territorials at that time and he had experience, but he was killed in Spain.[283] I thought about goin' tae Spain masel', I really thought about it. It widna ha' took much, you know. If there had been a boy there that said, 'Right, get on wi' it,' we might ha' been on it.

When we left Blantyre on the March we jist made our way tae Uddingston. We had a flute band. It wis the Hibs' band, they were fluters, tae go tae Uddingston. Then we got the tramcar tae Glasgow. We stayed in the City Halls and the next mornin' we a' assembled, the West o' Scotland, and Kerrigan he was there. He took the West and Harry McShane took the East, that's the Edinburgh March. I think it wis either Kilmarnock or outside Kilmarnock we stopped. And then we went frae there tae Sanquhar and I think tae Annan. There was a pretty good turn-out at Dumfries. But there was no money, no money – we never got anythin' in the boxes, very, very little.

We slept in any place we could get – an old hall, an old church hall, schools. We made our own meals. We got a plate o' porridge in the mornin', and maybe a couple o' rolls. I enjoyed the March very much, after we went out o' Scotland I enjoyed it. I never had a blister, never had a blister.

We went intae Warwick and the police were there. We were a' ready for a meal. There were nae meal. We had tae march right away oot the toon. We were a' gettin' yon wey, ready for wer bed. At the finish up they had tae negotiate wi' the police tae get a place tae lie down. No, they widnae give us it: 'Get out, and if ye're not out by a certain time...', the batons were goin' tae be used. Kerrigan got buses and away we went.

I don't know where we went tae efter that. But I remember entering London. I'll never forget it – millions, millions, millions turned out. The greatest scene ever you seen in your life. Hyde Park – ye wouldnae ha' got a dog in at that time, crammed. We attended the meetins – Harry Pollitt, Willie Gallacher, and Wal Hannington. And Guy Bolton, he was the quartermaster, and here we were in this place we were stayin'. He has a look at me, and I had on the same boots, the same shirt, the same trousers that I left wi' – and that was sleepin' in them. 'Oh,' he says, 'come on in here, young fellow.' I went away in and they were packed wi' clothes. Big Guy fitted me out wi' a suit, a pair o' brogues, socks – stripped me, threw oot the auld claes. 'Right!' – shirt, tie, suit, and, och, everythin'. 'There,' he says, 'ye're fit tae go out now.' And away I went, away down tae the East End. And I got into tow wi' Jews and they were takin' me tae parties and everythin'. They were Left, very, very Left. In fact, they were Communists, in the Party.

I wis in London only a week and then we come back by train tae Glasgow. I visited a lot o' places in London, like Westminster Abbey, the Houses o' Parliament. But I didnae look for a job, I didnae look. I wis a bit homesick. I wanted tae get back hame tae my mother's. So I stayed the night in Glasgow in the City Halls and attended a rally there the next day.

Efter I come back home I sterted right away carryin' the coal again for a few months. And then I got a job at Clydebridge steelworks. When the War came I was still at Clydebridge and I wis called up. Then I was deferred for aboot two or three months – my ears were kind o' dischargin'. Then they sent back for me again and they passed me A1. I went tae the Royal Marines at Chatham. I didnae go overseas. The only place I went tae was Belfast, tae guard an I.R.A. prison.

After the War I went tae work in the tyre factory at Inchinnan and I wis there till I took the early retirement when I was sixty in 1978.

So the 1936 Hunger March was an important episode in my life. I felt quite proud I had taken part in it. We gained self-respect and a kind o' education, how tae get through life. The March had its implications. Well, they took notice, put it that way. I think there were a change in the circumstances. I never joined a political party after the March. But I wis always Labour. After the War, I used tae canvass the likes o' the elections but I never joined the Labour Party. I always had every intention but I never got to it. Oh, the Hunger March was an education, it was an education.

Tony Brown

Well, I was born in a place called Auchintibber, a mile and a quarter frae Blantyre. Auchintibber wis jist a small minin' village. They were all miners. Ye kent everybody that was in it. There were nae other work. There were one public hoose and my granny used tae wash it oot. And she got so much – it wisnae very much.

Ma faither worked in No. 1 of Dixon's colliery in Blantyre. I don't know what my grandfaither Brown done. But I ken my mother's father – that's him that I'm ca'ed efter, Anthony McDonald Brown – was an old preacher and he worked in the pits. When the Dixon's explosion happened he was doon the pit prayin'. That wis the Blantyre Disaster in 1877. He was in that but he survived it. I don't remember him: he was dead afore I wis grown-up.[284]

I had brothers and sisters. There were twelve o' us: six sons and six daughters. I'm the second oldest o' the family but the oldest son. I was born in March 1906. There were two died when they were quite young. One he got drooned. He ta'en fits and he'd fell. It wisnae that deep o' water, jist a puddle. An' he fell and his face went in first. That was it. That's when they got him.

The house we lived in wis paraffin ile lamps. There were two rooms, well, room and kitchen. and it was a' stane flairs, nae widden flairs. I can mind my mother used tae buy thae big roond chalks tae make patterns on the flair. It wis an outside toilet, nae bath. They were maybe coal company's hooses because I cannae mind o' a rent man comin' roond. I ken in Blantyre that they were a' coal company hooses. So maybe in Auchintibber it wis the same.

I went to school in Auchintibber. I left school when I wis thirteen. I was the first son. You got exempt frae the school a year afore yer time was up. It wis a while efter I left school before I got a job. I wis jist runnin' aboot and then I went tae a ferm and got a job at singlin' neeps or liftin' tatties, odd jobs. That was for a few months. Even afore I left school I was singlin' neeps in a place at East Kilbride when the first Zeppelin came ower. We seen the Zeppelin that plain, the first Zeppelin ever I seen. That was 1918.

Afore I left school tae ma mother used tae gie us soup tae cairry tae a deserter frae the British army. I remember him awfy weel. Benny Latimer, that was his name. He was a miner. He lived three doors away in the same row as me. He was called up tae the War. He was at Ypres and he deserted that big battle in France, I think it wis the Somme. He got leave frae France

363

and he didnae go back. I expect he was feart, that's the whole thing aboot it. He was a married man. He lived in the glen at Auchintibber, just up on the tap side o' the rows. It was thick wi' sma' trees. He had a hut and he lived in the hut. He was there for aboot eichteen month. Ma mother and the man's wife used tae gie us soup for him and we used tae cairry his soup up in a can, and his tea, and a' this. They kep' him goin' wi' cigarettes. And we used tae watch for the polis. There were two polis, well, they used tae sift aboot and sift aboot but he was aye on his gaird. The miners kept the secret, naebody betrayed him. An' he was awfy active, he could jump ower gates, jump hedges and run. He used tae come tae his ain hoose if it were a cauld night. And that's when they got him. They got him in the hoose near the end o' the War. He was taken away. I never heard o' him again. I never seen that man frae the day I left him, takin' his meals up.

My uncle he'd a steel plate in his skull. And Benny Latimer was there wi' him when he got it at the Somme, I think it wis. Ye kent the want was there wi' my uncle. It affected him a lot. He got a full pension though. He lived a guid long time after the War.

I was thirteen year auld when I got my first job doon the pit, in No. 2 o' Dixon's in Blantyre. I got a job there drivin' a powny. Its name wis Sandy. My wage was three shillins a day. And I got a sixpence aff o' a' the men for cairryin' their water cans. Ye had tae cairry big flasks. So that wis another half-a-croon a week. It wis an eleven-day fortnight. That wis in 1919 when I began.

I wis drivin' tubs wi' Sandy the powny. There were two men and it wis what they cried a dook.[285] That was a single tub at a time. If the chain broke, the tub would run back tae the joke gripped it. And the joke was that heavy I could hardly lift it – I was light built an' that.[286] Well, I used tae drive the tubs oot o' this dook. And when ah got tae the tap then I had tae make a race, maybe ten tubs at a time. And I had tae run the cowsy. The full yins ta'en the empties up. The cowsy was a steep incline brae. When I got ten tubs on, ye drew the pin and opened the block. If I was away drivin' a tub oot the dook I used tae pit a bit o' stick in the wire. Harry Jones, a Welshman, was the bottomer and when he pulled the bell I kenned he was ready if I come oot and the stick was oot. I jist knocked the blocks oot and I come up wi' my last tub. Well, this day the stick was oot but there were nae empty race o' tubs on. And it run away. When I opened the block it started tae run. Ah says, 'Oh!' And I run and I drew the pin and I sat pressin' the lever doon tae stop it. Somethin' dawned on me. Ah says, 'I'd better get oot o' here.' It was richt tae the pit bottom and the peeweep – the empty chain – come up. If I had sat there tae try and stop it I would ha' got melted – right in the face. That wis the first week or two I wis workin'. Wi' the race runnin' afore I was ready, the powny got killed. And the dook was closed. I wrecked the place! But I never got intae trouble. The manager gied me a tellin' off. I telt him what wis wrang, I explained the situation tae him. And he says it wis a bad omen because a stane could drop frae the roof and hit the wire and release your stick. It's quite right, what he said.

Efter two or three year I left Dixon's and went tae the Clyde. And I had tae walk it. There were nae transport. I was still livin' at Auchintibber. I walked a mile and three-quarters to two miles goin' and comin' – four miles. Hamilton Accies Football Club wis next door tae the Clyde pit in Hamilton. I was still only aboot fifteen year old and I was on backshift, at night. The wage was jist the same, three shillins a day. I think ma faither was tae blame for me gaun tae the Clyde. He thought there were mair money in it. But there werenae mair money in it. I went tae the Clyde on my own, ma faither was still workin' in Dixon's No. 1 at Blantyre.

At the Clyde pit I was drivin' a powny again. A man called Snowball Fram was my neighbour. Snowball Fram was a great boxer. I think he had fought for the world's championship. And he was drivin' his powny wi' his bare feet. The water! And the rats! When ye went intae thae stables in the mornin' the rats were jumpin' oot the box. Oh, oh, it would ha' frightened ye! Snowball had bare feet because o' the water. He didnae wear Wellingtons. He'd ta'en his boots aff and come oot, drivin' oot this road wi' the powny. Oh, it wis well named, the Clyde! Jist as wet as the river! I didnae work in ma bare feet, I wore Wellingtons. But I wisnae very long in the Clyde pit, two years.

I'd been in Dixon's in the 1921 lock-out. Ye were out for three month. Then I went back. I wisnae victimised. Efter the Clyde I went back tae Dixon's. I was in Dixon's in the 1926 strike. Ye were oot thirty-two weeks. But I got my job back at the end o' the strike, I wisnae victimised. And I was in Dixon's tae I come through here tae Fife in 1930.

My father was a machineman and he had a job on the machines in Dixon's No. 4 pit. His wages wasnae big. My mother had a hard time o' it. Ma faither and me tae begin wi' were the only two wage-earners. And there were a' ma younger brothers and sisters comin' along. Oh, it wis haund tae mooth! A Thursday: a piece on sugar – that was your breakfast! No' every mornin', but when it come Wednesday or Thursday ye were jist destitute. Oh, we were hard-up. And ma faither kept whauppets. And we used tae dip our pieces in the sheep's heid that he was makin' for the dugs tae eat.

And ma faither was awfy strict. We'd tae be in at nine o'clock. Right up tae I wis married he never let us smoke in the hoose, never let us smoke at a'. I never smoked forenent him till I was aboot twenty-eight. Frightened o' him? Oh, he was an awfy man. Ma faither was strict. He was in the union but he wasnae active, and he wisnae active politically or in the church. I joined the union masel' when I went doon the pit and I've been in the union a' my days. But I wisnae active.

I got married in November 1929. My wife had worked on the pitheid at Dixon's where I wis. But that wisnae where we met; I knew her in the village. She come frae Blantyre, Dixon's Raws. When we got married I was twenty-three and she was eighteen. Her family were a' miners. She had five brothers, a' miners, and her faither was a machineman in the pit. She had two sisters tae but the wife was the only one that worked on the pitheid.

Up tae 1930 I worked in Dixon's. I was neebourin' a man, a qualified man, fullin' his tubs and that. But in 1930 I lost my job and I signed on the dole. I didnae get the sack in Dixon's. I think I was there tae Dixon's closed. I'd been married about six or seven months at the time, and I lost my job. But I'm no' certain the pit closed. Well, there were a guid lot o' men come through here tae Fife. They a' drifted through here.

The wife wisnae workin' efter we got married. We lived in a single room. Ah couldnae get a hoose. We lived first wi' ma mother at Auchintibber. Then ma faither he wisnae agreein' wi it. We had tae look for another place. So we went tae the wife's mother's. And as things come oot, ye ken what like it is, steyin' wi' their mothers and a' this an' that. We went tae a cisin o' mines in Blantyre, it wis a room there as well. We never had a hoose tae ah come tae Fife.

The dole was interviewin' ye: wid ye go tae Fife, wi' experience o' the pits, an' a' this an' that. 'Are ye a face worker?' Well, we said we were a face worker. Ah wisnae a face worker but ah said ah wis a face worker, tae get work. The dole peyed oor wey through here tae Fife, peyed oor furniture flittins an' that, and ta'en us through. And it wis a room we went tae in Valleyfield. That would be roond aboot the autumn o' 1930.

We got a room in a miner's house at Valleyfield. The miner was Patty Hands. He was older than me. He had one youngster. By then we had one bairn tae. The child wasnae that auld. Noo we steyed there in Patty Hands' room till the rats come on the scene. Patty Hands' wife used tae tell us. She says, 'The marks o' the claws on some o' ma furniture,' she says, 'and it was the rats.' It had been gaun on for some time, years maybe. They were feared o' them. Well, the hoose was infested wi' rats. An' it was through the rats that ah left and the wife and bairn tae. I remember it well. I wis lyin' in ma bed one night and the press door was oot and in, ye ken, gettin' bowf bowf. I heard it as plain. And ah says, 'There's somethin' wrang here.' Ah thocht it wis the neebours next door, Paddy Devlin, because they were a great pair for fun, ken, playin' jokes on ye. So ah says tae the wife, 'Get up and see what that is.' She wis feared tae get up. So I gets up. And I sat at the fireplace. And the bang! bang! bang! 'Oh,' ah says, 'I'm gaun tae be on ma gaird here.' So I gets the poker. Ah says tae the wife, 'Noo you open the press door and I'll be ready.' And it wis a rat. It was half in the hole in the press, the rest o' its body couldnae get in. Ah got the poker and ah jammed it. An' I kept that poker there. Ah says, 'Gie me thae shoes ower.' I pits ma shoes on and I got a cloth. I got the rat wi' ma hand on the cloth. And when I went tae pu' its tail the skin o' the tail come away. But ah got that rat and I pressed on its heid and killed it. And it wis a fit long, a fit long. I put it on the windae ledge. And I wis terrified when I seen whit it wis. We had the bairn at the time. And I think it wis a Thursday. The pey was on Friday. And we had nothin'. But ah says, 'Right, we're off.' And we walked through the night frae Valleyfield tae here at Methil. That's aboot thirty mile. We had shot aboot cairryin' the bairn. But we'd only got as far as a wee place cried Torryburn aboot half a mile frae Valleyfield and a boy stopped us on this wee brae. He says, 'Whaur are ye gaun at this time o' night?' We telt him Methil. The wife's mother by that time had moved there frae Blantyre. If she hadnae been there I don't think I would ha' ventured walkin' that, ye ken. And this boy gave us ten shillins. We had nae money, we had nothin'.

Between thumbin' lifts we very near walked a' the road. The wife come tae Kirkcaldy, her heel was a' skint. It wis a long road. I think it wis at Rosyth there were a bus conductor, she was awfy good. She says, 'Jist sit in,' till we went tae Dunfermline or Kirkcaldy, 'cause we had nae mair money tae pey. We got some lifts. And it wis a godsend, gettin' a lift, because ye were feart tae stop onybody. There were very little cars, an odd one – but they jist went on. It wis in the mornin' when we got tae Kirkcaldy. The wife's mother lived in Donaldson Road in Methilhill. So when we got there on the Friday ah had tae go back on the bus tae collect ma wages at Valleyfield. The wife's mother gied me the fare.

But I didnae get a job at Methil here. I couldnae get intae the Wellesley pit. I couldnae get into the Michael. I couldnae get intae Wells Green. I tried all the pits, the whole lot. I went tae Muiredge pit, and tae the Rosie. I didnae go tae Lochhead but I went tae a' the other pits and ah couldnae get a job. I had been aboot a year at Valleyfield so this would be aboot 1931. I was on the dole. Oh, I went up tae the pit gates two or three times a week. I couldnae get a job. I tried tae get a job through the Labour Exchange. It was Leven Exchange I signed on at. I walked doon tae Leven frae Methilhill, a mile and a quarter, and back, three times a week. And in between times I was aye walkin' oot tae the pits as well. Oh, it went on for months and months. I couldnae get a job. My faither-in-law spoke for me, this yin speakin' for ye, but they couldnae get me a job either. I was unemployed a' the time afore I went on the Hunger March in 1936 – aboot five years.

In 1934 I joined the Territorial Army in Leven. Well, ah had nothin' else tae dae. Ye jist got browned off, fed up. Ah swithered whether tae jine the Regular army or the Terries. So I jined the Terries. You only got a bounty every year. The bounty was £30, I think. That wisnae what made me join the Terries – jist browned off, fed up, nothin' tae dae. Graham Robertson, a friend o' mine, an auld Celtic player, he was already in the Terries. He encouraged me tae jine it for somethin' tae do. By that time I had two bairns.

I joined the Leven branch of the National Unemployed Workers' Movement. But I wisnae active. I didnae attend meetins or go roond wi' leaflets or anythin' like that. I wis jist a payin' member. And I never was a member o' any political party.

Well, I remember siftin' oot wi' the Hunger March and what they were gaun tae London for. I heard aboot the March at a meetin' and also frae friends. 'Well,' ah says, 'ah'm gaun tae go jist tae see.' Because I thought the Means Test at that time was very drastic. We were still livin' wi' the mother-in-law at Methilhill. Well, it wis the Means Test that I went on that March wi'. It wis through it. That's what the March was fur. The wife didnae object tae me goin'. Oh, she was keen, she was keen. So ah says, 'Well, pit ma name doon.'

I think there were aboot twenty-odds o' us frae this area, East Fife. We were the East Fife contingent: Methil, Buckhaven, Leven, Methilhill, Denbeath. There were a few other boys I kenned on the March: big Harry Paterson frae Methilhill. But Harry was one o' the ones later on that packed up. He had blistered feet. And there was Chick Watson frae Methil. Well, we got the bus frae Buckhaven tae Kirkcaldy. When we got to Kirkcaldy we got issued wi' boxes, collectin' boxes. The band played us a' roond Kirkcaldy. It wis at night. Now we bid in Kirkcaldy, in the big hall that night. We got the bus tae Glasgow. There were a guid few frae Kirkcaldy. There were Pinder MacQueen.[287]

Now I can very near vouch for how many left Glasgow. That's when we started tae walk, from Glasgow Green. There were about 400 on that March, because I mind o' them saying the figures an' that, frae the various parts o' Scotland.

I went through four pair o' boots on the way to London. I started off wi' my ain boots, pit boots. They were guid for walkin' an' I was never bothered wi' blistered feet. And I walked every inch o' that road. The hardest walk was at the Shap. Then the Co-operative in England gave us boots, each man a new pair o' bits.

When we left frae Buckhaven I had a big coat, my boots and socks, jist my usual claes. We had nothing special. We didnae even take a change o' underwear. Ye washed it at night when ye got the chance, dried it on the hot plates. I had nae pack. But I had a bunnet. I never carried a stick. We got a briefin' aboot it. The stick was tae help ye on the road. We were told not to carry any weapons or anything like that. And we didnae, we didnae. And if we had had sticks or weapons gaun intae Hyde Park I believe that we wid ha' come aff second best. We had meetins on the road, briefly tellin' ye what tae dae an' things no' tae dae. If a stick helped ye – and walkin' wi' a stick helped some o' them, but they hadnae tae hae sticks gaun intae London or Hyde Park: no weapons o' any kind. The sticks were a' surrendered, somebody came and collected them. I don't know who it wis, but there were nae sticks tae be used.

There were some o' them right bad wi' their feet an' a' that. Some dropped out and they got transport, some o' them wi' packs. The biggest pack ever I seen a man cairryin' – and he cairried it a' the wey – wis Peter Kerrigan. What a pack he had! He was one o' the leaders. And ye ken there were sometimes ones destitute, destitute. But they got well warned, well tutored. They spoke to them and that, had the meetins, telt us whaur we were goin' next an' a' this. And some days you were ninety-seven miles off o' London. Ye'd set oot the next mornin' ye'd come tae signposts again and it wis gettin' longer every time. I don't know why that was, whether it was routes they were takin'.

Dumfries was an awfy place. Well, they were tryin' their utmost I think tae destroy the March. Ye ken, two or three scuffles. The Marchers didnae get involved in it. It wisnae the police, it wis what I term hooligans. And there some good people ready tae help ye. The hooligans in Dumfries werenae students, maybe Blackshirts. They were oot tae destroy the March anyway – provoking, roarin' and shoutin' frae the pavements, but the Marchers didnae pey heed tae them. Ance ye got intae England it wis different a'thegither, different atmosphere, different people. And they were helpin' ye every way they could. They gave ye things that ye werenae lookin' for, maybe fruit, eatables, and cigarettes. I got tins o' meat from people watchin' the March. Ye got tins o' meat and ye had a box that they were drappin' money intae. I've seen them giein' ye ten shillins for a *Daily Worker,* ten shillins. And they were really good. The Co-operative was marvellous.

Oh, there were some o' the places we went tae was wicked, wicked. Ye were up and ye were killing these big beetles. The flair was full o' them. And flies, thae big spider flies, Oh! That wis the grubbers, the poorhouse. I was in a few workhouses and I had to chop sticks before I got my breakfast. I jist dinnae ken the name o' the place. An' ye got an awfy thick slice o' pan breid wi' two squares o' margarine. And they come roond and seen how much sticks ye chopped afore ye got yer breakfast! Oh, I was in a guid few workhooses. And they werenae one ony better than the other. We got porridge in one, an' they even put cheese in the porridge, chunks o' cheese, intae the porridge! Oh, ah wis shocked wi' that. Ah jist couldnae eat it. We used tae go oot at night after we were lowsed, well, efter we haunded in wer boxes an' a' that. So we went intae a big fruiterer's. It wis a market and we got a bag o' ingins that they couldnae keep. The hall that we were in was a big massive hall and they're a' lyin' heid tae heid. We opened this bag and we started flingin' these ingins jist abune their heids and they're burstin'. We had them a' greetin' wi' the smell o' the ingins. Och, it wis jist a bit o' fun.

I don't think we got a penny off the Co-operative in Fife – no' that I mind o'. But the Co-operative in England were helluva good. And at that pub or hotel, whether it's Penrith or Kendal, but it's at the bottom o' the brae afore ye enter the Shap, they were helluva good. They gave every one a cooked meal, sausages and eggs and a'thing. I don't remember ever being really hungry on the March. Ye were well fed – the best that ye could expect. Onything ye got ye ate it. It wis good. We used tae go in for a pennyworth o' stale buns – a penny, and they'd fu' maybe aboot three pokes for ye! And they widnae take the penny. Each village ye marched tae ye had a rest, a night's sleep and away the next mornin'. Well, at night we used tae go tae a baker's an' that – stale buns, onything we could buy. We had nae money tae buy onything.

On the way doon tae London there were twa boys collectin' wi' the boxes. There were a string on the box. They went in tae the lavatory and seemingly they must ha' been tryin' tae open the box. The money fell on the flair in the lavatory! They werenae sent home – they werenae caught. Oh, they done it. Maybe even a person comin', a dressed gentleman or a dressed woman: they come and ye'd gie them a *Daily Worker*. They'd slip ye ten shillins, a ten shillin' note. Some o' them was gettin' that, keepin' it. And they were even goin' buyin' a tin o' soup, they'd fling the soup oot then rig the tin up, make a hole in the tap, collectin' their ain box first, then they started on the Marchers' box. They were daein' it. I didnae see them masel' but I kenned they were workin' wi' two boxes. Somebody telt me they were daein' it.

We were away aboot five weeks, I think. I wisnae in touch wi' the wife, no' as far as mail was concerned. I didnae write home and she didnae write at a'. But ones did. There were somebody that wrote sayin' that they were gettin' charged wi' desertion, Hunger Marchers was gaun tae get charged for desertin' their wives and kiddies. There were ones wis charged, because the police was there, met them, chargin' them for desertin'.[288]

When we got tae London the soup kitchen was in Hyde Park and ye got a bowl o' soup. They were haudin' meetins, a platform there and maybe one awa' ower here, when a' o' a sudden these mounted police made one charge. There were nae violence – they jist made one charge. Ah said, 'Ah'm gettin' oot o' here.' They wid ha' run ye ower at Hyde Park. After that we got rigged up again and organised tae march tae the House of Commons. And the first twenty men got in and ah happened to be one o' the twenty. There were a tea laid oot for ye. There were cigarettes, jougs o' water – nae beer, nae drink! And Pinder MacQueen frae Kirkcaldy he started tae sing *The Rid Flag*. He only got aboot four words oot and we were grabbed – right doon that stair, out. But I met Jimmy Maxton, he sat wi' us for the tea. Well, we remained in London for aboot four days, I think, four nights. And the London County Council decided that they were gaun tae pay our fares back. It wis them that sent us back by train frae King's Cross straight tae Edinburgh. Then we came on a train frae Edinburgh tae Kirkcaldy. There were a group tae meet us there. The platform was full – police an' a'. They were there tae charge the boys that had left wi' desertin' their wives and kiddies. I wisnae charged wi' desertin' mine.

I thought the March wis a success, because if we hadnae went there and drew their attention that we were interested in the drastic things they were gaun tae dae they would ha' still went through wi' it. I wid dae it again if I went for one thing – tae put Maggie Thatcher oot o' that 10 Downing Street. I'd volunteer the morrow.

Efter the March I got a job at the Wellesley pit at Methil. It wis ma guidfaither that got me the job. I had collected a steel hat, boots, and my check number. This first day I was tae stert work the manager, Gemmell, sent a boy up wi' a bike tae tell me tae come doon. This was about twenty minutes to one and I was gaun oot backshift. He says, 'You've to go down to the Wellesley office at once.' 'Oh,' ah says, 'at once?' Ah says, 'Ah'm gaun on the backshift the day.' 'Ah, well,' he says, 'ye've tae go down at once before ye go.' 'Ho,' ah says, 'this is it.' So I went doon. And there were four policemen in the check box. When ah goes in Gemmell comes tae me. He says, 'Bring that steel hat, boots, and check number down here at once.' He says, 'We're no' wantin' any violent rebels in these premises.' So I was victimised oot the Wellesley wi' bein' in the Hunger March. He had learned that I wis on the Hunger March. This was a few months after the March that

I wis to ha' sterted. And he wouldnae let me speak tae the police – 'Out!'

Andrew Gemmell was the manager before that in Auchinraith pit in Lanarkshire. I had an uncle in that pit. Afore the pit inspector came they had the place wide open – nae screens up nor nothin'. An' it was fu' o' gas. So when Gemmell got word that the inspectors was comin' – and this is true – he got them tae pit screens up on every road in that pit to purify the air. When the inspectors inspected the pit it was a'right. Then he pulled the screens back doon again and there were men gettin' hame, sent hame wi' gas – 'cause they tested the gas whenever they went in. The place was fu' o' gas. The explosion happened a fortnight efter the pit inspectors had been, when he ta'en the screens doon. And see if the mob had got him! They had tae pit him oot the back windae and he'd never been seen in Blantyre since. There were seven men killed in that explosion. My uncle Matha Maclean was one o' them. The miners knew tae this day whit like the pit wis. And he wis camouflagin' it tae get the output oot. And that's what Gemmell did. They even published that he was a murderer. Gemmell was tried and he was found guilty o' negligence in runnin' Auchinraith pit and he was fined £23. The Wemyss Coal Company then gave him a job as the agent for the pits through here in Fife. The agent had two or three pits under his control, above the manager. Gemmell immediately operated a policy o' victimisation. I was victimised for goin' on the Hunger March, nothin' surer than that. That's the only reason that he gave me. He wouldnae listen tae me.[289]

I wis unemployed for maybe a year efter that, then I got a job in Wells Green pit and I wis there till the War broke oot. Then I wis called up tae Perth Barracks 'cause I wis a Territorial in the Black Watch. Well, we marched tae the station at Perth and arrived at Aldershot. One day when there were 1,600 men on parade at Aldershot I wis picked oot as the smartest. We were there for a few months then we landed in Le Havre in France. We were there for a guid few months. Then we were gaun intae battle. We ta'en up position at the Albert Canal. Ah wis a commander o' the Bren gun. At ten o'clock the barrage opened oot an' each Bren carrier – there were ten – run oot o' ammunition. I bet ye I shot 500 Germans at that Canal. There were jist mass formations. They were jist fa'in' as ye pressed that trigger – thirty-six bullets a second comin' oot o' there. We run oot o' ammunition and he chased us. Ah wis seven days on the beach at Dunkirk. Ah couldnae wade out 'cause I was committin' suicide: I couldnae swim. He didnae bomb us. He bombed the ships. But he never bombed the beaches. He strafed us wi' gunfire aff his planes, tracers. If he had made one move tae bomb thae beaches there wouldnae ha' been a man got oot. Well, I got off the beach. I got on tae a wee boat then we were ta'en on tae a boat cried *The Kingfisher*, a destroyer. And I was mair terrified on that boat. When I got on tae it and they gave us life jaickets I mind o' sayin' tae the old captain, 'Are there ony sharks in this water?' I wis feared o' the sharks! I got back and I landed in Margate. We got bombed at sea but they missed us.

We were ta'en tae Yeovil. We were examined and I was put intae hospital. I lay thirty-two weeks in Basingstoke. It was worse than the front line. Ye were cairried tae the shelters every night, every night. When I come oot o' Basingstoke I was put back tae the Black Watch. So I wis drifted tae the Isle o' Wight, jist gairdin' for invasions. Then they shoved me intae hospital in the Isle o' Wight and that's where ah got ma discharge in 1942, on medical grounds. The doctor says, 'Ah can't cure ye but we'll hae ye fit for goin' home. An' if ye have any trouble aboot yer pension,' he says, 'don't be frightened tae write tae us.' Ah never claimed a pension.

I got a job on a lorry, coalman wi' Lawson o' Leven aboot 1943. And I left him in 1945–46 and ah went back intae the pits – the Michael colliery at East Wemyss. I wis there tae I retired in 1962.

John Lennox

The street where I grew up in Aberdeen, Clarence Street, down near the shipyards, was only a short street. There were seven blocks of tenements, six houses – room and kitchen – to each block. The families were a' big in Clarence Street. We had six in our family – my five brothers and me – and my faither and mother was eight. The McCallums, who lived above us at No. 35, had eight in their family. The Pratts at No. 31 was fourteen o' a family – seven of that men. So there was a lot of menfolk in our street but oot of all the menfolks there was only three that was working: Pratt and McCallum worked in the docks, and my father was a butcher.

I lived in Clarence Street from 1915 until 1928. I wisnae actually born there. I was born in Arbroath in October 1906 but came to Aberdeen in 1915.

I come of a family interested in politics. It was not my father, it was my mother who was the driving force in our political activities. Even as a schoolboy I went with my mother on a Sunday night to a local cinema, when Davie Kirkwood, Jimmy Maxton, George Buchanan, Neil Maclean, Rev. Jimmy Barr come up and were speakers. And there was Gallacher and Saklatvala M.P. That was the sort of background we had.[290]

My mother was a bit o' a suffragette. She wisnae actually in the suffragette movement but she had that tendency and always worked for women's freedom. She wasn't a feminist in the modern sense but she was keen on women's liberation. So it was her that introduced all the family to this political activity. In Aberdeen we were the first ward – St Clement's Ward – to return a Labour councillor about 1920: George Catto. The Lennoxes were all engaged in that campaign.[291]

I lefts St Clement's School at fourteen. I just had an ordinary education. I played football. Miss Taylor the headteacher said one day when I was in trouble at school, 'If you had as much brains in your head as you have in your feet you'd do well.' After I left school, when I was about fifteen or sixteen I joined the Independent Labour Party Guild o' Youth. I was in that for a wee while. The I.L.P was a strong propaganda force. It was up and doon the whole o' Scotland. Aberdeen was no exception and there was quite a strong branch here. As a boy I used to sell the *Labour Leader, New Leader* and Tom Johnston's paper *Forward*.[292] Bob Cooney, a Communist Party activist, who was a year younger than me, he'd be sellin' the *Worker's Weekly* or some o' these papers. We had a cinema on a Sunday evening where we held this meetins and on a winter's night we would be inside and we did allow Bob to stand in the doorway if it was really wet. But we kept him at arm's length. Well, in Aberdeen the Communist Party did eventually come tae be capable o' gettin' meetins. But at that time in the 1920s they werena the propaganda force the I.L.P. were locally.

Well, when I left school I was idle for six months. It was the time o' the miners' strike, 1921. And the painters in Aberdeen were also on strike. They were out for twenty-one weeks. They went out for three ha'pennies an hour extra and unfortunately they had to settle for a ha'penny less. Then I got started my time as an apprentice painter.

We did six years then in our apprenticeship. I wanted to join the painters' union when I become an apprentice but they said no: you waited till your last year of apprenticeship and then you joined the union. You were the boss's property when you were an apprentice. Apprentices had really no rights at all, none. Ten shillings a week was the starting wage and I ended up after six years with twenty-four shillings a week.

The firm I was with, Donald's, did a lot of the toff's shootin' lodges up in the North-East. So I spent half my apprenticeship on country jobs. The lodgin' allowance was twelve shillins a week. Bein' in the country you did about fifty hours a week instead o' the normal forty-four hours. That was wi' the agreement o' the trade union. You were jist paid the normal rate for that, you didnae get time-and-a-half.

The painter's bible at that time was *The Ragged Trousered Philanthropists*. Conditions that book was describin' were familiar to me. Anyway in 1928 I got working with the firm I had served my apprenticeship with. But of course painters was a seasonal job. It was March or thereabout before you were taken on. And you could be paid off as early as July. The season could be as short as that. So we were well used to being unemployed. When a painter got paid off his world didnae collapse aboot him. That would have been the experience maybe of many other workers who'd never experienced it before. But if you were a painter you just simply accepted that.

So as far as Aberdeen was concerned – and the same would apply to painters in any provincial town – ye either went to Edinburgh or you went to London. It was London I went to in 1928. I went back and forth like that to London for a couple o' years. Then I got in with a London firm. Oh, we had many a hard time in London lookin' for work all the different places and big furnishin' companies. They all jist had a little season and ye got in for the season and then you were paid off. In between times comin' near New Year time we hoped to get paid off – it wasnae difficult to get paid off! – so then we come up here to Aberdeen and had an extended six weeks' or thereaboot sort o' holiday at New Year. That was quite deliberate, that was how we worked it.

The painters had a strike somewhere in about 1932 and big Sandy Bannochie, my mate, and me travelled up. I had served my apprenticeship along wi' Sandy in Aberdeen. So big Sandy and me did posters and was active in the strike. Finally, I got in with this London firm, Clark and Fenn's of Clapham. It was the time the luxury cinemas were bein' built all over the country and we went out all over wi' them. Then in 1935 I come back to Aberdeen.

By that time I was a member of the Communist Party. I joined it in London in 1928 in the Wandsworth Road. While I was in London and comin' back and forth to Aberdeen I'd quite a lot o' association with Bob Cooney. So when I come back in 1935 we sort o' picked up where we had left off. In Aberdeen the Communist Party met in what you called the All Power Hall. The locals called it the All Power Hallie. It's still there in Loch Street, an old buildin', dilapidated. It had an old rickety stair. Of course they did their best to paint it up and make it as attractive as possible. The ceiling was liable to collapse at any time so there was a beam supporting it. And on this beam was the slogan 'All Power to the Workers!' It was really funny. So that was the All Power Hallie. Bob Cooney and his brother George used to perform on all the social occasions. It wasnae jist Party members, the public come in an' a'. So Bob and George used to do sketches and things and took the opportunity to put across propaganda.

The National Unemployed Workers' Movement was quite strong in Aberdeen. They had an old church hall, the front entrance of which was in Prince Regent Street. The N.U.W.M got the rent fairly cheap. It was quite a good hall but it was a bit dilapidated. After all, life was a bit dilapidated in these days. People werenae used to the plushy lights and the standards nowadays. But the N.U.W.M. Hall was a focus, people were attracted there. Anybody who had a claim or was in trouble they come to the N.U.W.M. wi' their cases. Johnny Mackie took up the cases for the unemployed.

Johnny was ages wi' me, I suppose. He was a tubby sort o' man and he was flat-footed so Johnny could never ha' gone on the Hunger March: he had enough to do to cross the road as far as walking was concerned. But he had a fatherly kind of appearance. He had left the school at fourteen same as me, so he didnae hae the advantage o' a higher education or anything like that. But he took up the cases for the unemployed and acted as a councillor for the workers. And by gosh he got results. It was petty, the sums involved, but it meant an awfu' lot to the people involved. Johnny wasnae an N.U.W.M. organiser and couldna have gone on a platform. He jist was a worker and he jist had this knack of being able to present people's cases and get an understanding about the whole thing.

On social occasions at the N.U.W.M. Hall it was really remarkable. The jiggin', the dancin', was right popular – many of the best dancers in the town went! Well, ye could say the unemployed got plenty o' time to practice! They got quite a good band together. So these unemployed fellows learned to dance and they could go up the town and at the Palais de Danse they could have held their own wi' the best o' them.

I forget exactly but it was only fourpence or something like that to get in to the N.U.W.M. jiggin'. So it didnae kill anybody if they wanted to dance. As a result we had a lot o' activities and this funded the other activities of the N.U.W.M. Now there was nobody made a fortune: it was jist a mountain o' pennies really, ye were dealin' in coppers. In lots o' ways, while it was hard to come by money you could live on the cheap. Across the road from the hall was a chipper and you could get a fish supper for four old pence – about 1^1/$_2$ new pence. But that was the foundation o' the N.U.W.M. That was why it was so successful in Aberdeen. Now that's where the 1936 Hunger March was organised, naturally in conjunction with the national headquarters. London was really responsible for it but the local people in Aberdeen organised the local contingent.

So there was all kinds o' appeals went out to the trade unions. You've got to remember the background: in the official Labour movement the Citrines and all these were in control, the right wing.[293] The Hunger March, because it was organised by the N.U.W.M was taboo officially. But there was a tremendous sympathy and understandin' on the part o' the workers, because they were living through this depression. They were all affected. If you were in a job you had a tremendous advantage: a grocer in the Co-op – thirty-eight shillins a week. A painter I knew in the Co-op he had £2 a week. He was runnin' an Austin car, petrol was only about 1/6d or 1/4d a gallon. At the same time you were affected by the unemployed because it wis awfu' depressin'. People were people. Ye see, it's difficult to understand but people werena dressed. Ye found the backside was really hangin' oot o' your trousers at times. That wis the sort o' conditions ye were livin' under.

How I got involved in the Hunger March was I come up, as I say, in 1935 to Aberdeen from London and I was engaged in politics. We were fightin' local elections and by-elections. We fought for Helen Crawfurd in North Aberdeen. She polled 12,000 votes against Tony Benn's father, Wedgwood Benn.[294] I was politically active and of course I was active in my trade union branch of the Scottish Painters' Society. It was a progressive branch politically and I got their official backing. Now I got nothing else of course: it was hard times and there really was no funds for anythin' like that. The proposed Hunger March was discussed for quite a while by the branch; it was proposed we participate and I was prepared to be one of the Marchers. So it was agreed and I was elected to go on the March. This was quite contrary to the national policy but it wasnae a rash nor instantaneous sort of decision. And I got a letter that I was the official representative of the Aberdeen painters' branch.There were only two of us on the March officially from a trade union: Tom Rennie was the other one, from I think it was the Transport and General Workers' Union. Of course I was definitely unemployed at that time but of course that wasnae unusual with painters.

We had set up the local March Committee and it was seekin' funds and support. If I remember correctly we got fifteen blankets, lovely black velour blankets, from Grandholm Mills. That's fifty years ago and I still have mine and I still use it on my bed! Ye cannae beat Grandholm cloth. But that was the only provision we really got in the way o' equipment. Later on, when we'd set off on the March from Aberdeen and had got as far as

Cowdenbeath, we were given copies of a typed list of instructions from London about what to take with us on the March and I've still got the paper. It said, 'Suitable boots, overcoat, army valise, blanket, change of under-clothing, plate, mug, knife, fork, spoon, shaving kit, towel, soap, etc.' Well, I had a valise or pack, like a 1914 War thing, wi' my blanket. But we jist wore what we had, wer ordinary clothes. I had a jacket, it wasnae leather it was a plastic sort o' affair. Then I had trousers and a jersey, vest and pants, a fork, knife and spoon, your shavin' gear, and an enamel kind o' mug. I had no pyjamas, I never had pyjamas. When we were kids we jist went to bed wi' wer shirt and that was that. And I had no cap nor cape on the March. Now other fellows some o' them had a bit o' an auld raincoat, well, probably frae a jumble sale or the Castlegate or somewhere. There's no use o' sayin' they had their best clothes on, their working clothes or anything else – jist the clothes they had.

When I heard I was to go on the March I bought myself a new pair o' boots. Now I was fond o' walkin', I always had been. But I thought I'd better do a bit o' practice for the March. So one day I walked tae Dyce and back again – a round trip o' twelve miles. When I come back there wis blisters on my feet. So I had an advantage or a handicap: I started off the Hunger March *with* blisters!

I had a walkin' stick. Oh, it was a very light yin. But tae tell ye the truth it wasnae any assistance as far as walkin' was concerned. Its assistance was it was something in your hand and it swung and you know it served that purpose. I still have that stick today. I didnae purposely go oot and buy it, it just happened to be a stick I'd had. Well, I suppose when the needs must the devil provides! Tae be honest, we were prepared for anythin'. We didnae know what to expect but we widnae ha' been caught unexpected. But the stick I had wasnae a lethal weapon. But still it could have helped to batter through if necessary!

The 1936 March actually started in Aberdeen. There wis one repre-sentative from Inverness and one – Kensitt – from Peterhead. But they come and joined us in Aberdeen. There was about thirty-two o' us set off from Aberdeen – I can't remember the exact figure but it was certainly in excess of thirty.[295] The March set off from the Gallowgate. It was the 26th of September. And we had, oh, hundreds, thousands really – the whole streets were lined. And then of course the Marchers were called to come into line. And I remember I looked round, I was watchin', just weighing up this and that, and I says tae mysel', 'Jesus, I'm bloody sure that half of us'll never make the Brig o' Dee.' That's the local boundary. I didnae give much for my own chances because o' my experiences wi' my boots tae Dyce! But you know what I mean: they were willin' but, oh no, no, there wis fellahs physically caved in after years o' unemployment. They never had been nourished. Yet I would have to eat my words because it's hard to believe but the majority of them all made it to London. So we set off and we were accompanied by the local people right to the Brig o' Dee.

It was a grand day, quite a good day. It wisnae rainin'. We were makin' for Stonehaven, that was wer first overnight stop. That was jist fifteen mile from Aberdeen. When we got to Port Lethen, about a third o' the way, we were caught up wi' the *Daily Worker* photographer. He took the only photograph of this March. [296]

Now as we started off on this journey ye wondered yersel': 'Good God, London!' It could ha' been on the other side of the world as far as you were concerned. It was a helluva distance at that time. We marched 700 miles. Directly to London you could go a lot shorter than that. But the March was organised to such a purpose that it took in the maximum that was possible. That was the reason it was decided upon. So it was considerably more than the direct mileage to London. And what was really remarkable too I think was the response – the amount of people prepared to take part in the March.

We had dates. We had a programme of stopping places and dates drawn up. I still have my copy of it. And we had to make these places on the dates shown because the reception committees had made arrangements for us to be fed at the different places. Now it didna apply in a' the places on the Hunger March. There was no reception committee in Stonehaven when we got there. So of course we had collectors who collected money. We had a bit o' an old car. It didna do anything other than act as a scout, go messages and get data aboot this and find oot that.

When I got on to the March I was elected to the March Council. Of course Bob Cooney, who was leading the March from Aberdeen, was that pleased I was officially from the trade union movement. So I got the honour o' bein' in the front rank o' the March. As I said, I started off wi' blisters and by the time we got to Stonehaven they were pretty raw. But of course as I was in the front rank and it's not for the captain to show any sign of weakness, I had to endure in silence!

At Stonehaven we had a meetin' to get the propaganda. The purpose o' the March was to arouse people to the consciousness of what unemployment really meant. So we had to take every opportunity to get them to respond. After the meetin' I went down to the sea and waded in to try and see if I could ease the feet. They were sore, oh, they were sore. I was very thankful when we got settled into this hut right down at the harbour. It was a dilapidated old hut. It had an open outside stone stair up to the door in the gable end. I think it must have been the loft of the place that we were in really. Anyway when I got there, oh, if you'd heard the groans. Ye see, it was the first stretch, it was only seventeen mile but on the other hand it was quite a walk. So there wis groans and moans. And I couldna find a place to lie doon. They were jist squeezed in as tight as sardines, except that sardines are actually on top o' one another. The room was eighteen feet by twelve feet. We wis a' sleepin' in there, just on the floor – no palliasse nor bags o' straw. We jist lay down on the floor and you didnae strip off but covered yourself wi' your Grandholm blanket. And actually you jist fell asleep wi' sheer exhaustion.

In the High Street in Stonehaven there was a restaurant. We got wer breakfast there. Who provided that I wouldnae rightly know. Stonehaven wasnae a politically conscious place but a rural backwater at that time, a sort o' Tory stronghold. Maybe churches provided the breakfast. In these kind o' areas it was the churches people that kind o' responded. We had to set off fairly early that morning to Montrose. We knew we had a big march in front of us. Seventeen miles had been bad enough but this was goin' to be a real test to go to Montrose because it was something like thirty miles from Stonehaven. They were all determined to carry on. It was fine weather. There was nothing of significance on the March, it was jist a question o' marchin' on and on. The motor went ahead and stopped in a pre-arranged place and boiled up and arranged for our midday bite – that wis sandwiches and a mug o' tea. We were quite enjoyin' oursels until we come to the latter stages and it began to really tell. There was quite a bit o' groanin' and moanin', not in protest but jist sheer physical discomfort. Of course we had wer stops and we had a bit o' a March Council meetin' and decided to ease up the pace a bit. We reached Montrose about eight o'clock at night.

The reception at Montrose was quite good. It was a Labour Party, officially a Labour Party. And that was a remarkable thing. Despite the official opposition on the part of the Labour movement there was all these branches in the different places up and down: what was true of Montrose was also true of many, many others. They did it, defying the national sort o' conception. They organised this reception committees. But of course they linked their efforts wi' churches. Ye see, there was a human aspect. Wherever we went we created an awful stir. There was an emotional sort of upsurge. People were sympathetic and responded.

So we spent the night in the Labour Party Halls in Montrose. We got quite a good meal. And we had a meetin' of course at night. Wherever it was possible we always had meetins at night. That was the purpose of the March of course, tae get the maximum of propaganda, effort and response. I was called upon to speak on mony occasions! I never considered myself a public orator but when you've to step in ye've to do your best. The meetins was confined to the question of unemployment. I mean the privation, the starvation and the horrible conditions that unemployed people lived under, the injustice o' people bein' committed to this way o' life. Oh, it was horrible conditions for working people at that time but the unemployed was excessive like. The message we tried to put across was unemployed or employed your struggle's the same. It was a song that we had, ye see: 'Yer struggle's the same and it can be won, Organise, Mobilise, Join Up!' It was along that kind of line – a joint effort on the part of the organised working class to alleviate unemployment. That was the propaganda and we confined it to that. We didna introduce the Abyssinian question and these sort of things that was going on.

The following day we went on a short trip – twelve or fourteen miles – to Arbroath. That wisnae too bad. When we reached Arbroath I got quite a surprise. Bess – she was to be my wife – had come down from Aberdeen. I couldnae believe my eyes! It was an Aberdeen holiday.[297]

Arbroath to Dundee's not that far – about seventeen mile – so that's where we marched the following day. I had the honour o' leadin' the March on that occasion. I think it was the first rain we really had. But by the time we got to Dundee we had time to be kind o' half dried out again. Oh, but the reception in Dundee! Oh, dear me, the response o' the people! Then they come out. And of course that's what happened in a' the places. The local people come to meet us, och, some o' them would come five, six miles. And actually we was a mighty army even although we started off about thirty strong. Every town ye approached ye'd an army of two or three hundreds really, och, even more than that. And Dundee, especially Dundee, was tremendous. And then right through into the City Square, and, oh, the cheering crowds! It's a terrific boost to your morale. You're slogging along for mile after mile, weary miles, nothing happening but an odd cow looking at you, and then a' this people are acclaiming you!

Now it was a Tory council that was in charge at Dundee at that time, though you had a good Labour movement and good support from the people. But when it come to gettin' accommodation, you know what the Tories did? They put us into a castle! Dudhope Castle wasnae actually a ruin but it hadnae been occupied for a considerable time. The furnishins was all gone, there was no fixtures. There was no lackeys, no wine cellar! I'll not say it was open to the sky but it was dilapidated. And that wis where we were housed in Dundee. [298] I addressed a meetin' in the City Square at night. It wis jist absolutely a mass o' people, a kind o' miniature version o' when ye see the Pope in Rome speakin' tae the crowds. The enthusiasm was there, the thing was flowing with you, it was easy there. It was a great feelin'. It was a tremendous reception.

Dundee was the first rest-day we had. And gie the city council their due, everything was laid on. Ye could go to the baths. Oh, I enjoyed that! It gave you that wee bit o' feelin' o' recreation as against sloggin' on. Oh, the morale was raised! The unemployed was jist in their ordinary rags but somehow or other they seemed tae create a sensation wherever they went: Marchers was gettin' the V.I.P. treatment.

When we left Dundee we got a big influx o' Marchers. The Dundee squad must have been forty or fifty, a big squad. But, oh dear, dear, dear. I mean Aberdeen was bad in a way, we were hit by unemployment. But, oh, Jesus, Dundee was murdered by unemployment. They were murdered wi' malnutrition. They were undersized. They were knock-kneed. Oh, I'm no' casting any aspersions: that was the condition they were in. Two or three miles out, when we left Dundee tae go tae Methil, they started fallin' out. Actually we lost – well, when ye say we lost them we never really had them – but there was a big drop-out on the part o' the Dundee members. The casualty rate wi' the Dundee was terrific that first two or three days, oh, it was a' the casualties in the Dundees. Quite honestly they werena physically fit for it. These fellows had been enthusiastic enough but they didna realise what exactly was entailed. But of course, mind you, there was a good, hard, solid core of them did stay with us.

When we left Dundee to go tae Methil we crossed over on the ferry, and we marched frae Newport right through Fife. I cannae remember now the different places, but Methil, Kirkcaldy. We come in among the minin' community. Well, the minin' places and areas was dilapidated. But, by God, the response o' the folk was amazin' really: rare reception committees and good food. It was amazin' jist how well they fed us. I think it's jist because the occupation o' the miners is so near to the earth – hard work, hard living, they've a human understanding these communities. It was no' only what they provided when these hungry Hunger Marchers come in – because after all, other places provided as well – it was how it was provided, the spirit behind the whole feeling. There was that homeliness aboot the reception, ye felt ye were at hame. Later on when we got into Yorkshire and these other minin' areas and got the same response that's what convinced me it's the occupation o' the miners, the danger and hardship o' their lives makes that fellow feeling. It was magnificent.

I forget exactly where it was in Fife but we met an auld pioneer o' the Labour movement. Bell was his name, I think, and, oh, he was ninety-four or of that age. We got word about him and made a bit o' a diversion. It was a fine day and they had him sittin on a chair outside his home. He was sittin' there waitin' for us to pass. He had been a big, big physical fit man, oh, he'd be well over six feet. And he had a big stick in his hand. As we were coming doon this hill towards where he was sittin' he was wavin' his stick. He was a real pioneer o' the working-class movement. It made oor day and I'm bloody sure it made his day. He thought it was the conquering armies of the working class coming doon the road directly!

I wouldnae say there were many miners or that joined our March in Fife, probably about four or five, I can't remember exactly. I mind somewhere in Fife we didnae get finished marching till about nine o'clock one night. The nights were fair comin' in – it was October by then – about half-past seven. In the gloaming you looked back and you just seen the shadows and the silhouette o' the banner marching right over you. It was like an army moving in the shadows. And we were singing this song:

> From Scotland we are marching
> From shipyard, mill and mine.
> Our scarlet banners raised on high
> We marchers are in line.
> We are a strong determined band,
> Each with a weapon in his hand.
> We are the Hunger Marchers
> Of the proletariat.

We went on to Kirkcaldy and we went through the long town. From Methil tae Kirkcaldy wisnae jis a great long hike but we had to march it at night and, oh, in the name o' God, the streets were cobbled. We marched a' round Kirkcaldy at night-time. Oh, my God, I remember my feet. It was awfu' sair. At Dundee the organising committee had had a whole pile o' boots and shoes. So I had traded in my boots, which were comparatively new, and got a size eight boot, a size bigger. By the time I had reached Dundee my feet had been kind o' seasoned, but wi' the new boots again at Dundee my feet were a problem at Kirkcaldy.

At Kirkcaldy there was a good Labour movement and an official Labour Party sort o' reception committee. We were being well fed. It consisted o' one big meal. Of course we had this provision wi' a drum up wi' tea, oh, about twice a day, and then the big meal at night.[299]

We marched on then tae Edinburgh, across the Forth on the ferry. I'm sorry to say it but Edinburgh oh, thon was the worst of a' the places we were in! It was a Tory-dominated place and it was a cold, cold reception we got officially from Edinburgh. I'm sayin' cold but maybe you could say it was a hot reception: the police were interferin' and guidin' us and directin' us and handlin' us and shovin' us here and shovin' us there. We were bein' controlled all the time and directed. That was what I mean by cold, it wasnae a very wholesome reception.[300]

We were in lodgins somewhere down in Leith. We had a reception committee. And we had a big meetin' in the Usher Hall, absolutely packed. And then we had meetins on the Mound. The local comrades were really good, they tried their best. We had good meetins and a lot o' good propaganda. And Edinburgh was another rest-day. We were there two nights. But the people in Princes Street just looked, there wisnae the standin' cheerin', the warmth o' the response o' the people in Fife or Dundee. In Princes Street we could ha' been selling newspapers and they wouldnae ha' taken much more notice. Oh, there was no question the people o' Edinburgh noticed us wi' our banners. But we were jist like something that jist passed by, that was the kind o' feelin' and response in Edinburgh. Oh, the baths were at our disposal. Officially they laid it on but there was nae enthusiasm. The facilities were there but there wasnae a real welcome like. I think the police were saying, 'Well, we'll get rid o' them as soon as we can.'

Before we left Edinburgh there was one good thing that happened; a change o' leadership. Now whereas it was masel' and Bob Cooney and Kensitt o' Peterhead on the front till we had reached Edinburgh, now there was a rehash of the whole control committee. So there was now the joint leadership: Harry McShane, Alex Moffat, Davie Chalmers and masel'. That formed the first row o' the March and that was the formation right till we reached London. Alex Moffat was an awfy nice fellah, one of the finest fellows that ever I really met. I liked Alex.

And another thing that happened at Edinburgh was wer soup kitchen. The local comrades gave us an old car, and where the back seat would ha' been they inserted a household boiler. I can't remember how they fired it but this was a mobile kitchen we used on the road. The idea was it charged on ahead o' us and then they stoked it up and fired it. Obviously, it took a few hours to get the water boiling, I'm quite sure o' that. But it made an awful difference to the March because after we left Edinburgh, oh dear, dear, that's when we were really on wer own and when we really had hard, hard times.

There was quite a number o' Marchers joined us at Edinburgh. When we left Edinburgh the March would ha' been about 200 strong. We didnae recruit any more after that really. That was the final make-up. The first stop was Gorebridge. Oh, there was no reception committee at Gorebridge. We were billeted in a scouts' hut. It was bad enough at Stonehaven but now them that had been on the March from Aberdeen had got accustomed to knowing if there was any advantage to get into a certain corner. So some o' the newcomers were scratching their head and saying, 'Well, where the hell do you sleep? – What do you do?' What was remarkable about Gorebridge was, oh dear, it was one o' the coldest nights. I remember wakin' and sayin', 'Oh, in the name o' God!' It wis freezin'. You could see daylight through the floor. The boards had shrunk. It wis good the scouts gave us the hut but we might ha' been as well sleepin' in the open really. That was my birthday the day we reached Gorebridge, the 6th October.

At Gorebridge one o' the members o' our Aberdeen contingent broke down. That was just sheer exhaustion. Actually in Edinburgh he had been to the doctor. So we got word by the time we reached Gorebridge and he had to leave the March for medical reasons. He was the first really to drop out from the Aberdeen contingent. His name was John Wilkie. He wept like a child really, he was that disappointed. His physique wasnae up to it. Now Bob Cooney had left us at Edinburgh. The Communist Party said they wanted him for other things. Poor Bob! He'd ha' loved jist to have carried on tae London. But, well, in a struggle individual likes and dislikes arenae of no consequence'.

When we left Gorebridge that wis the start of our lean times. They really started then. Now we had a big march to Galashiels. Oh, we walked and walked, it seemed to be never endin'. It was quite late at night afore we got to Galashiels. And in Galashiels we had a bit o' trouble. There was an effort to get a reception committee really goin' but it didnae get very far. And the local council were Public Assistance Committee and a' that. I jist don't remember exactly where we did sleep. Oh, the response o' the public was very good. They were sympathetic and concerned right enough. But right through from Galashiels tae Hawick tae Langholm,[301] Carlisle, Alston, Middleton-in-Teesdale, Barnard Castle, Richmond – oh, that was a real Tory place, Richmond – Ripon and Harrogate, right until we reached Leeds – oh no, no, no!

It was lovely country, oh, it was beautiful! And it was lovely weather. And ye ken the mounds and the hills was like a great velvet pad. And the changes o' colours o' the autumn: oh, if you'd seen thon, it really was awfy impressive. But, oh dear, dear, dear, there was no habitation. Ye could walk for miles. There was no life, no customers, no collections, and there was no food. Ye see, that was the problem that was worryin' us really. It certainly was worryin' the March Council. We were really hungry. As a matter of fact

we had to send oot an appeal to the country. Supplies run oot a'thegither.
We were the best part of seven or eight days on that particular route before
we got back into habitation. We sent oot an SOS and what a response we
got. The Aberdeen Committee responded and so did the rest o' Scotland.
A truck arrived, it was tinned stuff and a' sort of food, and augmented the
rations.

I remember three things aboot these days. It was the climbing up these
hills, up hill and down dale. It wasnae rough goin', the roads were quite
reasonable. Well, as we swept down one hill and went up on to the other
side here's a Rolls Royce comin'. It come and went past. More for
something to do than anything else we gave it an 'Oh!!!' – a real raspberry
and shoutin'. He got past maybe two or three hundred yards and he drew
up and stood up in his car and waved. Jock Winton, one of the official
collectors, away and caught him. And he got a pound! The boy gave him a
pound! That was right in the middle o' the desert, as it were, so we got a
good drink of water!

Then Jock Winton. We walked 750 miles thereaboot tae London but
Jock must have done another 300 besides because he'd a' these other
journeys. There were other collectors besides, but Jock Winton and
McDonald were the two that really put their heart and soul into it, and Jock
in particular. You would see a farmhouse right away over there, a mile there
and a mile back again. And Jock would come back wi' a bloody hen. Now
he swore blind that he was given it. He never come back empty-handed,
and he's rattlin' his collectin' box.

And then the soup kitchen was in operation. Paddy the cook had
joined us at Edinburgh. He was actually an Englishman. He'd been a
seafaring man, his cooking had probably been on trawlers. And Paddy had
one sort of all-in recipe: everything went into the pot. I don't suggest for a
minute that the hen went in with the feathers, but that was the sort of thing.
Whatever we got – going through the Borders the local butcher would gie
ye a chunk o' meat, a farmer would gie ye potatoes and grains – Paddy put
them a' in the boiler. I tell you, by God it was good to get a real hot meal!
You were so hungry and so active.[302]

When we had crossed over the Border, well, of course being Scots
they made the most o' the actual crossing – a conquering army come across
wi' the banners wavin'! Now we were still on politically virgin ground. It
was an area that had never been moved before in that sense. And we come
right down into England and right through that whole area. When we come
to Leeds that was where our hunger and hardship ended. Leeds has – or had
at that time – a tremendous Jewish community. An awful lot of them was
interested in the Left politics. And, by gosh, it was a wonderful reception in
Leeds. It was a bit like the response o' the Dundee people. You seemed to
be surrounded by people. We caused tremendous stir. It made you feel
awfu' important like, a' the people that was interested. Of course the feeding
was jist overwhelming. I think the tables had cloths, and we had individual
chairs: you werena squattin' on the ground, ye werena lyin' on the floor, ye

were sittin' doon in a civilised fashion. Ye had forks and knives and ye had to recall your manners! And they gave us clothes – the boys were a' getting new trousers: after all, their boots and their claes wis, well, they were sleepin' in them, walkin' in them. So we got newly dressed in Leeds. Leeds was the one place that really made a tremendous difference.

Then we went through Wakefield and Barnsley. From Wakefield to Barnsley, sure it's not very far. But it poured o' rain. We were absolutely soakin'. When we got to Barnsley the miners' wives had us stripped off and they had towels! They must have organised it when they seen the weather because they couldnae ha' had all that towels normally there. They had pit oot a call for towels. So we were a' rubbed in this towels and then we were set a great big dinner down to us. We just had the towels round about us: it was a wee bit kind o' embarrassin'. And they had big roarin' fires and they put wer claes there and dried oor claes. The lovely feed we got – I always remember Barnsley. Noo that's a minin' area: these people were used tae emergencies and copin' wi' circumstances. They dinnae panic, these people. They've a practical approach. And by God it was great, it was really good.

Rotherham wasna that far from Barnsley. Well, most o' these places were comparatively easy as far as distance for marchin' was concerned. The really big journeys were behind us. The lean times were really behind us, and there were quite a number o' reception committees. Rotherham was a Labour-controlled council at that time. Now they had a different attitude. What they did, they fragmented us! They laid on baths and cinemas and we had a rest-day. But the thing was this, we was outmanoeuvred. Of course I'm speakin' as a member o' the March Council. We was wantin' the propaganda value, the maximum value out of it. That's what we were after. We got no meetin'! And no march through the town at all! We was outmanoeuvred! So that was Rotherham. That was a Labour council.

Then we got on to Sheffield. It was quite a big centre but there was a local situation, this one was wanting this and this one that. So what happened was Councillor Fletcher, a Labour councillor and a businessman, he stepped in and paid for the reception and for the meal for the whole March. It was a bit like Leeds: a real reception in some official place and real waitresses servin' ye.

Then we come to Chesterfield. What happened all through the March was the local comrades come out and acquainted us with the local situation. And we always had a meeting a mile or two out and weighed up the whole situation and discussed our tactics. So they told us it was market day in Chesterfield but that we werenae goin' tae be permitted to go through the High Street where the market was held. Well, it was put to the Marchers and the Marchers decided that they were goin' to go through. By this time there would be 200-odd on the March. So we formed up and jist marched in. Right across the road was about fifty policemen, a double row o' them. So we jist ppphhhhhhhh – jist swept the police aside. That was a real victory for us. The applause that we got from the people – it was market day and the place was crowded! There was applause and cheerin': the whole crowd was with us. As a gesture, later that night the chief constable come and gave us two pound and he also donated leather for the shoemaker to repair the boots. We had a cobbler on the March an' a' and he used to patch up, oh, rough and ready, the shoes, soled them or heeled them.

In the main the whole conception o' the police was, 'Get them in and get them out as quick as possible and withoot any fuss.' But then other policemen had adopted a diversionist, deroute-them policy. I mind one particular day we were bein' guided by the police round this way. We looks across and here's a small town over here. I cannae recall the name o' the town but Harry McShane says, 'Goodness me! Halt! About turn!' Now we added three mile to wer walk. But there's one thing : we went through that town and the people knew we were there and knew where we were goin'. That was a tactic of the police, a' this kind o' tricks that they played. As a matter o' fact, as we got further and further south they become more provocative, particularly in Tory areas. And quite honestly we nearly reached open conflict on two or three occasions. We were really prepared for battle at Chesterfield like. I suppose it was a sense of relief it went through as easy as it did. But we were expectin' to get the batons and naturally we'd ha' been fightin' back. The poles o' the banners would ha' been used in that way.

The Aberdeen contingent had a banner. It said, 'Aberdeen to London. United against the Means Test.' It was carried all the time except if we were out in the country and out o' contact wi' the general public, then the banner was rolled up. But the banner always come out two or three miles from our destination and then the same when we were leavin'. It was just a very plain, ordinary kind o' banner: ye couldnae carry a great wind-resisting thing.

What was lacking at first was music. The nearest approach we got to that was a gazooka, a toy submarine sort of thing that you hummed into. Oh, ah forget just where it would have been when we started getting these things. But anyway we had this gazooka band and that helped a lot. And then it must have been in Fife or somewhere thereabout miners came in and formed a kind o' fife band. You couldn't ask the fellows to play and carry their kit so as a concession their kit was put in that truck we had. One day we were marching along, the band in front of us. This bandsman hadnae been lookin' and he just carried on marchin' by hissel' away from the rest o' us. But the thing was this: there was not a sound, not a note, coming from him! He had joined the band and had been impersonating them. Next day he was back carrying his kit!

Och, there wis a' kinds o' songs the boys sang on the March. They would strike up tunes and hummin' songs, popular tunes o' the day. And then of course a lot o' revolutionary songs, *The Internationale*, and:

Our March is nearing done
With the setting of the sun.

We didnae get that jingoist sort o' thing associated wi' the First War, *Pack up your Troubles*.

Oh, they would never stay dumb. There was whistlers and there was jokers. It was lively – short of occasions when you were goin' through the drivin' rain, when everybody was more or less muted and it was heads down and just get on. But otherwise there was all kinds o' larkin' and jokin' – efter all they werenae marchin' like the Guards. We didna really march in step. We prevailed upon them to try and march into a town in style from about half a mile out.

Oh no, you couldnae hae a crowd o' fellahs thegither without, och, fun and chaffing and all sorts of cairry-ons. I remember Joe Craib at Chesterfield. Joe was rotund. He wasn't a good advert for a Hunger March, being so fat. But Joe was a jovial character. He wasn't the brightest fellah you would have met in your life but he was a rare likeable fellow. But when we were in Chesterfield workhouse we were in the cells. It was just one long passage and real bars on the doors, and this dim lights and it was lights-out at nine o'clock. Joe had fell asleep in his cell and the boys crowded in and started singing hymns, slow and harmonising. Joe woke up and, oh, the expression on his face! He thought he was away to heaven wi' the singing o' the hymns and the soft music.

But at that workhouse we had done about fifteen miles that day and, oh, there was awfy reluctance to give us accommodation. Finally they decided to give us the workhouse. So the workhouse master he gave us a mug of cocoa and a slice of bread and marg. And then the lights wis oot at nine o'clock. And in the morning we got a mug of tea and we got a slice of bread and one sausage and that was the meal. And we had aboot twenty miles to march on that.

The Aberdeen contingent were essentially all unemployed. Now I admit as time went on we realised that we had one or two who were there just for the ride. It was something to sort of occupy their time. Mind you, we didnae have trouble wi' them. They stuck it because they had nowhere else to go, they jist would have starved – especially goin' over the Borders and down through that part of the country. But the bulk was jist unemployed fellows that were seekin' to do something about it. The determination was there: no humans would endure the privation and hardship and the tremendous physical effort unless ye had conviction! It was a conscience conviction. It wasnae a question o' being political in any sort o' party sense. It was a question that they felt there was a necessity to do something and this was something that they were doin'. And I think they felt quite proud o' doin' it really. They were standard bearers, I suppose. They kind o' felt they were on a kind o' crusade. There was something really drove them on. That was right through the March. Even the one or two that were there for the ride they never caused trouble. They maybe werenae particularly enthusiastic as far as demonstratin' went. But they werena trouble-makers and werenae sabotoors. And I'm quite sure even while they were there they felt they were really part of something that was really needing done.

Out o' the thirty in the Aberdeen contingent I don't think there would be any more than six who were Communists. No, there wasnae a lot o' Communists. I think there could ha' been members of the I.L.P. there, but they werenae there officially like, on behalf of the I.L.P. I wouldn't say there was anybody frae the Labour Party as such, not officially. No, it was jist about the six members of the Communist Party and the others were jist all genuinely unemployed. Bob Cooney was of course a leadin' member o' the Communist Party in Aberdeen and in Scotland at that particular time. Now Kensitt from Peterhead was a member of the Party. Kensitt was nominated as a Communist candidate for the local Peterhead council. So he come on the March. And it was a funny thing that he had never worked for years and then he got a telegram and here was an offer of a job! It was obviously a ploy o' the authorities, the kind o' things they do. So the March Council had tae be wise and realise we had to free him so that he could go back because o' this, to take up this job. I don't know how long the job lasted. That wis jist beyond Edinburgh he got the telegram. So that wis the authorities gettin' him out o' the March when he was a Communist candidate: if he didnae come back he was a workshy, he wasna interested in work.

While we had the longest march and the best organised march – it was over 700 miles from Aberdeen – we got the least publicity because it clashed wi' the Jarrow March. Ellen Wilkinson, the M.P., was leadin' their march. They had official backin': the corporation was behind them, the whole Labour movement was behind them. And they got issued wi' capes, groundsheets, ex-army surplus from the '14-'18 War. We didnae have that, we'd no ground sheets or nothin' like that. We were comin' doon the centre o' the country. The Jarrow March was doon there direct to London. Now they did 250 mile. And good luck to them – I mean the fellows did well. But it was only 250 mile. But they got tremendous publicity: the Movietone News, the Gaumont Newsreel, they all followed the Jarrow March. Ours didnae have the official backin'. It was organised by the N.U.W.M., Wal Hannington, Harry Pollitt, and they were Communists – in other words, it was Communist inspired. That was the interpretation placed on it. The remarkable thing was in many o' these places you were through there was joint reception committees, Labour Party members, no party members at all – anybody. People responded. Church people: a parson on one occasion was responsible for givin' us a ten-gallon churn o' milk. Now the Jarrow March had the official backin' o' the Labour movement and the powers that be. And ever since then, whenever there is any reference to unemployment or hunger marches, what you see on the telly is the Jarrow March. It's always the Jarrow March. Now we were filmed once if I recall right jist north of St Albans, only once. So there is on record a film of our March but I've only ever seen it once on the telly.

When we were filmed jist north of St Albans, what happened was we were marching on and we looked to our right. It was open country. About two or three miles away we could see this mass. We had expected them and we were on the look-out for them and likewise they were on the look-out for us. We were the Scottish East March and they were the Scottish West March. As they approached and approached and approached, oh, the cheerin' and the counter-cheerin', the flag wavin'! We'd probably marched for an hour, the best part o' five or six miles as the roads we were on converged. That was the West o' Scotland linkin' up wi' the East o' Scotland. Oh, it was a tremendous sight. Peter Kerrigan was leadin' the West, Harry McShane and Alex Moffat were leadin' the East. We must ha' been about 800 strong or probably nearer a thousand, I should imagine. It's a sight you would never forget.[303]

The final place was Willesden. This was the sort o' assembly point for the final march into London. And because we had been the longest on the road, the East o' Scotland got the honour o' leadin' the March into London. It was followed by the West o' Scotland and so on. We all knew what was expected of us. Everybody was keyed up. Everybody then was marchin' in step, maybe not like guardsmen, but they really marched. And, oh, thousands o' people! The crowds o' people on the pavement were jist simply continuous right through. They werenae jist passive: there was the cheerin' and the response frae the people.

Now Paddy the cook had died on the March, away aboot Chesterfield. He was taken to hospital and there he died o' pneumonia. We got notified that Paddy was dead. So N.U.W.M. headquarters sent us this banner, a tribute to Paddy who gave his life for the cause of the working class. So of course we had this banner wi' us when we into London. And that caused a tremendous impression – oh, the hats a' come off.

In Hyde Park there were jist a mass o' humanity. There wis different platforms and the demonstration was bein' addressed by this one and that one, national figures. I was on the platform with Sir Stafford Cripps and S. O. Davies.[304] This was an official Labour Party rally in support o' the March and I was delegated to go as a guest speaker. I was jist to make a ten-minute contribution. But, oh, the reception! I had never experienced onything like that before.

Then of course the activities in London was occupyin' them. We had calling on your M.P. at the House o' Commons and all that sort of thing. Ye ken, that reception jist made it all worth while really. It made an awfy impression on me anyway. I think the other fellows must have felt the same. The Hunger March was one o' the highlights of my life really. There was conviction behind it, ye see. There was a real purpose. We did gain. There was changes in the Means Test and there was concessions the Government did make as a result o' the March.[305] It was the March that generated the public enthusiasm, the public awareness and the public conviction. The Government at that time was mair conscious o' what the public were doin', what the public were sayin', and they responded to that. I never thought that fifty years after, the same problem would still be with us. Oh, the forces o' evil are strong, aye, they're cunnin' and they're formidable. But we've had the Welfare State since that time. We've had a better education. We've had better housin'. We've bathrooms: we didnae have bathrooms when I was a boy. A new generation has been born and they've been born with a different conception o' life. And I jist don't think that these people are goin' tae accept any lowerin' o' that standard.

We was taken back home by train from London. It was the railway unions that provided the train, I'm nearly sure that was it. The other comrades dropped off at the different places but when we finally got to Aberdeen we got a great reception. It was stirrin' times really. It was a question of 'Form up' again and we marched through the centre of the town to Beaton's Ballroom, just across the road from where the March actually started from, seven weeks previously. We had covered in excess of 700 miles. I had kept a diary on the March and I had the mileage between each point recorded. Unfortunately, the diary got lost: a friend o' mine was very interested in it and sent it to the *Morning Star* a few years ago and it got lost.

When I went on the March I had been staying with my mother. I had been married two and a half years but my first wife died in 1935. As I mentioned, Bess, who was to be my second wife, had come down to Arbroath for the day when the March was there on the way to London. From that time we were writing letters to each other till the March reached London, and she kept all my letters. There's not a lot of sentiment in the letters. We thought we were hardened fighters for the working class at that time and we didnae indulge in too much sentiment, although we had genuine feelings for one another. Most of my letters were an apology for being short of time. Being on the March Council I would do the marching then I had to supervise. I only did my share, to see that the Marchers were fed and had somewhere to lie down. You had all these jobs to do and then even afore you got your meals sometimes and even when you were having your meal there was a March Council meeting called to consider the next day's activities. But the letters describe quite a number of the experiences and I think I've described to you pretty well mostly what was in the letters.

After the Hunger March, the next stage was to go to the Spanish War. I volunteered for the Spanish War. Well, Bess had waited through the Hunger March and had fully supported me going on the March. Now I was going away to Spain. She said if I went to Spain that's it. So love triumphed over political conviction! We were married the following year. Och, I don't regret it really, because we had a remarkable life together. Worldly wise we never achieved very much but we had a tremendous companionship.

David Anderson

I left Oakbank School in Aberdeen in 1928 when I was sixteen year old and I joined the army. I joined because of unemployment at that particular time. Oakbank School was a reformatory. I got put there when I was twelve year old for stealing out of this baker's van.

I was born and brought up in the slums of Aberdeen. I was born in the Shiprow and brought up in Jack's Brae and Denburn which was slums then. My mother died when I was seven years old. My oldest sister was sixteen when she left home and got married. And my brother joined the army as soon as he was sixteen.

I was left with my father and he was just a drunkard. I was left to make my own breakfast when I was seven years old. I went to Skene Street school and I didn't feel out of place there. I mean I had a retentive memory when I was a kid. I could read over a poem and learn it and I had no difficulty at school. I was a year in front, I was always the youngest in the class. Before I was twelve years old I passed for the Central School Higher Grade.

As I said, when I was at Skene Street I didn't feel nothing. I was ragged, like. I had an old jersey that had been white once upon a time. I tried to dye it blue and it came out mottled colours. It was torn at the sleeves. I goes to the Central School and I became an oddity right away. All the kids turned up in their nice ties and the girls were in nice dresses and here was me with an old jersey and my trousers all patched at the back. I used to try and overcome this inferiority complex with bravado. For the first time in my life I am at the front seat for observation. And then I was sent to the Trust.

The Trust in Aberdeen was where the poor had to go and get meals. You had to clock in. It was just benches. You went down for your breakfast. You got watery porridge and skimmed milk and that was your breakfast. Then for your dinner you went down, you got a sheaf of bread and a plate of soup made without meat, just vegetables. And I used to hate this place. It went against my grain.[306] Instead of that I used to go round the new market and steal out of bakers' vans. Of course I got caught, and that was when I was put to Oakbank School, the reformatory.

You weren't allowed out during the week. You were allowed out on a Saturday about two-thirty but you had to be in by seven. You got a certain amount of marks and the better marks you had you got out till nine o'clock. So Saturday afternoon and evening was the only time you got out, apart from sometimes we were out with the school pipe band. We went to all the games like Fochabers, Craigellachie, played at the matches on a Saturday, and things like that.

But that was what I done, I joined the army. I was a Regular in the Gordon Highlanders from November1928 to November 1935. Out of that time I was in Ireland for about a year and from Ireland I went to India. I was in India for about three and a half years. For most of my time in India I was stationed on the North West frontier. I was in Lundi Kotal, seven miles from Afghanistan, on the Khyber Pass a year and a half, I think, and then I came down to Peshawar for about another two years.

I became interested in politics before I came out of the army because of things that had happened, things that I had seen, things that had influenced me in quite a number of ways. When I came back home I was twenty-three years old and I thought that a person who was unemployed was simply unemployed because he didn't want to work. But I changed my opinion because I tried hard for ten months to get a job and didn't succeed.

I was a member of the Gordon Highlanders' Association. We all paid two guineas to join the Association. The prime purpose of the Association was to find us employment on our return to civilian life. The Association's headquarters was in King Street, Aberdeen, and there was very seldom a day passed that I wasn't there seeking employment. Eventually, through the Association, I got a job as a waiter at £2 a week, for a fortnight, at the camp of 5th/7th battalion of the Gordon Highlanders at Inverurie.

At that camp was a Colonel Bruce who was the owner of the Adamant works in Aberdeen which made precast stone and things like that for the building trade. I approached the Colonel and asked him if he could give me employment after the Camp was finished. He gave me a card he signed for me to take to his manager. I went to the manager and the first thing he asked me was what I had done before. Of course I told him I had just finished seven years in the army. He just gave a laugh and said, 'Oh no, no, you'd be no good. Your hands would be too soft.' I practically begged him to consider giving me a job, but 'No, no, no.' But I still hung around and persisted and he said, 'Look, come with me,' and he took me around the works. There were fellahs there on the precast stone that was being scrubbed with scrubbing brushes. They were using the scrubbing brush to clean the stone of sand and to me it looked definitely a hard job and would be hard on the hands. But at the same time I still wanted a job. I said, 'Look, can I be given a chance?' And he says, 'No, no chance at all.' That was it. I had to leave.

It was round about this time I began to go to meetings with my brother. My brother had been in the army too. He was seven years older than I was and he'd done seven years as a Regular before me. He'd come home and faced unemployment. He'd got jobs here and there but he had experienced unemployment for quite a long time too. So he and I went to different meetings of different political parties. At the Belmont cinema we went to a meeting of the Communist Party. The main speaker was

Pete Kerrigan. And to me what Peter Kerrigan had to say was just sheer common sense. And it was then that I joined the Communist Party, round about August 1936.

It was just after this when I was called up to the army to the Class 'A' reserve. There was trouble with the Arabs and Jews in Palestine. In October we went over to Palestine. All the kilted regiments went to the West Yorkshire Regiment and I was with a platoon of the West Yorkshire Regiment billeted in a Jewish colony just outside Tiberias. After approximately three months the trouble was quelled and we returned to civilian life.[307]

Now prior to going over there, we were informed by our commanding officer of the West Yorkshire Regiment that all those in employment were not to worry because their employers had been approached and their jobs would be kept open for them. For all those who were unemployed the Government would do everything to find employment when we returned home. When we did return home each of us who were unemployed got a big form to fill up what sort of occupation we would care for. I filled in for the Post Office, prison wardens, and jobs of that nature where no real arduous labour was required. But there was no response.

When we were going over to Palestine in October 1936 we had had a ship's newsletter posted every day and we got all the information about the war in Spain, the people in overalls fighting against the Fascists. Despite the fact that I had no real political convictions I had developed a hatred of Hitler's methods. So when I came back from Palestine and didn't get a job, I made application to join the International Brigade in Spain. I left Aberdeen on the 12th February 1937 and arrived in Figueras in Spain two days later.[308]

I came back from Spain about late October or early November 1938. I was a member of the Communist Party but I didn't feel I was a Communist when I went to Spain. But I was a convinced Communist when I came back. And naturally the first people I went to when I came back was the Communist Party headquarters and took up activities. At that particular time we were active in a great many ways. Anything that cropped up I was prepared to take my part in it and do the utmost I possibly could.

Now just shortly after I came back from Spain the Hunger March had been proposed and I volunteered to go on the March. It was in November 1938. It was from Aberdeen to Edinburgh. We started off wi' about thirty-four or thirty-five from Aberdeen. That was includin' the ones that came frae further north – Inverness, Elgin, Fraserburgh, Peterhead and so on. Well, I just went along with the others. Then we made our way to Stonehaven and were joined by a couple more. We stopped the first night at Stonehaven. Everything was organised perfectly. And then on to Inverbervie, Montrose, Dundee, and so on.[309]

It was the Co-operative that provided most of the hospitality as far as we were concerned. They put us up in premises that they had. Every one of us had a blanket along with us and we slept on the floor. But the Co-operative provided meals. The rest of the meals – intermediate like – were provided by one lad, Neil Kane, from Aberdeen who had a car. He used to speed into the next town and get organised, get a tea-urn filled up and sandwiches provided and then he'd come back and meet us on the road. Actually, we ate better than we would have been able to at home.[310]

What surprised me most was the organisation. It must have been prepared beforehand, because everywhere we stopped we were met and accommodation, food, everything was provided. Every night where we halted we were met by people who had taken part in the organisation of the March. I don't think there was anything, apart from the marching, that was bad. Well, the marching wasn't bad either. We covered about seventeen or eighteen mile every day. I had been accustomed to marching as a Regular soldier and I didn't take it too bad. But some of the fellows must have found it pretty hard to carry on. But apart from their feet everybody seemed to put up with the March no bother at all.

Dave Campbell was the leader of the March from Aberdeen. Dave Campbell was a great speaker. I enjoyed listenin' to him and I learnt a lot from him. When we got to Dundee, Stalker went co-leader with Dave Campbell right until we got to Edinburgh. Stalker was a fairly old person. I'd reckon he'd be well on in his fifties. The Marchers were young, in their twenties and thirties.[311]

Stalker was a member of the Communist Party, I think. I would say maybe about a third, maybe less, were members of the Communist Party or I.L.P. or Labour Party. But the biggest majority were people who were out o' work and were wantin' to do something to push on the fight for work. That was the main thing that they were marchin' for, was to fight for work. It may be that some had political affiliation, I don't know. But I don't think there were that many that were.

Well, we stopped at Dundee and we gathered quite a lot more from Dundee. We got crowds turning out to welcome us everywhere we went. I think Dundee was the biggest crowd we met. But everywhere we stopped we were met with friendliness and help. Not great masses of people but sufficient to take notice. We'd quite a crowd in Dundee that watched the March.

I had played a penny whistle, a tin whistle, when the contingent was smaller coming down from Aberdeen. And then when we got to Dundee we'd a good meeting of the Communist Party there and somebody provided a set of bagpipes. So I played from Dundee to Edinburgh on the bagpipes. I didn't play all the time! But I played as much as I could. And then in between, if I wasn't playing there was singing. Everybody sang, oh, different tunes, revolutionary songs the most. They sang *The Internationale, The Red Flag*. They sang any other song that was a marchin' song – *A Long Way to Tipperary,* everything was mixed up. I mean, after all's said and done everyone wasn't revolutionaries or Communists. They were people that were wantin' to find work and they were marching to find work and you can't say that they were all revolutionaries.[312]

The object of the March was to protest against the unemployment that was rife in Scotland at that particular time. It was an attempt to rouse the public to the fact that there was something that could be done about it. When we got to Edinburgh we formed outside the Government offices and we put in our protest. A deputation went forward to speak on behalf of the unemployed. I didn't go on the deputation. We just remained outside. Dave Campbell was one of the deputation and there were a few more, from Glasgow, Dundee, and others.[313]

It was the last Hunger March that took place because it wasn't long after that that the War started. Looking back on it now, well, my thought is that any fight at all that is for the advancement of the working class never disappoints me even although it meets in failure. We must go on fighting, that is the only thing that we can do.

Well, I came back home from Edinburgh with Neil Kane in this little car of his. The rest came back with the train. Neil was the fellow that went on beforehand on the March with this wee two-seater car. There was a wee space in the back where you could sit. Well, I went back with him and I was sorry about it because it was four or five hours and it was an open car, a sort of sports model. I was frozen stiff!

Well, when the 1939 War broke out, not long after that Hunger March, I went back into the Gordon Highlanders. I spent six weeks in France and then I was at the depot of the Gordon Highlanders in Aberdeen for about two years. I was an instructor there. Then I transferred in 1941 over to the R.A.F. Regiment and I was an instructor there for the rest of the War. I had a very, very easy time during the War. After the War I was an assistant warden at the community centres in Aberdeen and then I worked in the building trade as a bricklayer until I retired.

Notes

192. John Monaghan was a member of the deputation that interviewed Scottish Office officials on the February 1932 Hunger March to Edinburgh. Scottish Record Office (hereafter S.R.O.) DD 10/246/1.

193. Ishbel MacDonald (1903-), eldest daughter of Ramsay MacDonald, acted as his hostess, his wife having died in 1911.

194. The N.U.W.M. office was at 183 George Street, but correspondence in the Scottish Record Office shows that in 1932 and 1933 Harry McShane was writing from an N.U.W.M. office at 69 Ingram Street, in 1935 (Scottish March Committee) from 167 Albion Street, and in 1938 from 29 Waterloo Street. S.R.O. DD 10/246/1, DD 10/246/2, DD 10/250, and DD 10/252.

195. Bob McLennan (1906-1981), assistant general secretary, 1955-61, of the Electrical Trades Union, was assistant organiser to Harry McShane in the Scots contingent on the 1932 national Hunger March to London. Harry McShane and Joan Smith, *Harry McShane: No Mean Fighter* (London, 1978), 188.

196. Tommy Flynn was killed at Cordoba in April 1937. Bill Alexander, *British Volunteers for Liberty: Spain 1936-1939* (London, 1982), 267.

197. P. Kingsford, *The Hunger Marchers in Britain, 1920-1940* (London, 1982), 196, presents a somewhat different account of the interview with Ishbel MacDonald by the women Marchers: 'They angrily rejected a suggestion from her that unemployed women in the textile and clothing trades and in office work should try domestic service. There was nothing more to offer and nothing promised.'

198. Glen Lee tunnel, work on which began in 1932, was part of a hydro-electricity scheme.

199. James Stewart, chairman of the Fife miners' Reform Union, died 1937.

200. Robert W. Service (1874-1958), author, educated in Glasgow, served apprenticeship with the Commercial Bank of Scotland, emigrated to Canada and settled on Vancouver Island, travelled extensively in Yukon.

201. There were separate contingents from Tyneside and Teesside, Lancashire and

Yorkshire, each with its own route. Wal Hannington, *Unemployed Struggles 1919-1936* (London, 1977), 287; S.R.O. DD 10/248.

202. It was not Nine Edge Street but Nynehead Street London County Council Centre, on the borders of Deptford and New Cross, where the Scots contingent was billeted and fed free of charge by the L.C.C. *Kentish Mercury*, 2 Mar. 1934.

203. Kielder was one of the Ministry of Labour instructional centres. See also below, note 313.

204. Randolph G. E. Wemyss, of Wemyss Castle, Fife, died 1908.

205. Dudley Stuart (1861-1939), sheriff substitute of Fife and Kinross at Cupar.

206. *The Spark* was published from July 1925 to *c*. 1932, until October 1930 as the organ of the Methil Branch of the Communist Party and thereafter as that of the militant section at Wellesley colliery, Methil. Most issues survive. The pit paper of the Militant Section, Muiredge Workers, Buckhaven, was titled *The Fan*, and four issues survive for March-May 1931. Though it may have been a different paper from the one mentioned by Hugh Sloan, *The Pan Bolt* was issued by the Peeweep Pit (Communist Party) Cell, Lumphinnans, and a single copy survives for August 1930. See I. MacDougall (ed.), *A Catalogue of some Labour Records in Scotland and some Scots Records outside Scotland* (Edinburgh, 1978), 131.

207. Thomas Kirkcaldy, a miner, was first elected to Fife County Council in 1929 and represented Buckhaven on it for many years.

208. William 'Mosie' Murray (1898-), fought in the 1914-18 War, was victimised for two years after the 1921 miners' lock-out, and after the 1926 miners' strike remained unemployed for five years, living on £1.20 a week for himself, his wife and two children, until he became a street-sweeper in Leven. He was branch secretary for fifty-one years of the National Union of General and Municipal Workers and fought cases for the unemployed as union representative on the local tribunal at the Labour Exchange at Leven, where he still lives.

209. Jimmy Hope (1890-1948), professional footballer with Raith Rovers, 1911-13, and Stoke City, 1913-15, returned to work in the pits in Fife in 1915. He was Fife County Councillor for West Wemyss and Coaltown of Wemyss from 1938 until his death.

210. Freddie Tennant, died 1987 age seventy-four, was Scottish flyweight champion boxer in 1938.

211. Philip Snowden (1864-1937), a leading figure in the I.L.P., Chancellor of the Exchequer in the Labour Governments, 1924 and 1929-31, and in the 'National' Government, 1931. The Snowden pint had, as Hugh Sloan puts it, 'a waist on it' and sold a penny cheaper than the standard pint.

212. Arthur Nicoll returned home from Spain for medical treatment after the battle of Brunete in 1937, then went back to Spain, taking his younger brother with him, and became commander of the anti-tank unit of the British Battalion in the International Brigades.

213. Bill McGuire went to Spain with Tom Clarke. I. MacDougall, *Voices from the Spanish Civil War* (Edinburgh, 1986), 57, 58.

214. This march to Cupar was almost certainly the one that arrived there on 26 January 1932. Its object, as Hugh Sloan goes on to say, was to protest against the Means Test. The points put by the deputation from the Marchers to Fife County Council were: that it should not co-operate with the Means Test; its Public Assistance Committee should make up cuts in unemployment benefits; work schemes or able-bodied relief, equal to the Labour Exchange scales of benefit in September 1931, should be provided irrespective of incomes of relatives; the feeding of schoolchildren should be taken in hand; there should be a 25 per cent reduction in rents, starting with those of County Council houses; workers with less than £2.25 a week household income should be exempted from payment of rates; and no County Council official should be paid more than £600 a year. The Council agreed to remit the matter to the Public Assistance Committee. *Fifeshire Advertiser*, 30 Jan. 1932.

215. Claud Cockburn (1904-1981), *Times* correspondent in New York and Washington, 1929-32; editor, *The Week*, 1933-46; diplomatic and foreign correspondent, *Daily Worker*, 1935-46.

216. This March to Edinburgh was in February 1932.

217. Tommy Bloomfield (1914-1987), Fife miner, went to fight in the Spanish Civil War, December 1936. Taken prisoner at Jarama, sentenced to thirty years' imprisonment but repatriated after some months, he then returned to Spain to fight again. *Voices from the Spanish Civil War*, op. cit., 47-55.

218. Edwin Scrymgeour (1866-1947), Prohibition M.P. for Dundee, 1922-31. Bob Stewart had been organiser of the Scottish Prohibition Party, founded by Scrymgeour in 1904.

219. See Volume I of the present work, note 135.

220. The Marchers passed through Cumnock on their way to spend the night of 24 January at New Cumnock, where half slept in the Town Hall and the other half in the Masonic Hall. *Cumnock Chronicle*, 26 Jan. 1934.

221. Hugh Sloan means the Lowther Hills, in which sits the village of Leadhills, about eight miles east of the Marchers' route. Of that stretch of their route, the *Glasgow Herald* reported on 26 January 1934: 'They faced a biting wind and shortly after leaving Kirkconnel they were overtaken by a fairly heavy snowstorm. For five and a half miles west of Sanquhar the road is narrow and consists of continual dips and hills. This was soon coated with a thin layer of snow, which made marching difficult, but all the party arrived at Sanquhar up

to time. It says much for the marchers that not one member fell out, and that there were no casualties reported during the evening. Accommodation was obtained in the Town Hall, the court-room, and a hut belonging to the Boy Scouts. The Temperance Association in the town also granted their hall for the use of the men ... the Provost gave orders to have all the rooms well heated during the evening (and) ... went over all the halls with Mr Harry McShane to ensure that each was comfortable.'

222. The route was by Dumfries and Annan, and the numbers about 400. *Cumnock Chronicle* and *Annandale Observer*, 26 Jan. 1934.

223. See Volume I of the present work, note 175. Reich Marshal Herman Goering (1893-1946), a leading Nazi, Prussian Minister of the Interior and president of the Reichstag at the time of the fire. At one point in the trial of Dimitrov and others accused, Goering had shouted at him: 'You wait until we get you outside this court, you scoundrel!' William L. Shirer, *The Rise and Fall of the Third Reich* (London, 1970), 193.

224. Joe Hill (1879-1915), born Joel Hagglung, a Swede, went to the United States in 1902 and became a songwriter and organiser for the Industrial Workers of the World. Executed by firing squad at Salt Lake City for an alleged robbery and murder, he became a martyr and folk hero. The ballad bearing his name was written in 1925.

225. *Cumnock Chronicle*, 26 Jan. 1934, alleged that at New Cumnock 'not a few casualties, mostly from sore feet, were sent home'. The *Glasgow Herald*, 25 Jan. 1934 reported that, 'The hunger marchers reached New Cumnock ... yesterday evening, and without having to record any casualties.'

226. Jimmy Beecroft was a Lanarkshire County Councillor from Blantyre.

227. Isaac Foot (1880-1960), Liberal M.P. for Bodmin, 1922-24 and 1929-35. Dingle Foot (1905-1978), eldest son of Isaac Foot: Liberal M.P. for Dundee, 1931-45; Parliamentary Secretary, Ministry of Economic Warfare, 1940-45; joined the Labour Party, 1956; Labour M.P. for Ipswich, 1957-70; Solicitor General, 1964-67. Nancy Lady Astor (1879-1964), first woman M.P. to take her seat in the Commons, Tory M.P. for Plymouth Sutton, 1919-45.

228. Edgar A. R. Cecil, Viscount Cecil of Chelwood (1864-1958), third son of the third Marquess of Salisbury.

229. For Hugh Sloan's experiences in Spain, see *Voices from the Spanish Civil War*, op. cit., 195-239.

230. Hugh Sloan, above, p. 283, and the *Courier and Advertiser*, 22 Jan. 1934, say there were thirty Marchers from Dundee. The paper says they were taken by bus from Ninewells, Dundee, to Glasgow.

231. *Glasgow Herald*, 23 Jan. 1934, estimated 2,000 supporters marched with the Marchers from George Square to the outskirts of the city.

232. See above, note 220.

233. Nancy Cunard (1896-1965), public figure and writer, who lived with black jazz pianist Henry Crowder, joined the 1934 Hunger March. She was an anti-racialist who helped organise in 1932 fund-raising for the black youths sentenced to death in Scottsboro, Alabama (see Volume I, note 90). She joined the International Brigades and went to Spain as a reporter for the *Manchester Guardian* and the Associated Negro Press.

234. The writer of the song about Jarama, sung to the tune of *Red River Valley* was Alex McDade, from Glasgow, who was killed at the battle of Brunete in July 1937. Alexander, op. cit., 106.

235. The Marchers in fact interviewed the Lord Provost and told him their demands, which included withdrawal of the Unemployment Act, abolition of the Means Test, rejection of 'slave camps', and provision of essential work by the government at trade union rates. They also sent a telegram to Sir Godfrey Collins, Secretary of State for Scotland, protesting against his decision not to receive a deputation of unemployed in Glasgow. *Glasgow Herald*, 26 Mar. 1935.

236. See above p. 380.

237. Tom Clarke almost certainly means not Kinross but Clackmannanshire, where some 250 Marchers, from Fraserburgh, Aberdeen, Montrose, Dundee and other towns, on their way to Glasgow arrived in Alloa from Dunfermline on 20 March. *Alloa Advertiser*, 23 Mar. 1935.

238. *Glasgow Herald*, 25 Mar. 1935, estimated the numbers taking part in the demonstration against the Unemployment Act by men, women and children the previous day in the city at 40,000, of whom about 3,000 were Hunger Marchers.

239. Less than two years after his participation in the 1935 Hunger March to Glasgow, Tom Clarke went to fight in the Spanish Civil War and was wounded at the battle of Jarama. See *Voices from the Spanish Civil War*, op. cit., 57-87.

240. Sir Henry Campbell-Bannerman (1836-1908), Liberal M.P. for Stirling Burghs, 1868-1908; Leader of the Liberal Party, 1899-1908; prime minister, 1905-08.

241. John Pollock (1893-1955), joined the Communist Party at age sixteen but left it 'disillusioned' six months later and joined the I.L.P. He was several times election agent at Kilmarnock and was consequently dismissed from employment as a boilermaker. He became a bus worker but was again sacked because of his work as election agent. He was sacked a third time from his job after speaking at a meeting. From about 1926 he was unemployed for five years then became a Co-operative Insurance agent at Ayr and moved there from Kilmarnock. He had been I.L.P. candidate at two by-elections in

Kilmarnock and was selected as Labour candidate but refused to sign the standing orders. He became an I.L.P. town councillor in Ayr. So long as James Maxton was alive, John Pollock remained in the I.L.P. After Maxton's death in 1946 he joined the Labour Party and was Labour candidate in Ayr but was never elected. He was chairman of the Scottish Division of the I.L.P. and was active in the Shop, Distributive and Allied Workers' Union. (Information provided by his son, John Pollock, General Secretary, Educational Institute of Scotland.)

242. The Scottish Socialist Party was formed in 1932 as a breakaway from the I.L.P. and remained affiliated to the Labour Party. Alexander (Sanny) Sloan (1879-1945), Ayrshire miners' leader, Labour M.P. for South Ayrshire, 1939-45.

243. Lt. Col. Sir Thomas Moore (1886-1971), in Regular army, 1908-25; on G.H.Q. staff in Russia, 1918-20; Tory M.P. for Ayr Burgh, 1925-50; and Ayr Division of Ayrshire and Bute, 1950-64.

244. Joe Stevenson died at Teruel in Spain early in 1938 of typhoid. *Voices from the Spanish Civil War*, op. cit., 221.

245. McGovern did not join the Tory Party but did advise electors to vote Conservative in the 1964 general election. See W. Knox (ed.), *Scottish Labour Leaders 1918-1939* (Edinburgh, 1984), 179.

246. Leon Trotsky (1879-1940), a leader of the Russian Revolution and founder of the Red Army, unsuccessful rival of Stalin after Lenin's death, murdered by Stalin's agents in Mexico.

247. The Scottish Labour Party was founded in 1888 by Keir Hardie and others, and merged into the Independent Labour Party in 1893-94.

248. *The Burial of Sir John Moore*, Charles Wolfe (1791-1823).

249. From *Death the Leveller*, by James Shirley (1596-1666).

250. Joseph Havelock Wilson (1859-1929), founder and leader of the National Amalgamated Sailors' and Firemen's Union, which changed its title in 1926 to National Union of Seamen.

251. The war, from 1932 to 1935, was over possession of the Chaco territory, most of which Paraguay gained by the subsequent peace treaty. See G. Pendle, *A History of Latin America* (Hardmondsworth, 1963), 207-8.

252. James Carmichael (1894-1966), I.L.P., 1946-47, and Labour, 1947-66, M.P. for Glasgow Bridgeton. Neil Carmichael (1921-), Labour M.P. for Glasgow Woodside, 1962-74, and Kelvingrove, 1974-83; Joint Parliamentary Secretary, Ministry of Transport, 1967-9; Parliamentary Secretary, Ministry of Technology, 1969-70; Parliamentary Under-Secretary, 1974-5, Department

of the Environment, and 1975-6, Department of Industry; created a life peer, 1983, as Lord Carmichael of Kelvingrove.

253. Fenner Brockway (1888-1988), imprisoned as a conscientious objector in the 1914-18 War, secretary, 1917, No Conscription Fellowship, organising secretary, 1922, and general secretary, 1928 and 1933-39; I.L.P., editor, *New Leader*, 1926-29 and 1931-46, chairman, I.L.P., 1931-33; Political Secretary, I.L.P., 1939-46; resigned 1946 from I.L.P. and joined Labour Party, M.P. for Eton and Slough, 1950-64; created life peer, 1964.   Campbell Stephen (1884-1947), M.D., B.D., B.Sc., I.L.P. M.P. for Glasgow Camlachie, 1922-31 and 1935-47.

254. Thomas J. Taylor (1912-), created life peer, 1968, as Lord Taylor of Gryfe, president, Scottish Co-operative Wholesale Society, 1965-70.

255. Engelbert Dollfuss (1892-1934), Austrian fascist Chancellor, murdered by Nazis.
A wave of strikes in India in 1928-9 led to the arrest throughout the country in March 1929 of many trade union and other working-class movement leaders, who were kept in custody at Meerut.   Among those arrested were two British Communist members of the Executive of the All-India Trades Union Congress, P. Spratt and B. F. Bradley.   A third Briton, Lester Hutchinson, a journalist, was arrested later after being elected vice-president of a militant union.   The thirty-two prisoners were charged with conspiracy to deprive the king of sovereignty of British India.   The trial, begun by a Conservative government but continued by a Labour one, dragged on for nearly four years, during which time most of the accused were kept in prison, bail being refused.   Seventeen of the prisoners, including Spratt and Bradley, were found guilty and sentenced to various terms of transportation, ranging from life to five years, or rigorous imprisonment of three or four years.   Four of the prisoners were acquitted or discharged and one other had died.   But the judge proceeded to sentence five of the prisoners who had been found not guilty, including Hutchinson, to three or four years' rigorous imprisonment, and six other prisoners, who had been found guilty by only one of his five assessors, to varying terms of transportation or imprisonment.   Protest demonstrations and meetings were held throughout Britain.   In August 1933 the High Court acquitted nine of the twenty-seven prisoners left, including Hutchinson.   Thirteen, including Spratt and Bradley, had their sentences drastically reduced, and five others, having already served their sentences in effect, were at once released.   Joan Beauchamp, *British Imperialism in India* (London, 1935), 139-59.   For the Scottsboro Boys, see Volume I of the present work, note 90.

256. Robert Tressell, *The Ragged Trousered Philanthropists* (London, 1914).   Pat McGill, *The Rat Pit* (London, 1915).

257. Dr Fred Reid, author of *Keir Hardie: the making of a Socialist* (London, 1978).

258. Only two copies, for April and November 1934, of *Youth Unity*, magazine of the Scottish Divisional Council of the I.L.P. Guild of Youth, survive – in the

Marx Memorial Library, London. See R. Harrison, G. Woolven, R. Duncan, *The Warwick Guide to British Labour Periodicals 1790-1970* (Sussex, 1977), 629.

259. The Fourth International was founded by Trotsky in 1938.

260. John Gollan (1911-1977), Assistant General Secretary, 1947-49, and General Secretary, 1956-76, Communist Party of Great Britain. Hector McNeill (1907-1955), Labour M.P. for Greenock, 1941-55; Glasgow town councillor, 1932-38; Parliamentary Secretary to Ministry of War Transport, 1942-45; Parliamentary Under-Secretary of State, Foreign Office, 1945-46; and Minister of State, 1946-50; Secretary of State for Scotland, 1950-51.

261. David Burke, an electrician by trade, became organiser for the Tobacco Workers' Union in Bristol in 1947, and general secretary of the Union in 1964. He died in 1967, aged fifty-five.

262. Hamish Fraser (died 1986) fought in Spain with the International Brigade in all the battles in which it was engaged, became a shop steward in John Brown's shipyard in the 1939-45 War, became disillusioned with Marxism and the Communist Party, and in the early 1970s became a Conservative town councillor at Saltcoats.

263. The rising of the Asturian miners and iron workers in October 1934 – 'the first battle of the Civil War' – against the right-wing government, was ruthlessly and brutally crushed by General Franco. See, e.g., Gerald Brenan, *The Spanish Labyrinth* (Cambridge, 1960), 280-9.

264. James Barke (1905-1958), novelist.

265. Plato (*c.* 428-348 B.C.), Greek philosopher. Albert Einstein (1879-1955), German-American physicist. Robert G. Ingersoll (1833-1899), United States politician and orator, known as 'the great agnostic'. William Morris (1834-1896), designer, craftsman, poet, socialist.

266. George Nathan had served in the British army as a sergeant-major in the 1914-18 War, later as an officer in the Guards. He became Chief of Staff of the XVth International Brigade before the battle of Brunete in 1937, in which he was mortally wounded. During his service in the British army he had been in Ireland and it has been claimed he was attached to the Black and Tans and was responsible for the murder of two leading Irish Nationalists.

267. André Marty (1886-1956), a leader of the French Communist Party and member of the Executive Committee of the Third International, was commandant of the International Brigades base at Albacete in Spain. He was expelled from the French Communist party shortly before his death.

268. At the outskirts of Kendal the Scottish West Marchers were met by the vice-chairman of the Divisional Labour Party, who was also pastor of the Unitarian Church. The Labour Party donated £3 and an individual collection from

their members raised a further £1.85 pence. An anonymous donor gave the
Marchers 300 packets of cigarettes, thirty-two ounces of tobacco and £6 in
cash. *Daily Worker*, 17 Oct. 1936.

269. Hannen Swaffer (1879-1962), journalist, editor, author. Ben Tillett (1860-
1943), trade union leader; a leader of London dock strike, 1889; a member of
the S.D.F. and the I.L.P. and British Socialist Party; supported Britain's entry
into the 1914-18 War; M.P. for North Salford, 1917-24 and 1929-31.

270. The Act of 1842 prohibited employment of women and girls and of boys
under ten years of age in collieries.

271. Bonafyin' – establishing *bona fides* as travellers so as to satisfy the licensing laws.

272. Barney (Bernard) McCourt, died in 1961 in his mid-sixties. He was a
Communist County Councillor for Mossend, Lanarkshire, from 1935-48.
'The late Sir Henry Keith, politically poles apart from Barney McCourt ...
once said of him that he was the finest man he had ever met in all his
experience in the County Council. A good administrator, he was a quiet
persuasive speaker rather than a rabble rouser.' Obituary in *Motherwell Times*,
20 Jan. 1961.

273. William Pearson (1896-1956), elected to Executive of National Union of
Scottish Mine workers, 1936, and later its secretary and treasurer; president
of the Lanarkshire Miners' Union, 1940; general secretary of the Scottish
Area, National Union of Mineworkers, 1945-56.

274. Tom Campbell (1901-), a noted Burns scholar and friend of the Soviet
translator David Marshak. The number of registered unemployed in 1936
was 1,755,000.   B. R. Mitchell and P. Deane, *Abstract of British Historical
Statistics* (Cambridge, 1971), 66.

275. *Glasgow Herald*, 6 and 7 Oct. 1936, estimated about 400 Marchers from
Glasgow, and between 200 and 300 from Edinburgh.   *Hawick Express*, 15
Oct. 1936 reported 'fully 300' arriving there; but *Eskdale and Liddesdale
Advertiser*, 14 Oct. 1936, counted only 'about 180' arriving at Langholm next
day.

276. See Volume I of the present work, note 10.

277. The British government decided in January 1937 to forbid, under the Foreign
Enlistment Act, 1870, recruitment of British subjects for service in Spain – in
effect, Republican Spain.

278. This was the Catholic orphanage at Smyllum, Lanark, run by the Sisters of
Charity. It closed in 1972.

279. Allan Chapman (1897-1966), Conservative M.P. for Rutherglen, 1935-45;
Assistant Postmaster General, 1941-2; Parliamentary Under-Secretary, Scottish Office, 1942-45.

280. John Bloom (1934–), Rolls Razor washing machines entrepreneur, went bankrupt, owing £2.5 million.

281. It was presumably John Carroll's contingent that, on Saturday, 10 June 1933, 'led by a flute band arrived at Stoneyburn. After being served with a meal through the kindness of the villagers they left bound for Edinburgh via Addiewell and West Calder.' And the next day, at Ratho, these '230 Hunger Marchers ... halted and had lunch in an enclosure off the main street ... The Company was made up of contingents from Ayrshire, Bellshill, Cambuslang, Wishaw and other places in Lanarkshire. Very orderly, all very grateful for any help or kindness rendered. After a frugal but refreshing repast and rest, they marched off jauntily with banners to the music of their pipe bands.' *West Lothian Courier*, 16 Jun. 1933.

282. See Volume I of the present work, note 157.

283. Tommy Brannan or Brannon and William Fox were killed at Jarama in February 1937; Willie Fleck at Chimorra in April 1937. Alexander, op. cit., 264, 267 (where Willie Fleck is given as 'Thomas Flecks').

284. The Blantyre Disaster, on 22 October 1877, caused by an explosion of fire-damp at Dixon's collieries, cost the lives of 207 men and boys. It was the worst disaster in the history of coal-mining in Scotland. R. Page Arnot, *A History of the Scottish Miners* (London, 1955), 60; Gordon M. Wilson, *Alexander McDonald, Leader of the Miners* (Aberdeen, 1982), 186–8.

285. A dook – an underground roadway driven downhill.

286. The joke or jock – an iron rod, usually pronged, attached to the back end of a group of tubs or hutches being drawn up an incline and that stopped them running back if the drawing rope broke.

287. Tony Brown was frankly uncertain of the year that he went on the Hunger March. In 1936 Marchers from Fife seem mainly to have gone to Edinburgh and then south through the central Borders. It may well be it was the 1934, not 1936, March he went on.

288. Seven West Fife Hunger Marchers were arrested on their return from London in early March 1934, and charged by Fife County Council as Public Assistance Authority with deserting or failing to maintain their wives and children while they were away on the March. All seven Marchers pleaded not guilty. At the trial at Dunfermline Sheriff Court the prosecution dropped the charge of desertion, and the men were charged only with neglecting to maintain their wives and children. Only one case, Walter Mannarn, aged thirty-seven, of Lumphinnans, was proceeded with, to stand as a test case for the others. Mannarn was found not guilty so the other cases were abandoned. *Dunfermline Press*, 10 and 17 Mar. 1934.

289. Six men lost their lives in the explosion at Auchinraith colliery on 30 August

406 Voices from the Hunger Marches

1930, and a further six received burning injuries. One miner injured in the explosion told the official inquiry that 'it was a common expression among the men that we would all be in the air some day'. The Chief Inspector of Mines concluded the explosion was due to the firing of a shot in the presence of inflammable gas and that there had been 'grave laxity', for which 'the manager [D. C. Gemmell] and under-manager cannot escape responsibility'. *Glasgow Herald*, 12 and 13 Nov. 1930, 20 Jun. 1931.

290. David Kirkwood (1872-1955), Clyde shop steward in the 1914-18 War, a leading figure in the I.L.P., from which he resigned after its disaffiliation from the Labour Party in 1932; M.P. for Dumbarton Burghs, 1922-51, then accepted a peerage as Baron Kirkwood of Bearsden. George Buchanan (1890-1955), M.P. for Gorbals, 1922-48; resigned from the I.L.P. in 1939 and rejoined the Labour Party; Minister of Pensions, 1947-8. Neil Maclean (1873-1953), secretary, Socialist Labour Party, 1903-08, Labour M.P. for Govan, 1918-50, expelled from the I.L.P., 1931. Rev. James Barr (1862-1949), United Free Church minister, Labour M.P. for Motherwell, 1924-31, and for Coatbridge, 1934-45.

291. George Catto was elected in 1919, along with four other Labour candidates.

292. Thomas Johnston (1881-1965), Labour M.P. for Clackmannan and West Stirling, 1922-24, 1929-31 and 1935-45, and for Dundee, 1924-29; Under-Secretary of State for Scotland, 1929-31; Lord Privy Seal, 1931; Secretary of State for Scotland, 1941-45.

293. Walter Citrine (1887-1983), assistant general secretary, Electrical Trades Union, 1920-23, assistant secretary, 1924; general secretary, Trades Union Congress, 1926-46; knighted 1935; created Baron Citrine, 1946.

294. Helen Crawfurd (1877-1954), militant suffragette, a leader of the Glasgow Rent Strikes, 1915; resigned from the I.L.P., 1921, and joined the Communist Party of Great Britain; a leading figure in Workers' International Relief; unsuccessful Communist Party candidate at Bothwell, 1929, and North Aberdeen, 1931, at the latter of which she polled a handful less than 4,000 votes.
W. Wedgwood Benn (1877-1960), Liberal M.P. for Tower Hamlets, 1906-18, and Leith, 1918-27, Labour M.P. for North Aberdeen, 1928-31, and Gorton (Manchester), 1937-42; Secretary of State for India, 1929-31, and for Air, 1945-6; created Viscount Stansgate, 1941.

295. *Aberdeen Press and Journal*, 28 Sept. 1936, reported there were thirty-five Marchers. One woman Marcher, who must have been on the separate women's March, returned with the Aberdeen contingent, said then to be twenty-seven strong, from London on 15 November. *Press and Journal*, 16 Nov . 1936.

296. Three photographs of the Aberdeen contingent in fact were published by the *Daily Worker* on 2 Oct. 1936 one showing the youngest Marcher, James Taylor, playing his mouth organ, another, with John Lennox clearly visible

at the head of the March, and a third with the contingent seated at the roadside during a tea-break. Other photographs of the Aberdeen and Dundee contingents were published in that paper on 8 and 20 Oct., with John Lennox at the front.

297. The Marchers held an open-air meeting in front of the public library at Arbroath and slept that night in the Good Templars Hall. One additional Marcher joined at Arbroath. *Press and Journal* and *Courier and Advertiser*, 30 Sept. 1936.

298. Dudhope Castle, a couple of centuries earlier the home of Graham of Claverhouse, 'Bonnie Dundee', had accommodated Hunger Marchers in March 1935 on their way to Glasgow *Courier and Advertiser*, 15 Mar. 1935 and 30 Sept. 1936.

299. The Marchers' arrival in the afternoon at Kirkcaldy was announced in the morning by a loudspeaker car that 'patrolled the High Street, playing at intervals *The Red Flag* and other ditties of a like nature.' The evening procession from Gallatown to the Port Brae was by torchlight and was led by the Dysart Colliery Band. Speeches were made by a local councillor and a representative from Kirkcaldy Trades Council. Next day a Kirkcaldy contingent joined the Marchers. *Fife Free Press*, 3 Oct. 1936.

300. The Marchers' arrival at Edinburgh on Sunday, 4 October, from the Burntisland to Granton ferry was the subject of a detailed report by Detective Lieutenant Sheed of the city C.I.D. The contingent, wrote Sheed, was between 150 and 200 strong, made up of Marchers from Aberdeen, Brechin, Dundee, Cowdenbeath, Lochgelly and Kirkcaldy, and accompanied by a flute band. Each group carried a red banner with the name of its district. They were met by Donald Renton and the Edinburgh N.U.W.M. flute band. Alex Moffat, their leader, told the Marchers they would not be allowed by the police to march to their destination but despite that they were going to do so, though they should not try to take any collection en route. The contingent and bands then marched to the Labour Party Rooms at Mill Lane, Leith. After a meal given by the Leith Provident Co-operative Society they marched to the Mound where they were joined by local activists from the Trades Council, trade union branches and the Communist Party, and all then marched behind a band to Leith Links to demonstrate against the Unemployment Regulations. They were joined there by demonstrators from Leith unions and Labour groups and also by a contingent of some thirty Hunger Marchers from Stirlingshire. The speakers at the Links meeting, which was chaired by Councillor A. H. Paton, I.L.P., president of the Trades Council, were D. R. Grenfell, Labour M.P. for Gower in South Wales, Councillor Mrs H. Inglis, Edinburgh, Bob Cooney, Aberdeen, and David Chalmers, Edinburgh Communist Party. The speakers 'denounced the National Government and particularly the Means Test', and evidently deplored the refusal by Ernest Brown, Minister of Labour and Liberal National M.P. for Leith, to receive a deputation from the Marchers in Edinburgh. Monday was a rest-day but on Tuesday the Marchers, who had been housed at Mill Lane, marched to the Mound, where a crowd of about

800 heard speeches by Harry McShane, Alex Moffat and Mrs Eva Gibbons, Edinburgh N.U.W.M. Harry McShane said the police were reporting him and Alex Moffat for holding demonstrations and taking collections in breach of a bye-law, but the Marchers would continue to do both. An Edinburgh contingent of about thirty joined the Marchers, who then marched along Princes Street, up Lothian Road and into Minto Street, where there was a halt for light refreshments, before the March to Gorebridge was resumed. Lieutenant Sheed's report lists the leaders of the March as Harry McShane, Alex Moffat, 'Advance Agent, Comrade Owens of Aberdeen, Treasurer, Comrade Noble of Kirkcaldy, Quartermaster, Comrade Donald Renton of Edinburgh', and Chalmers and Jones, Edinburgh, Spence, Aberdeen, and Stalker, Dundee. Sheed adds that 'Donald Fraser Renton and David Chalmers are two well-known Edinburgh Communists, the latter being a criminal deportee from Canada. The known persons taking part in the march and likely to commit a breach of the peace are Donald Fraser Renton, David Chalmers, John Dalgleish, Thomas Ford and John Bigham.' The police-record serial numbers of Dalgleish and Ford were given in the report. Sheed described, and listed the registration numbers of, five motor cars and a van being used by the Marchers. Three of the cars, one with a trailer containing provisions, and the van with a loudspeaker, left Edinburgh with the Marchers. Sheed admitted that 'The temper and conduct of the marchers,' the majority of whom carried walking sticks, 'were exceptionally good during the whole time of their stay in Edinburgh.' S.R.O. DD 10/246/2. See also *Glasgow Herald*, 7 Oct. 1936 and *Edinburgh Evening News*, 5 and 6 Oct. 1936, both of which estimated the Edinburgh contingent at 'about 50'.

301. At Galashiels, where they were joined by one local volunteer, the Marchers were accommodated in the Town Hall, where they were given a 'substantial supper and breakfast' by the Provost's Committee. At Hawick the Marchers were welcomed as at Galashiels by local branch members of the N.U.W.M., accommodated in the Town Hall, and entertained by a local concert group. Speeches were made by Harry McShane, Alex Moffat and John Lennox. At their last overnight stop in Scotland, at Langholm, the Marchers, who 'marched into the town with banners flying and to the music of a drum and fife band', slept at the Buccleuch Hall and Town Hall. The feeding arrangements which 'were in the hands of their own organisation', left an indelible impression on Harry McShane: 'We were met by the whole town; they brought long tables out to the streets and spread them with food they had prepared. It was a tremendous surprise – I had never known it happen before. There was a great atmosphere among all the people and all the marchers.' Harry McShane, op. cit., 216; *Eskdale and Liddesdale Advertiser*, 14 Oct. 1936; *Border Telegraph*, 13 Oct. 1936; *Hawick News*, 9 Oct. 1936.

302. For Patrick Halpin, cook, see Volume I of the present work, note 27.

303. Kingsford, op. cit., 211, says that on arrival in London the Scottish West contingent numbered 276, the East 185.

304. S. O. Davies (1886-1972), a coalminer at twelve years of age, Arts graduate,

University College, Cardiff; vice-president, South Wales Miners' Federation, 1924-32; Labour M.P. for Merthyr Tydfil, 1934-70; Independent Labour M.P., 1970-72.

305. The Minister of Labour Ernest Brown was forced by the wide support for the Hunger Marchers to receive a large deputation from them accompanied by their constituency M.P.s. The deputation included Alex Moffat and Mrs Harley of Greenock. Brown 'listened in silence to the most damning indictment he had ever heard levelled against his Government. At the end he announced that the new Unemployment Assistance Board scales, due to come into operation four days later, would again be suspended, for a period of two months for reassessment, that no cuts in the scales would then be immediately operated, and that there would be a spread-over system covering 18 months, during which the Government would only gradually apply the new scales, and that the full scales would not therefore be in operation until July 1938. Further, in no case would there be any re-assessment or cut in the scale of any applicant without a two weeks' notice after re-assessment.' Wal Hannington, *Ten Lean Years* (London, 1940), 146; *Daily Worker*, 13 Nov. 1936.

306. The Aberdeen Educational Trust, King Street, was a charitable institution that provided free meals for poor children.

307. Britain was the mandatory power, under the League of Nations, in Palestine from 1920 onward. Trouble between Jews and Arabs had already erupted there in 1929 with loss of 250 lives. The increase in immigration by Jews, mainly from Nazi persecution, from 1933 brought further conflict which continued, contrary to David Anderson's recollection, more or less until the outbreak of the 1939-45 War, reaching a height in 1938 when those killed totalled, 1,785 and when British forces carried out 'a virtual military reoccupation' of Palestine. C. L. Mowat, *Britain between the Wars 1918-1940* (London, 1956), 376, 624-5.

308. David Anderson's recollections of his experiences in Spain are in *Voices from the Spanish Civil War*, op. cit., 89-99.

309. The North-East contingent of Marchers, some of whom wore their war medals, was one of several making their way from various places in Scotland to Edinburgh to put the demands and grievances of the unemployed before the Secretary of State. The local press variously estimated the number leaving Aberdeen on 15 November at twenty-one and twenty-four. Three cases of these came from Inverness and one, William M'Leod, from Fort Augustus, from which he had set out several days earlier and walked the thirty-five or so miles to Inverness to join the three local Marchers to Aberdeen. M'Leod, who belonged to Edinburgh but had been working on roads at Fort Augustus since early in the year, had already walked 200 miles by the time the North-East contingent reached Dundee on 20 November. By that point three additional Marchers had joined at Montrose and two at Arbroath. At Dundee a further thirty joined the March. *Press and Journal*, 16 Nov. 1938; *Courier and Advertiser*, 21 Nov. 1938.

310. Overnight stops from Aberdeen included the Cross Hall, Stonehaven, Town Hall, Inverbervie, and Beach Pavilion, Montrose. In Dundee they were accommodated at the N.U.W.M. Hall in William Lane. *Press and Journal*, 16 and 27 Nov. 1938; *Courier and Advertiser*, 21 Nov. 1938.

311. The youngest Marcher was Stalker's fourteen-year-old son George. Stalker himself was a councillor and Angus District organiser of the N.U.W.M. Dave Campbell was vice-president of Aberdeen Trades and Labour Council. *Courier and Advertiser*, 28 Nov. 1938; *Alloa Journal*, 26 Nov. 1938.

312. After leaving Dundee, the North-East contingent marched via Perth, Kinross, Alloa, Falkirk, Bo'ness and South Queensferry to Edinburgh which, about a hundred strong, they reached on Sunday, 27 November, along with the other contingents 'a considerable number' of whose members had recently returned from fighting with the International Brigade in Spain. *Edinburgh Evening News* and *Courier and Advertiser*, 28 Nov. 1938; *Alloa Journal*, 26 Nov. 1938; *Falkirk Herald*, 3 Dec. 1938.

313. The deputation to the Ministry of Labour office at Drumsheugh Gardens was led by Harry McShane, and included Wal Hannington, Bob Selkirk, M. Linden and J. Laird, Glasgow, J. Morris, Alloa, William Campbell, Ayrshire, Charles Lennox, Lanarkshire, John C. McEwan, Inverness, and three others, as well as George Stalker and Dave Campbell. Government officials present represented the Scottish Office, the Department of Health, and the Unemployment Assistance Board, as well as the Ministry of Labour. The proposals submitted by the deputation were intended to reduce unemployment by repealing the 1934 Act, which would abolish the Means Test and consequent investigations; reduction in working hours, increased old age pensions to 'take men off the labour market'; raising of the school-leaving age; and increasing scales of benefit. Harry McShane urged more Government contracts should be placed in Scotland, speeding up of house-building, building of Forth and Tay bridges and in the Highlands piers, roads, bridges and drainage schemes; afforestation; and building of air-raid shelters. He protested against afforestation by inmates of government 'slave camps' – which it was said the Home Secretary, Sir John Gilmour, by 'a slip of the tongue' had described in 1934 as concentration camps. Harry McShane presented complaints about three government camps – Glenbranter, Redesdale and Kielder – that he had himself recently visited. At Glenbranter there were complaints about a local policeman, McInnes, known as Strachur Dan, who it was alleged beat up men at the camp. At Redesdale camp a Coatbridge man who had been taken ill had had to wait thirteen hours for medical attention, and was then taken to Newcastle late at night in a waggon used for carting stone. He had died a few hours later. At Kielder 'a special type of bug' seemed to have appeared from among secondhand clothing issued. There were also complaints about the camp manager. Most of the other members of the deputation, including George Stalker and Dave Campbell, also spoke on points in the submission. Several hundred Marchers waited in the street outside singing *The Internationale* and, according to the *Scotsman*, 'a number of parodies of popular numbers, including *The Lambeth*

Walk, which was made the vehicle of a ... chorus which introduced the name Ernie Brown in a manner which clearly showed that the present Minister of Labour was not, in the vocalists' view, the right man in the right place.' Accommodation for the Marchers overnight had been arranged by Edinburgh Trades Council and Burgh Labour Party at the Waverley Market. S.R.O. DD 10/252; *Scotsman*, 29 Nov. 1938.

Some further reading

Croucher, Richard, *We refuse to starve in silence: A History of the National Unemployed Workers' Movement* (London, 1987)

Gilbert, Bentley B., *British Social Policy 1914-1939* (London, 1970)

Hannington, Wal, *Unemployment Struggles 1919-1936* (London, 1977)

Hannington, Wal, *Never on our knees* (London, 1967)

Hannington, Wal, *Ten Lean Years* (London, 1940)

Kingsford, Peter, *The Hunger Marchers in Britain 1920-1940* (London, 1982)

McShane, Harry, and Smith, Joan, *Harry McShane: No Mean Fighter* (London, 1978)

Mowat, C. L., *Britain between the Wars 1918-1940* (London, 2nd ed. 1968)

Pollard, Sidney, *The Department of the British Economy 1914-1967* (London, 2nd ed. 1969)

Stevenson, John, and Cook, Chris, *The Slump: Society and Politics during the Depression* (London, 1977)

INDEX

This index covers *Voices from the Hunger Marches*, Vol I & II.

(1932), 60, 81, women's, 53, 208, (1934), 109, 195, 263, 296, women's, 109, 238, (1936), 36, 37, 370
  transport on, 5, 53, 368, boat, 5, buses, 5, 19, 191, 230, 231, 245, 259, 260, 284, 292, 293, 338, 342, 354, 362, 368, 399, car, 378, 379, 382, 394, 395, 407, 408, chuck waggon, 32, 33, ferry, 73, 81, 210, 281, 380, 382, 407, lorry, 19, 44, 192, 206, 295, 323, 342, 343, motor, 150, train, 51, 259, 298, tramcar, 177, 353, 361, truck, 383, 386, van, 32, 44, 206, 260, 285, 288, 339, 340, 341, 342, 345, 408
    victimisation of, 165, 370, 371, 405
    washing and bathing by, 18, 59, 110–11, 143, 148, 284, 285, 298, 344, 368, 380, 382, 385
    weather during, 81, 263, 293, blizzard, 285, cold, 7, 281, 383, fine, 379, frost, 232, good, 34, 130, 178, 260, 377, 383, miserable, 292, sleet, 292, snow, 7, 75, 152, 210, 296, 398, warm, 143, 214, windy, 285, 398, wet, 7, 46, 60, 73, 141, 292, 296, 297, 323, 380, 385, 387
    winter relief sought by, 75, 113, 129, 143
    youth section: women's, (1934), 231, 232, 233, 235, 236, 237, 238, 239, 246, West of Scotland, (1936), 318, 320, 321, 326
Hunter, Jimmy, 331
Hutchinson, Lester, 402

Ilford, 240
ILP, *see* Independent Labour Party
imperialism, 92, 209
Inchinnan, 362
Independent Labour Party (ILP), 43, 91, 92, 207, 208, 215, 227, 249, 316, 400, 402, 406; and British Socialist Party, 206; and Communist Party, 45, 206; disaffiliation from Labour Party by, 206, 225, 302, 315, 406; Guild of Youth, 8, 228, 229, 235, 236, 251, 302, 314, 315, 373, 402; and Hunger Marches and Marchers, 8, 22, 136, to Cupar, (n.d.), 110, to Edinburgh, (1933), 144, 199, (1938), 158, 394, to London, (1932), 45, 59, (1934), 149, 192, 195, 201, 260, 262, women's, 229, 235, 236, (1936), 26, 166, 321, 325, 353; leaders of, 21, 201, 213, 397, 404; in localities: Aberdeen, 373, 374, Ayr, 302, 303, Bridgeton, 315, 316, Cambuslang, 59, 75, Clydebank, 185, 189, 227, 228, 229, Cowdenbeath, 117, Dundee, 283, 296, Glasgow, 215, 249, 314–16, Greenock,

156, 173, 174, Kilmarnock, 400, Kirkcaldy, 126, Lesmahagow, 335, Lochgelly, 92, 258, Maryhill, 43, Possilpark, 43, 45; and NUWM, 3, 22, 318; Scottish Division, 400; Scottish Labour Party and, 401; Scottish Socialist Party and, 400; Second International and, 211; Socialist Sunday School and, 50; Third (Communist) International and, 93, 206, 211; unemployed organisation of, 22, 201; and United Front, 117, 211
India, 160, 161, 169, 170, 283, 291, 300, 392, 402, 406; Trades' Union Congress, All-, 402
industrial unionism, 217
Industrial Workers: of Great Britain, 183, 185, 186, 217; of the World, 186, 207, 217, 399
Ingersoll, Robert, 319, 403
Inglis, Councillor Mrs H., 407
Ingram, Ned, 59, 60
Inkpin, Albert, 93, 211
insects, *see* creatures; Hunger Marches and Marchers, rats and insects
Internationa Brigades: Irish Battalion, 322; Thaelmann Battalion, 319; *see also* War, Spanish Civil
Inverasdale, 181
Inverbervie, 393, 409
Invergordon, 88; naval mutiny, 225
Inverkeithing, 73, 99, 117, 181, 281
Inverness, 4, 181, 291, 377, 393, 409, 410
Inverurie, 392
Ipswich, 399
Ireland, 48, 207, 300, 306, 392, 403; see also Easter Rising, (1916)
Irish, 21, 83, 84; Battalion, International Brigades, 322; Citizen Army, 16, 197; immigrants, 56, 83, 84, 111, 147, 185, 227, 243, 244, 249, 303, 306, 330, 348, 357; Nationalists, 403; potato famine, 84, 348; Republican Army, 229, 362; Socialist Republican Party, 217; Troubles, 322; tunnellers, 255, 333
Iron and Steel Trades Confederation, 207
Irvine, 302, 305; Valley, 305
Iscourt (Ycourt), 56
Isle of Wight, 372
Italy, 145, 169, 224, 226

Jaccanelli, Ernesto, 263
Jack, J. L., 213
Jackson, Andy, 161, 169
Jamaica, 181
Japan, 145, 226
Jarama, 168, 218, 279, 283, 320, 326, 398, 400, 405